Collaborative Family Law

Another Way to Resolve Family Disputes

Richard W. Shields

Judith P. Ryan

Victoria L. Smith

THOMSON ™

CARSWELL

National Library of Canada Cataloguing in Publication

Shields, Richard W.

   Collaborative family law : another way to resolve family disputes / Richard W. Shields, Judith P. Ryan, Victoria L. Smith.

Includes bibliographical references and index.
ISBN 0-459-24043-9

   1. Family mediation—Canada. 2. Domestic relations—Canada.
I. Ryan, Judith P.   II. Smith, Victoria L.   III. Title.

KE569.S55 2003   346.7101'5   C2003-900458-9
KF535.S55 2003

THOMSON

CARSWELL

One Corporate Plaza
2075 Kennedy Road
Scarborough, Ontario M1T 3V4

Customer Relations
Toronto 1-416-609-3800
Elsewhere in Canada/U.S. 1-800-387-5164
Fax 1-800-298-5094
World Wide Web: http://www.carswell.com
E-mail: orders@carswell.com

Foreword

In the sixties, divorce reform cracked the encrusted nut of family law. In one blow, parliament took Canadians from the centuries-old offence-based theories for divorce and spousal support to revolutionary new no-fault concepts. This let loose forces for radical change that affected all areas of family law. Property was first in line. Starting from the concept of marriage as an equal partnership, new legislation in the late seventies ordered an accounting of property acquired during the marriage. This ended a long struggle for recognition of a spouse's non-monetary contributions. Next, was child support. In the nineties, it went from a case-by-case analysis of needs to the use of guidelines based on statistics, a completely foreign approach. In the same decade, spousal support was overhauled. It expanded from awards at subsistence levels to—when it could be afforded—comfort levels. Here the courts, which led much of the reform in every area, pumped meaning into what were once considered innocuous objectives of the support legislation. The forces of reform are still swirling. The whole idea of marriage, for instance, is undergoing profound change with the recognition of same-sex relationships and a drive for equal rights with heterosexual couples.

These reforms have created remedies in some areas, such as in property division and child support, that are more-or-less certain in their application offering relatively little choice. In other areas remedies have been created that rest largely on judicial discretion making them uncertain and allowing an abundance of choice; spousal support for example, with its alternate models and divergent opinions on quantum, and care of children with the test of best interests and a wide variety of parenting arrangements. And the way in which different remedies may be combined increases the range of choice. Child support can have a different outcome, for instance, when it is considered along with the remedy of exclusive possession of the matrimonial home and credit is given for the benefit to the child of living there. Viewed negatively, this array of remedies laced with discretion leaves the lawyer with a sense of being at sea with a broken compass. Predictability is gone. The positive perspective, however, is that the variety of remedies and the liberal use of discretion produce flexibility that promotes the desirable goal of individualized justice.

However, there is a problem when we think of the courts taking responsibility for putting all this together. Although we have case management and settlement conferences built into the court system, it is still an adversarial process relying on the development of an outcome through confrontation by claim and counterclaim. It is a process that is possibly the best that can be designed for issues that are capable of either/or, yes/no, I am right/you are wrong, determinations. Or that can be cast in the form of a debate where the issue is one-pointed and the verbal cut and thrust trims the case to the one clear logical answer.

However, family issues are usually much messier, and do not yield to these simple formulations. They require a more multidimensional process; a process that can work with the complicated sprawl that is the nature of many family matters; a process that is able to delve into the needs and concerns below the surface; a process that is then able to build satisfaction of these needs and concerns into the solution.

The solution must dovetail the respective interests of the parties and make sense as far as they are concerned. Each party should feel that by his or her own standard each has treated the other party fairly and has been treated fairly in return.

The standard of fairness employed by the parties may not be the legal standard. In fact, the central thesis of this book is that the legal standard – or what the lawyers think a judge might do in a given situation – is not the sole test, or even the main test of fairness or acceptability. The legal standard is only one standard among many. To believe otherwise runs the risk of reducing the discussion around the table to talk about rights instead of interests, and of having the legal template confine the solution to precedent that does not satisfy the parties' more fundamental needs and concerns. The standard must be more resilient than the legal standard, therefore, and may involve a subjective component based on notions such as personal ideas of entitlement, equality, moral right and wrong, and of the regard in which the other person should be held. The parties' standard of fairness must be respected in the same way that all choices affecting outcome are respected, and part of the collaborative process is the joint search for, and the adoption of the parties' particular standard.

The domain of the search, however, while not confined to, certainly does involve the law. One of the benefits of the collaborative process is that the lawyers are involved in the process from the beginning. As well as offering their skills at analyzing problems and guiding the negotiations along an interest-based plane, they are expected to advise on the law as the matter progresses. Legal options are considered in a timely way and are not allowed to pop up unexpectedly at an awkward moment to derail the settlement. The lawyers advise their clients of the client's rights and obligations under the law mindful that the legal option does not have to be implemented, but must be known. The clients are free to compromise and substitute their own standards of acceptability and reasonableness for the legal standard – they do this all the time, even in the traditional process – but they need to do this with their eyes open. They may depart from the legal standard and adopt some other standard, if their own good sense tells them that this is the right thing to do; for example, where the wife's inheritance is used to purchase the matrimonial home, both wife and husband may say that the value should not be shared as prescribed by the law, but should be credited entirely to the wife. The important point is not what they do, but that they do it with full knowledge of their legal options. Information about these options is fed into the collaborative process at appropriate moments, and the beginning of the discussion of any issue might not be the time. Indeed, premature advice-giving may put a chill on the negotiations and discourage a broad canvassing of interests and of the trades or other means that can be used to satisfy them.

However, the separation agreement or other contract that concludes the negotiations will be within the law in the sense that it will contain a settlement entered into with all important information on the table and all compromises knowingly made. It will be reasonable in view of the standards adopted by the parties and will not be susceptible to an application at law to set it aside.

While not necessarily so, it is most likely that the agreement generated by interest-based negotiations and settled according to the parties individual standards, will be within the range of the specific and discretionary remedies provided by the law. But even so, it is doubtful that the same provisions could be devised in the process administered by the court system.

An adversarial or confrontational process, like the court process, which sends the parties into their respective corners to come out fighting, is not up to the task. Any kind of contest, hard-fought or friendly, causes parties to take positions. Positions narrow the scope of the engagement leaving many of the larger needs and concerns, that may matter most to the parties, hanging on the other side of the ropes.

Another way to look at the problem is to recognize that the range of remedies now available under the law, and the huge discretion that has developed to make adjustments and put the pieces together, has outgrown the capacity of the traditional legal process. The substantive law has developed, by and large, to keep pace with the demands of modern society. It is the delivery system that has lagged behind.

A totally different kind of delivery system is required; one that is as radical as some of the substantive law reforms that we have seen. Such a system, Collaborative Family Law, is described in this book.

The practice of Collaborative Family Law is confined to settlement without threat of litigation. Collaborative Family Law lawyers disqualify themselves, in advance, from going to court or from using any of the litigation procedures. They avoid confrontation. They are trained problem-solvers using cooperative methods that have been developed by mediators and interest-based negotiators working in many different settings over the past two or three decades. This book describes these methods and how collaborative lawyers put them to use.

All significant negotiations are conducted in meetings with both clients and both lawyers present. In these meetings and throughout the collaborative process, the lawyers climb down from their pedestals and encourage the clients to control the agenda and the outcome. They help the clients see down the road, trying not to get in the way. Rather than acting as the mouthpiece *for* the clients, they work *with* the clients, respecting their intelligence to think and speak for themselves. They act as legal advisors, negotiation coaches, and guides in the process. They help the clients assemble and exchange all important information and show them how to use that information to generate settlement options.

Information, advice and counseling beyond the competence of the legal team are often required. A child specialist, for example, may be engaged to work independently with the clients to develop a parenting plan; a valuator may be jointly retained by the clients to appraise property or value a business; or a financial planner may be asked to work with both clients to prepare financial statements and budgets, and to recommend how to best conserve and share the family's financial resources. These experts are neutral in their relations with the clients and work as part of the settlement team.

The collaborative process is new, exciting, and calls for the best from the lawyers. When the light dawns, the lawyers feel as though a great discovery has been made, and their enthusiasm for practice rekindled. They enjoy going to work in the morning.

This book describes how to make it happen for you. The theoretical background necessary to understand the process is clearly explained, and each stage of its implementation from the first interview through to final agreement is described step-by-step. With attention to the book you are able to change hats from litigator to collaborative negotiator, harness new-found skills in empathetic communication and conflict management, and by doing so help the clients identify and reconcile their interests in a mutually satisfactory way. Both you and the clients will be the better for it.

The authors, Richard W. Shields, Judith P. Ryan and Victoria L. Smith are well-qualified to give you this instruction. They have solid backgrounds in family law and mediation, the forerunner of collaboration. They are enthusiastic promoters of Collaborative Family Law and since its beginnings in Ontario have been involved at both the practice and training levels. Thus, they are able to speak not only from first-hand experience, but also with the clarity of a teacher's analysis and preparation. By writing this book they are sharing their experience and knowledge in a way that allows the rest of us to catch up quickly on a movement that is as significant to family law practice as the reforms of recent years has been to its substantive development.

James C. MacDonald, Q.C.

About the Authors

Richard W. Shields is a lawyer and mediator. He was admitted to the practice of law in Ontario in 1976 and, for several years, he practised exclusively as a lawyer in civil litigation and family law. Rick completed the Certificate in Dispute Resolution program at Pepperdine University in California in 1994, following which he began his mediation practice under the firm name, "Another Way Mediation." He obtained his Master of Arts in Conflict Resolution from Antioch University in Ohio in 1996 and his Master of Laws in ADR from Osgoode Hall Law School, York University in Toronto in 1998. Following his own training in collaborative law in 2000, Rick transformed his practice. He now restricts his professional work to family mediation and collaborative family law. Rick received his Certification from the Law Society of Upper Canada as a Specialist in Family Law, his Certification from Family Mediation Canada as a Comprehensive Family Mediator, and his Designation from the ADR Institute of Canada, Inc. as a Chartered Mediator. He is a member of several ADR associations including the Canadian Bar Association and Ontario Bar Association (Family Law and ADR Sections), the ADR Institute of Canada, Inc.(past president of the ADR Institute of Ontario, Inc.), Family Mediation Canada (past Certifying Administrator), the American Bar Association (Dispute Resolution Section), the Association for Conflict Resolution, and the Association of Family, Court and Community Professionals. He is also a founding member and an active participant in the Hamilton/Halton Collaborative Family Law Association. Rick is also an educator and trainer. He teaches Family Law in the Bar Admission Course in Ontario, Family Law and Negotiation at McMaster University, and Mediation at York University and the University of Guelph. He received his Certificate in Adult Education from St. Francis Xavier University and he is a candidate for a Doctoral Degree in Adult Education from the Ontario Institute for Studies in Education of the University of Toronto.

Judith P. Ryan has dual professional qualifications as a social worker and a lawyer. After receiving her Master of Social Work degree, she began her professional career in Kingston, Ont. While working as a family therapist, she was among the first in Canada to develop a mediation model for the resolution of custody and access disputes. Thereafter, Judith enrolled in Queen's law school. She was admitted to the practice of law in Ontario in 1982. In 1986, she obtained her Master of Laws degree from the University of Toronto. Her thesis was on the ethical implications of mediation for the practice of family law. Since then she has published several articles on both mediation and the practice of law. Judith established her own law firm in Toronto that she restricted exclusively to the practice of family law. For many years, Judith practiced her own form of nonadversarial, interest-based family law. At the same time, she developed a comprehensive model for the mediation of all kinds of family disputes. She subsequently incorporated J.P. Ryan & Associates Limited, a full service dispute resolution firm which offers mediation and arbitration services, dispute resolution systems design, and mediation training. With over twenty years experience as a dispute resolution practitioner, Judith has now mediated over a thousand cases across a broad spectrum of disputes, and has designed and conducted hundreds of ADR workshops and training programs across Canada, the United States, Australia, and elsewhere, for judges, lawyers, and health care professionals, as well as for government agencies and private businesses. Judith received her Designation from the ADR Institute of Canada, Inc. as a Chartered Mediator and her Certification from Family Mediation Canada as a Comprehensive Family Mediator. She is a member/board member of several ADR associations including the ADR Institute of Canada, Inc. (past vice-president of the Arbitration and Mediation Institute of Ontario, Inc.), Family Mediation Canada (past national president), the Association for Conflict Resolution, and the Association of Family and Conciliation Courts. She is currently a member of the Board of Governors of Seneca College. Finally, Judith has been a regular consultant on dispute resolution for federal and provincial governments, the Law Society of Upper Canada and other professional associations, and major corporations. She is a panel member of the Toronto and Hamilton Collaborative Family Law Groups.

Victoria L. Smith is a partner in the law firm Simmons, da Silva & Sinton, where she practises family law exclusively, and she is a principal of Im-mediation Inc., which offers family and civil mediation and arbitration services. She was admitted to the practice of law in Ontario in 1983. Victoria participated in extensive negotiation and mediation training workshops in Canada and the United States including those offered by Family Mediation Canada, York University, the Law Society of Upper Canada, CDR Associates in Boulder, Colorado, and the Harvard Negotiation Project. She has been a practicing mediator since 1990. Following her training in collaborative family law in 2000, she has restricted her practice to collaborative family law and mediation. Victoria received her Certification from Family Mediation Canada as a Comprehensive Family Mediator and her Designation from the ADR Institute of Canada, Inc. as a Chartered Mediator. She is a founding director and supervising mediator of Peel Mediation Services, which provides mediation services and internships in the Peel Family Court. She is a member of several ADR associations including the Canadian Bar Association and the Ontario Bar Association (Family Law and ADR Sections), the ADR Institute of Canada Inc., Family Mediation Canada, the American Bar Association (Dispute Section Subsection), the Association for Conflict Resolution, and the International Association of Collaborative Professionals. She is co-chair and a founding member of the Peel/Halton Collaborative Law Association, a founding member of the Ontario Collaborative Family Law Federation, and a panel member of the Toronto CFL Association. Victoria is a part-time instructor in mediation and negotiation at Osgoode Hall Law School, York University.

Richard, Judith, and Victoria, in addition to writing this book, have worked together to train lawyers throughout Ontario in the Collaborative Family Law process and the skills required to be an effective practitioner. They have also been actively involved in the formation and development of Collaborative Family Law Associations in Toronto, Peel, Halton, and Hamilton.

About this Book

Collaborative law is a revolutionary new way to practice family law that is spreading like wildfire across North America. It is reframing the experience of separation and divorce for a growing number of families and transforming their lawyers as well.

The traditional process offered to divorcing couples has been the adversarial legal system. Whether or not they eventually wind up in court, negotiations conducted under the implied or overt threat of litigation often inflict personal and financial devastation on families. Despite sincere efforts by lawyers to help, resolution usually comes too late, costs too much, and falls below expectations. The intangible interests of the parties – to preserve relationships with extended family and mutual friends, to co-parent amicably after divorce, to be treated with respect, and to control the process and the outcome – are ignored altogether.

Three decades ago, interest-based mediation was heralded as the answer to the litigation process for families. Indeed, mediation was the first dispute resolution model to recognize the capacity and authority of the parties to determine their own settlements and it continues to be a powerful process option. However, in mediation, the parties work with one neutral facilitator and that approach is not appropriate for everyone. Furthermore, mediated agreements sometimes break down in the hands of lawyers operating in the adversarial paradigm.

In 1990, Stu Webb, a lawyer in Minnesota, spoke out on behalf of divorcing spouses and disillusioned family lawyers. He created an enlightened alternative to the adversarial process that he called Collaborative Law. The concept is simple and profound: tailor the process to the parties, not the other way around, and give lawyers a joint mandate to empower the parties to create their best possible agreement, as they define it.

In the collaborative law process, trained collaborative lawyers represent and support the parties throughout each stage of the process. The parties agree to act in good faith, make full disclosure, put their children first, and consider each other's perspective and interests. Lawyers act as negotiation coaches, information resources, and advocates for the interests of their clients and the integrity of the process. The underpinning of collaborative law is the written agreement between all participants that the collaborative lawyers are retained solely to facilitate the negotiation of a mutually acceptable agreement. If either party decides to go to court, both lawyers are disqualified from further representation.

With the option of drifting to court waived, the creativity and problem-solving skills of all participants are unleashed. Over and over again, collaborative clients confirm the wisdom of Stu Webb's concept by creating customized, *outside-the-box* agreements. Clients take away an improved ability to communicate and co-parent and a process for resolving future issues. They achieve closure of their relationship with dignity, at reasonable cost.

The collaborative process not only benefits clients, it changes the lawyers as well. As we develop the skills and attitude required for effective collaborative practice, we become more self-aware, more skillful communicators and more sensitive to the real needs of our clients. Collaborative Family Law allows us to reconcile our personal and professional values and to discover deep personal satisfaction in our work. Stu Webb is right about something else as well: Collaborative Law is just plain more fun.

The authors of this book have joined the revolution. Designed to complement process and skills training, our purpose is to provide the theoretical and practical knowledge to begin collaborative practice. We do not intend to be prescriptive. There are many ways to do this work effectively and all of us have much to learn. We hope you will find this book a sound beginning.

What do we cover in this book? Parts one and two offer a contextual framework within which to place Collaborative Family Law. In chapter one, we consider the meaning of *collaboration* from related dispute resolution literature. We then contrast two ways to resolve family disputes: the adversarial way and the collaborative way. The paradox of client expectations and experiences encountered in the traditional litigation process is described in chapter two. In chapter three, we offer a brief history of the responses to the problems inherent in the adversarial way and conclude with our own definition of Collaborative Family Law.

In part three, we provide a detailed, phase-by-phase description of the Collaborative Family Law process. We begin with an overview of the process in chapter four. The client-centred approach to interviewing is described in chapter five, as is the conduct of the first client meeting, which focuses on helping the client make an informed choice as to process. In chapter six, we review the two agreements that are fundamental to Collaborative Family Law: the Participation Agreement and the Collaborative

Retainer Agreement. The first contact with the other spouse or lawyer and ideas for effective interaction are considered in chapter seven. Chapter eight focuses on preparing the client to participate effectively in the collaborative process. We conclude this part with a discussion in chapter nine of the settlement meetings and, in particular, the first.

The skills incidental to effective practice are described in part four. We begin with communication skills in chapter ten. We emphasize the importance of questioning and listening within a collaborative environment. In chapter eleven, we review the interest-based negotiation model developed initially by Roger Fisher and William Ury and subsequently refined by the Harvard Negotiation Project. We adapt this process into a seven-step negotiation model for application in a Collaborative Family Law setting. A consideration of appropriate interventions to overcome impasse is the subject of chapter twelve. We discuss what collaborative lawyers can do both at the negotiation table and during private meetings and also interventions by various third party experts and neutrals.

In part five, we describe the application of the Collaborative Family Law process to resolve substantive issues that arise following a separation. We suggest how our seven-step negotiation model might be used to resolve parenting issues in chapter thirteen, child support in chapter fourteen, spousal support in chapter fifteen and property division in chapter sixteen.

We conclude this book in part six with our final thoughts on the way to collaboration. In chapter seventeen we open a conversation with our colleagues about becoming a Collaborative Family Law lawyer, forming a Collaborative Family Law association, creating public awareness of Collaborative Family Law, and collaborating beyond the Collaborative Family Law model described in the book.

The appendices include useful material and precedents to start a collaborative practice, and a sample Collaborative Separation Agreement.

This book could not have been undertaken, let alone completed, without the contributions of others. Stu Webb, Pauline Tesler, and Chip Rose led the way in developing the collaborative law process, instilling passion for this work among lawyers, creating a community of collaborative professionals, and sharing their thoughts about the skills and mindset necessary for excellence in practice. While Richard and Judith are sole practitioners, Victoria is a member of a law firm. She is grateful to her partners for supporting her time away from practice to work on this project and to her former assistant, Kim Agnew, and her current assistant, Rajinder Johal, for their tireless help preparing the manuscript. We express our gratitude to our publisher, Carswell, and in particular, our agent, Fred Glady. His insights and suggestions, as well as his considerable patience with three busy authors were greatly appreciated. In a book about families, it is appropriate that we offer our deepest appreciation to the members of our own families, without whose continuing love and support this book could not have been written: from Richard to his wife, Mary Lou Shields and their daughters, Erin, Alison, Meghan, and Caitlin Shields; from Judith to her husband, Ted Andrews, and her mother, Eileen Ryan; and from Victoria to her husband, Craig Turner and their children, Alexa and Jameson Turner.

Richard W. Shields
rshields@anotherwaymediation.com

Judith P. Ryan
jpmryan@aol.com

Victoria L. Smith
vsmith@lawcan.com

Acknowledgements

In addition to the acknowledgements provided in the endnotes of each chapter, the authors would like to thank the following publishers for material referred to in this book:

Reprinted from Richard E. Walton and Robert B. McKersie: *A Behavioral Theory of Labor Negotiations: An Analysis of a Social Interaction System*, Second Edition. Copyright © (1965) Richard E. Walton and Robert B. McKersie. Introduction © 1991 by Cornell University. Used by permission of the publisher, Cornell University Press.

Reprinted from *The Resolution of Conflict: Constructive and Destructive Processes*, by Morton Deutsch, 1973, Copyright © 1973 by Morton Deutsch, with permission of the publisher, Yale University Press.

Reprinted from *Negotiation Behavior*, Dean Pruitt, Copyright © 1981, with permission from Elsevier.

Reprinted from *Legal Negotiation: Theory and Applications*, Donald Gifford, 1989, with permission of the West Group.

Reprinted from *Disputes and Negotiations: A Cross-cultural Perspective*, P.H. Gulliver, Copyright © 1979, with permission from Elsevier.

Reprinted from *Bargaining in the Shadow of the Law: The Case of Divorce, Yale Law Journal*, Volume 88, Pages 950-997, by Robert H. Mnookin & Lewis Kornhauser, by permission of The Yale Law Journal Company and William S. Hein Company from The Yale Law Journal.

Reprinted from *The Causes of Popular Dissatisfaction with the Administration of Justice, Federal Rules Decisions*, Volume 35, Roscoe Pound, 1906, with permission of the West Group.

Reprinted from *Getting to Yes: Negotiating Agreement Without Giving In*, Second Edition, by Roger Fisher, William Ury, and Bruce Patton. Copyright © 1981, 1991 by Roger Fisher and William Ury. Reprinted by permission of Houghton Mifflin Company. All rights reserved.

Reprinted from *Getting Together: Building Relationships As We Negotiate* by Roger Fisher and Scott Brown. Copyright © 1988 by Roger Fisher and Scott Brown. Reprinted by permission of Houghton Mifflin Company. All rights reserved.

Reprinted from *The Adult Learner*, Fifth Edition, by Malcolm Knowles, Copyright © 1998, with permission from Elsevier.

Reprinted from *The Skilled Facilitator: Practical Wisdom for Developing Effective Groups*, Roger Schwarz, Copyright © 1994 by Roger Schwarz. This material is used by permission of John Wiley & Sons, Inc.

Reprinted from *Barriers to Conflict Resolution*, edited by Kenneth J. Arrow, et al. Copyright © 1995 by the Stanford Center on Conflict & Negotiation. Used by permission of W.W. Norton & Company, Inc.

Reprinted from *Getting Past No: Negotiating Your Way from Confrontation to Cooperation* by William Ury, Copyright © 1991 by William Ury. Used by permission of Bantam Books, a division of Random House, Inc.

Reprinted from Source: *Parents Forever: Making the Concept a Reality for Divorcing Parents and their Children*, Justice Canada, Dept. Of, 1989. Reproduced with the permission of the Minister of Public Works and Government Services, 2003.

Reprinted from *Wrestling with the Model, Collaborative Review*, Journal of The International Academy of Collaborative Professionals, Chip Rose, Copyright © 2002. All rights reserved.

Reprinted from *Resolving Social Conflict and Field Theory in Social Science*. Kurt Lewin, 1997, Copyright © 1997, with the permission of the American Psychological Association.

Table of Contents

APPENDICES

NOTICE TO READER

This Separation Agreement was prepared by two Ontario lawyers in accordance with the laws of the Province of Ontario and a suggested form of agreement offered by the Law Society of Upper Canada. It is presented in this text as a sample agreement negotiated in the course of a Collaborative Family Law case. The authors and publishers accept no responsibility for its use by other lawyers. Canadian lawyers should be aware of the pending decision of the Supreme Court of Canada in *Miglin v. Miglin*, which may affect the content of the future such agreements. The authors and publishers recommend to the parties to a family dispute that they not simply adapt this agreement for their own purposes. They should obtain independent legal advice before signing any agreement of this nature.

Part One:

The First Word

- *Collaboration*

1

Collaboration

- *The Word*
- *The Nature of Collaboration*
- *The Literature*
- *A Synthesis*

THE WORD

We begin with the *Word*. Our word is *collaboration* and it is the subject of this work. The verb, *collaborate*, as a derivative from two Latin roots, is itself a collaboration of words. *Collaborare*, to work together, derives from *com-*, with, and *laborare*, to work. Our English word, *to collaborate*, means to work with.

Collaboration has two faces. For the generation that lived through the Second World War, collaborators were conspirators. Veterans and other survivors of that great conflict recall the betrayal by the Norwegian Minister of War, Vidkun Quisling, the duplicity of the Vichy regime that governed unoccupied France, and all those other war criminals who gave aid and support to the enemy. To the innocent victims of their war crimes, collaboration was treason. It was an abominable act comparable to that of Judas. When we speak of collaboration as working with an adversary in this fashion, we describe one of its two faces only.

We turn to the other face of collaboration in support of our model for another way to resolve family disputes. We collaborate with those with whom we are in conflict not for the purpose of obtaining a beneficial outcome for one party only. Rather, we intend that our collaborative efforts should secure a result that is to the mutual advantage of the parties. The goal of collaborators is not the satisfaction of *self-interest* alone but *other-interest* as well.

THE NATURE OF COLLABORATION

What do we mean by collaboration? To some, working together means no more than engaging in a process in which the disputing parties voluntarily disclose and exchange all of their information and remain civil and respectful toward one another. They refrain from resorting to destructive behaviour and communication. Their discourse is both informative and pleasant. However, each remains steadfast in his determination to secure the best outcome for himself. That it should likewise be beneficial for the other is incidental to his primary purpose. This view of collaboration might more properly be described as *cooperation*. Does collaboration mean no more?

For those disputing parties who recognize that to commence or continue contentious litigation will be disadvantageous to them both, collaboration promises something else. They recognize that self-destruction is antithetical to the objectives of any dispute resolution process. To avoid that outcome, they collaborate to arrive at some mutually acceptable point between their apparently incompatible positions. They seek a *compromise*. The end result will almost certainly be less for each than what was sought and what might have been realized through litigation. Is this all that we intend through collaboration?

Whether we consider collaboration to be synonymous with either cooperation or compromise, it appears to occupy a place at the opposite end of the conflict resolution continuum from *competition*. When we compete, we seek to win and that goal serves to rationalize any strategy or tactics. A more vigorous exchange between competing forces may be referred to as a *confrontation*, an interaction often associated with provocation. Whatever collaboration is, it is neither competition nor confrontation but, its opposite. Are competition and confrontation everything that collaboration is not?

Before we can move ahead to describe this alternative dispute resolution process, we must first be clear as to our understanding of collaboration. Are we talking about something more than cooperation, something other than compromise, and something quite unlike either competition or confrontation? The literature offers guidance. We begin there.

THE LITERATURE

Dominance, Compromise, Integration

Mary Parker Follett, an early contributor to both organization management and conflict resolution, said that "(t)here are three main ways of dealing with conflict: domination, compromise and integration."[1] Domination is self-explanatory. One party uses personal power to prevail over another. The dominant gets everything; the subordinate receives nothing. With compromise, each party gives something to obtain peace or to permit the resumption of whatever activity was suspended or disrupted by the conflict. Both of these ways involve at least one of the parties surrendering something of value in the pursuit of resolution. For Follett, that result is not good enough; she prefers the third way, integration. Integration offers solutions that do not require either party to sacrifice anything.

Follett's words open our discussion of what is found in the literature. Each contributor to this collective scholarship invariably offers choices. In some of these works, the distinctions are framed in terms of social behaviour while, in others, as negotiation strategies or styles. Behaviour suggests a predisposition that will prevail in the absence of some overt exercise of self-control. We may be able to modify or transform these behaviours, although, to accomplish this task is no simple undertaking. Choice is implicit in the selection of an appropriate strategy or style. We may not be able to change our behaviours; they may be transcendent. However, we can choose our strategies and styles and we can do so wisely or poorly. Whatever accounts for our conduct in the course of dispute resolution, distinctive alternative orientations appear in the literature subsequent to Follett's introduction.

Distributive and Integrative Bargaining

Integration is the way preferred by Follett. Richard Walton and Robert McKersie distinguish between *distributive* and *integrative* bargaining.[2] Both are joint decision-making processes. However, the similarity ends here.

"Distributive bargaining is a hypothetical construct referring to the complex system of activities instrumental to the attainment of one party's goals when they are in basic conflict with those of the other party."[3] The goals in conflict may relate either to the allocation of resources or the apportionment of a loss. Game theorists classify distributive bargaining in its purest sense as *zero-sum*: a gain by one party represents a corresponding loss to the other. A fundamental and complete conflict of interest between the parties prevails. This approach may be more appropriate for the determination of single issues and, also, where there is little likelihood of any future relationship between the parties.

"Integrative bargaining refers to the system of activities which is instrumental to the attainment of objectives which are *not* in fundamental conflict with those of the other party and which therefore can be integrated to some degree."[4] These objectives define an area of common concern or a *problem* that requires a *solution*. If solutions to common problems exist which benefit both parties, the conflict is amenable to resolution through integrative bargaining. Within the integrative bargaining paradigm, the discussion is not rooted to the potential for gains and losses as in distributive bargaining. It is not a zero-sum exercise; a gain for one party does not represent an equal loss by the other. Walton and McKersie characterize integrative bargaining as *varying-sum*.

Promotive Interdependance

Morton Deutsch distinguishes between *cooperative* and *competitive* processes.[5] He states that "the crux of the differences between cooperation and competition lies in the nature of the way the goals of the participants in each of the situations are linked. In a cooperative situation, the goals are so linked that everybody 'sinks or swims' together, while in the competitive situation if one swims, the other must sink."[6] For Deutsch, the goals of the participants in a cooperative process must be so linked that any of them can attain his goals. He offers the concept, *promotive interdependence*, to describe the positive correlation between the goal attainments for each of the linked participants.

If we apply Deutsch's definition, cooperation extends beyond the conduct or disposition of the parties within the process. To be candid and informative, civil and respectful will certainly be more conducive to goal attainment by a party. However, for a process to be truly cooperative, it must also bear some relation to the outcomes realized by the participants. It cannot be so if either party fails to attain the objectives sought. Also, when one party behaves so as to increase his chances of goal attainment, the likelihood that the others with whom he is promotively linked will attain theirs as well is increased.

Assertiveness and Cooperativeness

Kenneth Thomas describes five conflict response behaviours.[7] He depicts them in a graph comprised of two dimensions. The vertical dimension represents *assertiveness* or the extent to which an individual attempts to satisfy his concerns. The horizontal dimension depicts *cooperativeness* or the extent to which an individual attempts to satisfy the concerns of the other person. At the axis or point of origin, the individual does not attempt to satisfy either his concerns or the concerns of the other. *Avoiding* is neither assertive nor cooperative.

Competing occupies the position at the extreme end of the vertical dimension. It is assertive and uncooperative. An individual pursues his concerns to the exclusion of those of the other. The outlook of the competitive person is entirely *zero-sum*; he gains in direct proportion to the losses sustained by the other. The extreme of the horizontal dimension is described

as *accommodating*. It contrasts with competing in every way. It is unasser-
tive and cooperative. An individual resolves to respond to the concerns of
the other while neglecting his own.

Any point along a line joining the extremes of the two dimensions
represents *compromising*. Compromising is neither entirely assertive nor
entirely cooperative. The concerns of both parties are satisfied in part. A
compromise may result from an expedient *split-the-difference* approach or
it may represent the best result that either party could hope to achieve in a
contested matter. If the extreme of the vertical dimension is extended hor-
izontally and the extreme of the horizontal dimension is extended vertically,
collaborating appears at the point of intersection. Collaborating is both
assertive and cooperative. The parties endeavor to satisfy the concerns of
both in full.

Competition and Coordination

Dean Pruitt observes that negotiators make demands and grant concessions.[8] He defines *demand level* and *concession rate*. "A bargainer's
demand level can be thought of as the level of benefit to the self associated
with the current offer or demand. A concession is a change of offer in the
supposed direction of the other party's interests that reduces the level of
benefit sought. Concession rate is the speed at which demand level declines
over time."[9] Logically, a lower demand level and a more rapid concession
rate by one or both parties will likely lead to agreement earlier than if the
opposite condition prevails.

Pruitt distinguishes between two negotiation behaviours and his distinction incorporates reference to demand level and concession rate. *Competition* consists of efforts to elicit unilateral concessions from the other
negotiator. Competitive negotiators make high demands. They attempt to
accelerate the concession rates of their adversaries. Their tactics and the
relative effectiveness of them are determined by the credibility of their
commitments. Pruitt offers, by way of example, the use of threats. This
tactic will only produce the intended response if the other party believes
that the party uttering the threats is committed to their implementation if
concessions are not made. Credibility is a function of the reputation of the
bargainer. In the past, has he fulfilled commitments of a similar kind?

Coordination is an alternative to competitive negotiation behaviour
according to Pruitt. When negotiators coordinate their behaviours, they
work together in search of a mutually acceptable agreement. Coordination
occurs in a negotiation when the parties exchange concessions. They may
either move toward one another along a single dimension or they may swap
concessions. It may also take the form of problem-solving discussions in

which they share information with a view toward finding an option that will satisfy the needs of both.

Competitive, Cooperative, and Problem-Solving Strategies

Donald Gifford offers definitions of tactics, strategies, and styles.[10] A *tactic* is "a specific negotiating behavior the lawyer uses when initiating the negotiating exchange with the other attorney or in responding to the other negotiator's behavior" and a *strategy* is "a series of tactics or specific negotiating behaviors that the lawyer uses to facilitate a resolution to the negotiation process that is favorable to her client's interests."[11] *Style* is "the lawyer's personal characteristics in interacting with other people."[12] We can be deliberate and conscious in the choice and development of our tactics and strategies. However, it is not so easy to alter our basic behavioural styles. If we are inclined toward being courteous and cooperative, we can not so easily be rude and competitive. We may be able to imitate other behaviours but only with difficulty and discomfort.

According to Gifford, there are three separate and distinct negotiation strategies: *competitive*, *cooperative*, and *problem-solving*. A *competitive* strategy seeks to undermine the confidence of the other negotiator in his position and thereby enhance a party's position at the expense of the other. The *cooperative* and *problem-solving* strategies are similar in that they both involve the use of *collaborative* negotiation tactics. *Cooperative* negotiators aim to advance their own interests although they believe that to do so they must also construct agreements that are fair and just to both parties. As with their competitive counterparts, they still consider that there is only a fixed quantity of resources to be divided between the parties. *Problem-solving* negotiators attempt to identify and exploit opportunities for joint gain. Gifford claims that a particular strategy will have a predictable impact upon a bargaining relationship. A *competitive* strategy fosters an *adversarial* relationship while *cooperative* and *problem-solving* strategies are conducive to *collaborative* or *accommodative* working relationships.

A SYNTHESIS

If we take this literature as summarized above, are we able to find therein the elements of a definition of collaboration, a *synthesis* that will fulfill our mission in this book?

Our model of collaboration in practice is integrative. Its purpose is to reveal solutions that do not require that either party sacrifice anything of significance to them. We agree with Follett. The proposition that, to achieve resolution each party must give up something, is not good enough. Negotiations need not be zero-sum. The integrative bargaining model described by Walton and McKersie is varying-sum. A gain by one need not mean a corresponding loss for the other. Again, we agree.

We also embrace the concept of promotive interdependence offered by Deutsch. Collaboration proceeds on the basis that there is a positive correlation between the goal attainments of both parties. The efforts of one party to attain his goals will invariably promote the likelihood of the other attaining his as a direct consequence.

The graph provided by Thomas describes best the distinction between collaboration and compromise. He extends the polarities of competition and accommodation to meet at collaboration. At that point, the parties in conflict are deemed to have maximized the interest satisfaction of each of them rather than simply for either of them. It stands in stark contrast to any point along the line of compromise that joins competition and accommodation, where the disputing parties achieve partial satisfaction of their respective interests only. Our collaborators seek the former rather than the latter. Compromise is not consistent with their mission objective.

If we place the goals of negotiators parallel with the descriptive characters assigned by Thomas to each axis of his graph, we might acquire some further appreciation of the collaborative outlook. To resolve most disputes requires achieving an acceptable balance between the resolution of the substantive *issue* in dispute and the maintenance of the *relationship* between the disputing parties The relative importance of each in relation to the other will most often determine the conflict response behaviours of the parties that in turn determine the conflict dynamic. A party will accommodate if he places a greater value upon the relationship than upon the issue. A spouse may defer to his partner on a matter that is a higher priority item for that important other. Similarly, if the importance of a decision on a particular issue outweighs any consideration of the impact it will have upon their relationship, they will be more competitive. With collaboration, the parties seek to resolve the issue while maintaining the relationship.

The coordinative negotiators described by Pruitt anticipate our collaborators. They work together for their mutual advantage. They make concessions not demands. Gifford's differentiation accords with our vision of collaboration. The terms, cooperative and collaborative, are not interchangeable. Negotiators can be cooperative within either of the distributive or integrative paradigms. However, collaboration involves more than simply the pursuit of agreements perceived to be fair and just to both parties. The disputants can do more for themselves than negotiate amicably. Each should be able to maximize the attainment of his goals without diminishing the prospect of the other doing likewise.

We return to the questions that we set for ourselves earlier. While collaboration incorporates all of the qualities of cooperation, it contemplates so much more. The primary focus of cooperation appears to lie with the *process* alone while collaboration addresses the *outcome* as well. Throughout this book, we approach our topic from these two perspectives. Compromise and collaboration are alike in that they both involve the satisfaction of the interests of both parties to a dispute. They differ in the degree to which they accomplish their task. Compromisers achieve partial interest satisfaction for each; collaborators maximize their combined interest satisfaction. Collaboration does not require that either participant forego the attainment of his goals. Collaboration is not accommodation; it does not involve sacrifice. Self-interest and other-interest need not be incompatible. The nature of collaboration is their reconciliation.

It is our premise that collaborative negotiation has the potential for creating the best possible agreements for both parties to a dispute in the best possible way. The purpose of this book is to examine why collaboration holds such promise and how to realize its profound potential.

The First Word

Collaborate – To work with others.
Collaborators are cooperative and more.
Collaborators do not settle for compromise.
Collaborators confront problems, not people.
Collaborators are not competitive.
Collaboration – People working together to solve their problems in a way that works for them.

ENDNOTES

1 Follett, M.P. (1925). Constructive Conflict. In H.C. Metcalf & L. Urwick (Eds.) (1940). *Dynamic Administration: The Collected Papers of Mary Parker Follett*. New York: Harper & Row, Publishers. p. 31.
2 Walton, R.E. & McKersie, R.B. (1993). *A Behavioral Theory of Labor Negotiations: An Analysis of a Social Interaction System* (2nd ed.). Ithaca, NY: ILR Press.
3 *Ibid.* p. 4.
4 *Ibid.* p. 5.
5 Deutsch, M. (1973). *The Resolution of Conflict: Constructive and Destructive Processes*. New Haven CT: Yale University Press.
6 *Ibid.* p. 20.

7 Thomas, K.W. (1976). Conflict and conflict management. In M.D. Dunnette (Ed.) (1976). *Handbook of Industrial and Organizational Psychology*. Chicago, IL: Rand McNally College Publishing Company, 889-935.

8 Pruitt, D.G. (1981). *Negotiation Behavior*. New York: Academic Press, Inc.

9 *Ibid*. p. 19.

10 Gifford, D.G. (1989). *Legal Negotiation: Theory and Applications*. St. Paul, MN: West Publishing Co.

11 *Ibid*. p. 13.

12 *Ibid*. p. 18

Part Two:

Family Dispute Resolution

- *The Adversarial Way*
- *The Collaborative Way*

2

The Adversarial Way

- *Expectations and Experiences*
- *The Adversarial Paradigm*
- *Adjudication and Negotiation*
- *The Adversarial Way Under Attack*

EXPECTATIONS AND EXPERIENCES

Family law is a *paradox* for our clients if we examine it from the parallel perspectives of their *expectations* at the outset and their *experiences* as they proceed. An imperative of judicial interpretation of statutory and case law is that all laws must be deemed *remedial*. The intended purpose of a law is to provide a remedy, to correct an unacceptable state of affairs – to make things better. When spouses separate, the nature of their relationship undergoes a radical change. Separation can be among the most traumatic of human experiences. The lives of the former life partners and those closest to them, their children, are thrown into chaos. The law should provide an accessible process that facilitates an acceptable outcome for their family. The expectations of the process are that it will produce this outcome. What are the experiences?

Expectations of Process

The parties to a family dispute recognize that some form of process is necessary to obtain a resolution of the issues in dispute between them. They seek a restoration of order in their lives and closure to their conflict. Those without any prior exposure with either adjudication or legal negotiation enter the process with certain expectations. There are at least four such goals.

First, clients expect their process to be *economical* and sensitive to their other competing financial needs. Each has a budget and each intends to remain within it if at all possible. In fact, most do not have a choice; their budgets are not sufficiently elastic to accommodate any undertaking at whatever the cost. Second, the parties expect the process to be timely and *efficient*. Once they decide to embark upon a course, they want it to move along at an appropriate pace relative to their other life experiences. Third, they want the process to be *empowering*; they want to be involved. Their active participation is a further expectation. Fourth, clients want the process to be *effective*. It should make a difference. They should arrive at a place fundamentally different from where they started.

Experiences with Process

Regrettably, the experiences of the parties to a family dispute are not always a reflection of their expectations. They incur expenses beyond all measure of reasonable projection. Their lawyers submit legal accounts based upon hourly rates to which the clients are totally unaccustomed. They are billed for all meetings, correspondence, telephone conversations, document preparation, and court attendances, irrespective of any meaningful or measurable accomplishment. In addition, there are the costs to obtain various reports from assessors, appraisers, accountants, and assorted other experts.

The process may extend over a period well beyond what they had expected. With each initiative undertaken by the one, there is the delay in awaiting a response from the other. With every court appearance, there is another to follow that can be weeks or months away. While they are sometimes present with their lawyers, the parties do not participate in a real sense. Rather, they instruct, they listen, they respond, and they react. They are more often like spectators than participants. They are disempowered.

At the end of the process, they often reluctantly accept a compromise. They might well ask the question their lawyers do not want to hear. *What was the point of all this work and expense if this is what we were going to be asked to accept in the end? We could always have resolved the issues in that way.*

Expectations of Outcome

The parties not only have expectations of the process but of the outcome as well. They expect that their lawyers will be able to offer reasonable predictions of what will happen. Again, there are at least four such expectations.

First, the parties have an expectation of *equity* or fairness. Each spouse seeks to be heard and to receive just treatment in accordance with the law. Second, there is an expectation of *enforceability*. Whatever outcome the parties should negotiate or obtain in court, they need the assurance that they can compel compliance with the terms of their agreement or order. Third, the parties expect their outcome to be *exhaustive*, that it will be clear, concise, and comprehensive, and that it will provide sufficient detail of what is expected of them. Finally, those who have been through protracted negotiations or litigation want to believe that it is over when they sign the agreement or receive the order. Their expectation is that the outcome represents an *end* to the process.

Experiences with Outcome

As with the process experiences, outcome experiences rarely mirror expectations. The parties often do not feel heard and they may not perceive the results obtained through the process as fair and equitable. Frequently, they feel that the outcomes unduly favour their spouses. As lawyers, we experience the frustrations of our clients who are unable to enforce the agreements and orders they worked so hard and paid so much to obtain. Instead of the outcome providing answers to all their questions and solutions for all their problems, it may seem too general and insufficiently tailored to meet their unique needs. They are compelled to seek further guidance from their lawyers or the court as to what their agreements or orders mean. Finally, no outcome ever seems to be final. There is no real end. Appeals and variation proceedings often follow in which a displeased party seeks to overturn an outcome previously secured.

Expectations of Process and Outcome

In summary, the parties to a family dispute hold expectations of process that their experiences reveal are often not realized.

1. The process will be *economical*; we will be able to afford it.
2. The process will be *efficient*; we will see movement and progress.
3. The process will be *empowering*; we will play a meaningful role.
4. The process will be *effective*; we will see it make a difference.

They have corresponding expectations that the outcome will possess certain attributes, which, again, their experiences do not always reflect.

1. The outcome will be *equitable*; we will each feel that we have been heard and that we received a fair and just treatment.
2. The outcome will be *enforceable*; we will receive what we negotiated or obtained.
3. The outcome will be *exhaustive*; we will know precisely what to expect and what is expected.
4. The outcome will be the *end*; we will be able to move on with our lives and this will all be behind us.

The disparity between client expectations and their experiences with both process and outcome is the paradox of family law. All too often, it is anything but remedial for those compelled to resort to and rely upon its principles and practices.

THE ADVERSARIAL PARADIGM

A paradigm is a conceptual framework or way in which we view the world. Our system for the resolution of family disputes is set within an *adversarial paradigm*. Family law is a part of a larger whole, the administration of civil justice. The adjudicative process is a fundamental component of that system. The structure of that process is adversarial. The parties are themselves adverse in interest. Each party seeks a favourable outcome that, by inference, is contrary to what is sought by the other. The advocates are adversaries. They are bound by their training and the rules of professional conduct to pursue the interests of their clients, to the exclusion of all others. With this approach to family dispute resolution, the process is adversarial, the parties are adverse, and their advocates are adversaries.

The premise upon which the adversarial approach is grounded is distributive, both as to process and outcome. It assumes that the resolution of a dispute involves the allocation or division of fixed resources. As distributive bargaining is zero-sum, there are *winners* and there are *losers*. This perspective considers the parties in conflict to be incapable of resolving their disputes themselves and assumes that they need lawyers to act as their protectors and champions in the adversarial arena. Their advocates rely upon competitive strategies and tactics. They take high opening demands, they hold back and limit information, they make threats and ultimatums, and they concede little. These lawyers engage in a deliberate program of attrition. They intend to wear down their opponents until they either accept their position or agree to some compromise favourable to their side. The proponents of an adversarial approach conduct themselves with the rationale that, to achieve what is best for their clients, they have no alternative.

ADJUDICATION AND NEGOTIATION

P.H. Gulliver states that there are only two generic dispute resolution processes: *adjudication* and *negotiation*.[1] "The crucial distinction then, between adjudication and negotiation, is that the former is a process leading to unilateral decision-making by an authoritative third party, whereas the latter is a process leading to joint decision-making by the disputing parties themselves as the culmination of an interactive process of information exchange and learning."[2] The degree of *control* exercised by the disputing parties in the decision-making process distinguishes one process from the other. With adjudication, there is far less control over the process than in negotiation.

Adjudication

A family law court proceeding begins with the issue of an originating process, a statement of claim or a petition for divorce. The originating process is served upon the other party, who must respond within a specified number of days. The respondent usually denies the factual allegations and the relief sought by the applicant and makes her own counter claims. At the outset of the proceeding, the lines are drawn between the two sides to the dispute. They are disputants; they are adversaries. One claims from the other who in turn denies the claims made. Each takes a position hostile to that of the other. There is no acknowledgment of any common purpose between them.

Early in a family proceeding, one or both of the parties may claim immediate relief by way of a motion. In this pre-trial proceeding, the evidence is limited to affidavits submitted by each party. Affidavits are often among the most incendiary of documents prepared for submission in a family law process. For the lawyers, effective motion advocacy demands that nothing relevant be omitted, however harmful it may ultimately be to the already tattered relationship of the parties. Some lawyers interpret this practice as a license for hyperbole and exaggeration. Affidavits are rarely restrained either in substance or in tone. Whatever the intention of the draftsperson and the deponent, affidavits are extremely one-sided. They inflict pain, they decrease the level of trust, and they escalate the level of conflict between the parties.

The lawyers may elect to conduct oral examinations of the parties upon their affidavits. In those interrogations, each of them seeks to draw out admissions and information from the other party beneficial to his or her client and damaging to the other side. While lawyers may ask any question on a subject relevant to the issues in dispute, they are careful in what they allow their own clients to provide. *Answer what you must but offer no more than what is required of you to comply.* Examinations at examiners' offices are combat zones, particularly if accusations and harsh language appear in the affidavits. They are not comprehensive information-exchange sessions. The advocates are quite deliberate in the development of their examination strategies and the deployment of their examination tactics.

On the return of the motion, the presiding judge hears argument from counsel and afterwards makes a decision. One of the lawyers prepares the order to be issued by the court and enforced. Invariably, the decision contains provisions that are partially or totally unacceptable to one or perhaps both parties. One or both of them will have lost on some critical issue. That sense of defeat can be pervasive. It may taint the remainder of the process to follow. The successful party attempts to hold onto what has been gained while the other seeks redemption for what has been lost.

In family proceedings, the lawyers are required to provide and obtain full particulars of the incomes and expenses, assets and liabilities of the parties. Production of exhaustive financial disclosure is an ordeal for clients. Many documents are unearthed and assembled – often without regard to their usefulness in addressing the issues in dispute. In particular, the financial statements required under the rules of civil procedure are ponderous. To compile and collate the data required to complete them requires a considerable expenditure of time and effort.

Prior to the trial, the parties and their lawyers appear before a judge on a pre-trial or settlement conference. Briefs are prepared and submitted. Each lawyer sets out the strengths of his or her case and exposes the weaknesses of the positions taken by the adversary. This conference is intended to offer a preview of what might occur in court; it is rarely a mediation. If a settlement is not negotiated, a trial date is set.

In the course of the trial, the rules of evidence prescribe a formal process to be followed by the lawyers and the court. A trial claims to be a search for truth, to determine which party is right and which is wrong. Despite this purpose, each lawyer attempts to limit the information received by the judge to that which supports his or her client's legal claims and, in turn, damages the position of the other. A lawyer attacks her opponent's credibility and character, further diminishing the possibility of a future relationship between the parties. On the basis of a limited amount of information, presented in an artificial setting, the judge makes a decision. She must limit her purview to the evidence tendered and apply the law to the facts so found.

A trial is in every respect a contest. There is no search for a mutually acceptable resolution of the disputed issues or even any common ground on anything. The lawyers may do whatever they consider appropriate and persuasive provided that they remain within the ethical framework of their code of professional conduct. They must pursue vigorously the interests of their respective clients to the exclusion of all else. Their mission is to win.

Negotiation

The adjudicative process would soon break down if all disputing parties chose to take their matters to trial. In fact, the vast majority of disputes are not resolved in this way. Approximately ninety-five per cent of all civil actions are resolved prior to trial. Most claims are resolved without the commencement of a court proceeding.

Negotiations may be undertaken in the course of an adjudicative proceeding already commenced. More often, litigation is clearly anticipated should the negotiations fail. In either event, it is likely that negotiations will assume the same adversarial character. Each lawyer has previously informed his or her client of the applicable law and his or her legal rights. This information provides the framework within which a negotiation takes place. What the parties have been told as to the likelihood of what a court might award determines their respective bargaining *positions*. The law casts its shadow over the negotiation.[3] In effect, the parties negotiate as they adjudicate. Negotiation, whether within a court proceeding or in anticipation of the possibility of litigation in the event of impasse, is imbued with the characteristics of the adversarial paradigm.

Gulliver describes two *processual models of negotiation*: a *cyclical model* and a *developmental model*. "One is the model of the repetitive, cyclical interaction between two negotiating parties, briefly characterized as the exchange and manipulation of information. The other is a model of the development of interaction from the initiation of a dispute to the conclusion of an agreed outcome."[4] We offer a summary of his developmental model, which is what we believe most lawyers contemplate as they embark upon a negotiation.

At the opening of a negotiation, each of the parties outlines his or her underlying complaints and demands. They articulate their initial positions on each of the issues. These early statements tend to represent the maximal limits of their preferences rather than a realistic assessment of their expectations. They do not comprise the real demands that they will ultimately make. At this point in the negotiation, the information each provides is likely incomplete and inconsistent. The parties are still exploring the extent of the bargaining range. They do not want to restrict themselves to particular courses of action or to narrow the range of their options. The parties attempt to extract greater precision and commitment from each other. They advocate their strengths and expose the weaknesses of their adversaries.

As the negotiation proceeds, the parties turn from what divides them to how they might come together. They may at first be tentative with their commitment to cooperation. Eventually, one of the parties makes a real offer on one or more of the issues. By a real offer is intended a possible outcome as opposed to an expression of that negotiator's preference set. The other party may respond with a counter-offer that may well be a modification of her earlier demands. On any single matter, there lies the potential for impasse. Where there are multiple issues to resolve, the task for the parties is far more challenging.

The parties search for a viable bargaining range of outcomes that are acceptable in preference to no agreement at all. Each of them may have to set aside or abandon those of lesser importance to move the negotiation along on matters of greater significance. One offers to reduce her demands on one issue in return for concessions by the other.

Often, what will ensue is bargaining by concession making and incremental convergence toward some point of agreement. The process may be as simple as marketplace haggling. More often, it is more complex. The parties may be dealing with multiple issues and criteria and, as such, they make concessions on different attributes and different issues. At some point, they may decide to take the easy route. In desperation, they may simply split the difference or take a neat round number. The irony of this final resort to a simple expedient is that it was always an available recourse from the outset of the negotiation.

If the negotiation breaks down or the negotiators reach impasse on one or more significant issues, the parties consider their alternatives: to give in or to give up control of the outcome of their dispute to a third party, either a judge or an arbitrator.

THE ADVERSARIAL WAY UNDER ATTACK

Awareness of the problems inherent in the adversarial paradigm is not new. On August 29, 1906, Roscoe Pound, later dean of Harvard Law School, addressed the American Bar Association assembled that day at the State Capitol in St. Paul, Minnesota. He drew the attention of his audience to the unique qualities of the Anglo-American adjudicative process. Of foremost concern to Pound was its contentious character.

> A no less potent source of irritation lies in our American exaggeration of the common law contentious procedure. The sporting theory of justice, the "instinct of giving the game fair play," as Professor Wigmore has put it, is so rooted in the profession in America that most of us take it for a fundamental legal tenet. But it is probably only a survival of the days when a lawsuit was a fight between two clans in which change of venue had been taken to the

forum. So far from being a fundamental fact of jurisprudence, it is peculiar to Anglo-American law; and it has been strongly curbed in modern English practice. With us, it is not merely in full acceptance, it has been developed and its collateral possibilities have been cultivated to the furthest extent. Hence in America we take it as a matter of course that a judge should be a mere umpire, to pass upon objections and hold counsel to the rules of the game, and that the parties should fight out their own game in their own way without judicial interference. We resent such interference as unfair, even when in the interest of justice. The idea that procedure must of necessity be wholly contentious disfigures our judicial administration at every point. It leads the most conscientious judge to feel that he is merely to decide the contest, as counsel present it, according to the rules of the game, not to search independently for truth and justice.[5]

Pound was no less critical of judicial organization and procedure. He described the system of courts as "archaic" and the procedure as "behind the times." "(U)ncertainty, delay and expense" not only discourage litigants but encourage "a deep-seated desire to keep out of court, right or wrong, on the part of every sensible business man in the community."[6]

In their seminal work on negotiation, *Getting to Yes*, Roger Fisher, William Ury, and Bruce Patton are as critical of traditional negotiation practice, which they call *positional bargaining*.[7] Positional bargaining is a process in which each party "takes a position, argues for it, and makes concessions to reach a compromise."[8] The inherent weakness of positional bargaining is that the negotiators lock themselves into positions which impedes progress toward a solution. Positional bargaining is inefficient. The parties begin with extreme positions and make small concessions. Significant time and effort is consumed in the process. Finally, positional bargaining is potentially destructive of relationships.

The response of some negotiators to the frustrations of positional bargaining is to opt for a more gentle style of negotiation or, put simply, to be *nice*. They see their adversaries as friends. They want to make agreements with them; they are not looking for victories. Are negotiators limited to a choice between soft or hard positional bargaining? Ultimately, the hard positional player prevails. "If the hard bargainer insists on concessions and makes threats while the soft bargainer yields in order to avoid confrontation and insists on agreement, the negotiating game is biased in favor of the hard player."[9]

Where two competent and effective positional bargainers negotiate and are committed to finding a settlement, they will most often move toward a mutually acceptable place somewhere between their opening offers. If those conditions do not prevail and neither party is prepared to capitulate, they may encounter an insurmountable barrier. An impasse of this kind may drive the negotiators toward adjudication, the process they were attempting to avoid, or they may instead opt for some face-saving, split-the-difference expedient settlement.

As a result of the gap between expectations and experiences with which we opened this chapter, clients and, in increasing numbers, lawyers as well, are no longer satisfied with the adversarial way. They seek another way – the Collaborative Way.

The Adversarial Way

Expectations and Experiences

Process of

Economical
Efficient
Empowering
Effective

Outcome

Equitable
Enforceable
Exhaustive
The End

The Adversarial Paradigm

The parties are adverse in interest.
The lawyers are adversaries.
The process is adversarial.

Adjudication and Negotiation

Adjudication is a form of warfare.
Negotiation in the shadow of the law leads
to entrenchment in bargaining positions.

ENDNOTES

1 Gulliver, P.H. (1979). *Disputes and Negotiations: A Cross-cultural Perspective*. New York: Academic Press, Inc.
2 *Ibid.* pp. 6-7.
3 Mnookin, R.H. & Kornhauser, L. (1979). Bargaining in the shadow of the law: the case of divorce. *Yale Law Journal*. 88:950-997. New Haven, CT: Yale University Press.
4 Gulliver, *supra.* p. 65.
5 Pound, R. (1906). The causes of popular dissatisfaction with the administration of justice. *F.R.D.* 35:273-291. St. Paul, MN: West Publishing Co. p. 281.
6 *Ibid.* p. 284.

7 Fisher, R., Ury, W., & Patton, B. (1991). *Getting to Yes: Negotiating Agreement Without Giving In* (2nd ed.). New York: Penguin Group Penguin Books USA Inc.
8 *Ibid.* p. 3.
9 *Ibid.* p. 8.

3

The Collaborative Way

- *A Paradigm Shift*
- *Alternative Dispute Resolution*
- *Mediation*
- *Principled Negotiation*
- *Collaborative Family Law*

A PARADIGM SHIFT

According to Thomas Kuhn, man assembles principles of understanding conceptually into frameworks or *paradigms*.[1] Aristotle's *Physica* and Newton's *Principia* are examples of paradigms that, for a time, provided a basis for observing and comprehending phenomena within their spheres of inquiry. These works were unprecedented and they attracted their adherents. Afterwards, others within the same discipline sought to fit new problems within those paradigms to find the solutions there as well. If a paradigm fails to provide answers to questions asked within it, the inquirer faces a dilemma. Is the familiar paradigm no longer valid or applicable? A challenge to an existing paradigm may strike at the core beliefs of the believer. The development and acceptance of an entirely new paradigm will often require a quantum leap of faith that, for many, will be difficult to make.

A paradigm shift occurs when a traditional approach is no longer capable of responding to all of the demands placed upon it. Either the problems remain unattended or another way must be found. Pound identifies the inherent deficiencies of the Anglo-American adjudicative model and Fisher, Ury, and Patton describe the pitfalls of positional bargaining. To overcome the problems associated with our adversarial tradition requires that we approach dispute resolution in an entirely different way. We must prepare ourselves to experience a paradigm shift.

ALTERNATIVE DISPUTE RESOLUTION

The Judicial Conference of the United States, the Conference of Chief Justices, and the American Bar Association jointly sponsored the *National Conference on the Causes of Popular Dissatisfaction with the Administration of Justice*. The conference was held on April 7-9, 1976 in St. Paul, Minnesota at the same site where Pound delivered his historic address seventy years earlier. The conference was named the *Pound Conference* in recognition of the continuing impact of the principles articulated by him.

The Chief Justice of the United States, the Honorable Warren E. Burger, delivered the keynote address. He defined the objective of the conference.

> Our task, then, once we review what has gone before, is to reexamine the "map" Pound drew, to assess the direction of the roads he laid out, and to consider whether we need, not just to tighten "nuts and bolts," but to begin work on the design of some new – even radically new – "vehicles" to take us where we want to go in the years ahead.[2]

Burger urged the delegates to probe for fundamental changes and major overhaul rather than simply "tinkering."

In his submission to the Conference, Frank Sander asked,

> 1) What are the significant characteristics of various alternative dispute resolution mechanisms (such as adjudication by courts, arbitration, mediation, negotiation, and various blends of these and other devices)?

> 2) How can these characteristics be utilized so that, given the variety of disputes that presently arise, we can begin to develop some rational criteria for allocating various types of disputes to different dispute resolution processes?[3]

Sander may have been the first person to employ the phrase, *alternative dispute resolution*, hereafter referred to as *ADR*.

Sander describes "the spectrum of the available processes on a scale of decreasing external involvement."[4] At the extreme left, he places adjudication, which includes court adjudication, arbitration, and administrative process. Mediation and conciliation appear to the right of adjudication. These processes also involve third parties but they do not have any decision-making capacity. Negotiation appears to the right of the third party intervention processes. It possesses a singular advantage over the others as it allows the parties to retain and exercise complete control over both the process and the outcome. Whenever the disputants involve a third party, they cede some of their authority over the process to the intervenor and, ultimately, they may assign the power to a third party to make the final decision.

Five criteria for selecting the appropriate process supplement Sander's ADR spectrum: the nature of the dispute, the relationship between the disputants, the amount in dispute, cost, and speed. Sander advocates "a flexible and diverse panoply of dispute resolution processes, with particular types of cases being assigned to differing processes (or combinations of processes), according to some of the criteria previously mentioned."[5] He states that by the year 2000 there will not simply be a court house but a *Dispute Resolution Center* at which a screening clerk will channel grievants to the process most appropriate for their cases.

In his Annual Report on the State of the Judiciary before the mid-winter meeting of the American Bar Association in Chicago on January 4, 1982, *Isn't There a Better Way*, Burger reminds the bench and the bar of the messages of the Pound Conference.[6] He speaks of the excessive costs and delays associated with litigation. He cautions his audience about the other destructive effects of the competitiveness of the courtroom. The adversarial contest distracts individuals and businesses from the pursuit of their personal and commercial activities. Burger challenges the members of the business and legal communities to use their inventiveness, ingenuity, and resourcefulness to shape new tools and to use other available techniques. He reminds lawyers of their traditional obligation, to serve as *healers of conflict*.

Frank Sander and Stephen Goldberg consider the questions that should be asked in making the determination as to which of the available processes to choose.[7] The parties to a dispute have goals that predispose them more to one process than another. If they seek to minimize costs, to obtain early resolution, to preserve privacy, and to maintain and improve their relationship, they will likely opt for mediation or negotiation. However, if their goals are to obtain vindication, to set precedent, and to maximize or minimize recovery, court is the proper forum.

MEDIATION

ADR represents a response to the inadequacies of the adjudicative model. Mediation is found within that spectrum of processes. Christopher Moore defines mediation in his book, *The Mediation Process*.[8]

> Mediation is an extension or elaboration of the negotiation process that involves the intervention of an acceptable third party who has limited or no authoritative decision-making power. This person assists the principal parties in voluntarily reaching a mutually acceptable settlement of the issues in

dispute. As with negotiation, mediation leaves the decision-making power primarily in the hands of the people in conflict. Mediation is a voluntary process in that the participants must be willing to accept the assistance of the intervenor if he or she is to help them manage or resolve their differences.[9]

Mediation was heralded as a favoured alternative to adjudication for family law cases. However, experience has shown that mediation is not appropriate for every situation. In some instances, the parties do not feel sufficiently safe or self-confident to proceed without their lawyers being present.

In most jurisdictions, lawyers do not attend mediation with their family law clients and do not participate directly in the mediation process. Clients who reach agreement in mediation attend upon their lawyers for independent legal advice before mediated agreements are ratified and concluded. At this juncture, mediated agreements can break down. Lawyers who have not participated in the negotiation may not comprehend the interests that the agreement was intended to satisfy. Without the benefit of counsel, the parties may have mediated without fully understanding their legal entitlements. The promise of mediation is not always realized in practice.

PRINCIPLED NEGOTIATION

Fisher, Ury, and Patton ask the question that confronts all negotiators: whether to bargain soft or hard. They respond with an unequivocal "neither." Negotiators should instead change the game. Fisher, Ury, and Patton offer *Principled Negotiation*. They do not actually define their model. Rather, they list their *Four Basic Points of Principled Negotiation*.

People: Separate the people from the problem.
Interests: Focus on interests, not positions.
Options: Generate a variety of possibilities before deciding what to do.
Criteria: Insist that the result be based on some objective standard.[10]

Principled negotiation combines conceptual originality with the elements of the integrative bargaining model earlier described by Walton and McKersie.

Principled negotiation provides an alternative to positional bargaining as ADR presented a spectrum of choice for those who seek to avoid adjudication. The two developments are complementary. Indeed, the mediation literature endorses principled negotiation as the preferred problem-solving approach. Mediators facilitate principled negotiation in practice.

COLLABORATIVE FAMILY LAW

Most family disputes are resolved through negotiation, whether or not court proceedings are commenced. The lawyers may engage in positional bargaining. Some practise principled negotiation. Others refer their clients to mediation, which they may attend on their own. If they are successful, they return to their lawyers for independent legal advice. Most often, these processes are conducted in the shadow of the law. Clients want their lawyers involved but they do not want to find themselves locked into an adversarial contest.

Stuart G. Webb is a sole family law practitioner in Minneapolis. Remarkably, the other of the twin cities, St. Paul, is the site at which Pound delivered his historic address. Like Pound, Webb had become frustrated with the traditional approach. He asked himself whether there was another way to resolve family disputes. Webb and a small number of local colleagues declared their intention to offer an alternative, *collaborative law*. They established the first collaborative law association. What is it they offered?

Webb describes their collaborative law approach.

> Collaborative law is a way of practicing law whereby the attorneys for both of the parties to a dispute agree to assist in resolving conflict using cooperative strategies rather than adversarial techniques and litigation. The commitment to working collaboratively is reflected in an agreement between both attorneys and their respective clients that, should settlement efforts break down, the attorneys will withdraw and not participate in actual proceedings.[11]

Within a relatively short period of time, the idea took root elsewhere. Soon there were collaborative law associations in several of the states of the United States and some of the western provinces of Canada.

Pauline Tesler is another family law practitioner who found the collaborative way. She also provides a definition of this process.

> Collaborative law consists of two clients and two attorneys, working together toward the sole goal of reaching an efficient, fair, comprehensive settlement of all issues. Each party selects independent collaborative counsel. Each lawyer's retainer agreement specifies that the lawyer is retained solely to assist the client in reaching a fair agreement and that under no circumstances will the lawyer represent the client if the matter goes to court. If the process fails to reach agreement and either party then wishes to have matters resolved in court, both collaborative attorneys are disqualified from further representation.[12]

Of significance beyond the commitment of lawyers and their clients to a negotiated settlement is the nature of the negotiations themselves. The negotiators do not engage in positional bargaining. They adopt the principled or interest-based negotiation model. Within the process, collaborative law negotiators utilize many of the same communication skills that mediators commonly use.

What are the common elements of this process that are consistent with our earlier discussion of collaboration and which resolve the dilemmas characteristic of the adversarial approach to family law process and outcome? First, the parties and their lawyers work together. Second, they agree that litigation will not be commenced while the process is ongoing and, to take the negotiations out from under the shadow of litigation, they agree that should they be unable to resolve the dispute, neither of the lawyers will be eligible to represent the parties in any subsequent litigation. Third, the negotiation process they follow is not adversarial. The parties apply the principled negotiation alternative. Fourth, with the facilitative skills of the lawyers to guide them, the parties communicate in a way that promotes the attainment of their mutual goals.

We offer this definition of *collaborative family law*.

> Collaborative family law is a dispute resolution process in which the parties and their lawyers commit themselves to the realization of a negotiated outcome. They agree that litigation will not be commenced while they are negotiating and that, in the event they are unable to negotiate a resolution of their dispute, neither lawyer will be eligible to represent his or her client in any subsequent litigation. In the process itself, the participants communicate to promote the maximum exchange of information, to reveal all concerns of the parties, to generate an array of creative ideas, and, ultimately, to agree upon the terms and conditions of a mutually acceptable settlement that satisfies the interest of both parties.

Those who practice collaborative family law no longer accept the assumptions and principles that underlie the adversarial paradigm. Experienced family litigators know all too well the turmoil and devastation experienced by their clients in contested divorce. We recognize that courts are not the appropriate forum for resolving family disputes, which are as much about feelings and relationships as legal issues. An adjudicative process that appears to be less effective today than before is a source of frustration for all lawyers. Many are alarmed by an emergent lack of civility among adversaries in the arena.[13] Others are weary of a process model that leaves them feeling disconnected from their personal values and drained by their clients who are often unhappy despite their best efforts and the results they obtain. For all of these reasons, lawyers are increasingly seeking another way to resolve family disputes, to restore satisfaction and pride in their work, to be appreciated for their efforts, and to provide a process and outcome of real value to their clients.

To become a practitioner of this approach requires a paradigm shift, a quantum leap for some, from adversarial to collaborative. It requires a radical change in our assumptions about the nature of conflict, the capacity of individuals to resolve their differences, our perception of our role as lawyers and our relationship with our clients, how we measure our success, and how we deliver the services we provide. It requires that we adopt new processes, attitudes, and skills, as we redefine the meaning of advocacy for our clients.

Lawyers who embrace the collaborative process become settlement specialists, leaving matters that must be adjudicated to litigation specialists. Collaborative negotiation is challenging and honourable. It restores integrity and value to the practice of law for those who feel alienated from it. Collaborative lawyers rediscover enjoyment and satisfaction as they heed the call of Chief Justice Burger to return to their role as *healers of conflict*.

The Collaborative Way

A Paradigm Shift
FROM Adversarial Adjudication and Negotiation
TO Alternative Dispute Resolution:
A Spectrum of Other Processes
AND TO Mediation:
A Negotiation Facilitated
by a Neutral Third Party, a Mediator
AND TO Principled Negotiation:
An Interest-based alternative
to Positional Bargaining
AND NOW TO Collaborative Family Law:
A Client-centred Interest-based Negotiation
Facilitated by Lawyers

Collaborative Family Law
Collaborative family law is a dispute resolution process in which the parties and their lawyers commit themselves to the realization of a negotiated outcome. They agree that litigation will not be commenced while they are negotiating and that, in the event they are unable to negotiate a resolution of their dispute, neither lawyer will be eligible to represent his or her client in any subsequent litigation. The participants communicate to promote the maximum exchange of information, to reveal all concerns of the parties, to generate an array of creative ideas,

and, ultimately, to agree upon the terms and conditions of a mutually acceptable settlement that satisfies the interest of both parties.

ENDNOTES

1 Kuhn, T.S. (1996). *The Structure of Scientific Revolutions* (3rd ed.). Chicago, IL: The University of Chicago Press.
2 Burger, W.E. (1976). Agenda for 2000 A.D. – need for systematic anticipation. *F.R.D.* 70:83-96. St. Paul, MN: West Publishing Co. p. 85.
3 Sander, F.E.A. (1976). Varieties of dispute processing. *F.R.D.* 70:111-134. St. Paul, MN: West Publishing Co. p. 113.
4 *Ibid.* p. 114.
5 *Ibid.* pp. 130-131.
6 Burger, W.E. (1982). *Isn't There a Better Way?* Washington, DC: ACR formerly SPIDR.
7 Sander, F.E.A. & Goldberg, S.B. (1994). Fitting the forum to the fuss: a user-friendly guide to selecting an ADR procedure. *Negotiation Journal.* 1:49-68. New York: Kulver Academic/Plenum Publishing Corporation.
8 Moore, C.W. (1996). *The Mediation Process: Practical Strategies for Resolving Conflict* (2nd ed.). San Francisco, CA: Jossey-Bass Inc., Publishers.
9 *Ibid.* p. 8.
10 Fisher, Ury, and Patton, *supra*, pp. 10-11.
11 Webb, S.G. (1996). Collaborative law – a conversation: why aren't those divorce lawyers going to court? *The Hennepin Lawyer.* August 1996:26-28. p. 26.
12 Tesler, P.H. (1999). Collaborative law: what it is and why family law attorneys need to know about it. *American Journal of Family Law.* 13:215-225. San Francisco, CA: Aspen Law & Business. p. 219.
13 Chief Justice of Ontario Advisory Committee on Professionalism, Working Group on the Definition of Professionalism (2001), *Defining Professionalism*.

Part Three:

The CFL Process

- *A Process Overview*
- *The First Client Meeting*
- *The Agreements*
- *First Contact with the Other Lawyer*
- *Client Preparation*
- *The Settlement Meetings*

4

A Process Overview

- *A Significant Undertaking*
- *Procedure and Process*
- *Principles of CFL*
- *Assumptions of CFL*
- *The Stages*

A SIGNIFICANT UNDERTAKING

To become a Collaborative Family Law practitioner requires that a lawyer make a radical shift in the way in which she practises law. Pauline Tesler describes the challenge for lawyers.

> In terms of malpractice prevention, professional responsibility, and "truth in advertising," it is the premise of this manual that no one should engage in collaborative representation without understanding that doing this work well requires undoing a professional lifetime of conscious and unconscious habits, and requires rebuilding from the bottom up an entirely new set of attitudes, behaviors, and habits. To do this work well, we must become beginners, and unlearn a bundle of old automatic behaviors before we can acquire the new, more conscious attitudes, behaviors, and habits of a good collaborative lawyer.[1]

The contemplated transformation is a significant undertaking.

In this chapter, we begin with an overview of the collaborative process. Throughout the remainder of this book, we refer to Collaborative Family Law as *CFL*, an acronym that is increasing in popularity as practitioners acquire greater familiarity with the process.

PROCEDURE AND PROCESS

For lawyers accustomed to the traditional approach to the resolution of family disputes, *process* is synonymous with *procedure*. Adjudication functions in accordance with a procedure fixed by statute and regulations as refined by judicial interpretation. The prescribed rules of practice and the law of evidence are not discretionary. Trial judges and litigation counsel are bound to observe and follow them. The parties are deemed adverse in interest. Each of their lawyers must pursue single-mindedly the rights of his or her client. There is no legal requirement for the lawyer to consider what the opposing side might need in order to resolve the dispute. The rules of engagement reflect this adversarial approach.

To be clear, we offer a definition of these terms. A *procedure* is a particular way of doing something, a sequence of steps to be followed. A *process* is a series of continuous actions to bring about a particular end or condition, a forward movement, a continuing development involving many changes. Procedure does not define process although it can lend a character to it. In the adversarial model, the formal rules of procedure formalize the process. Process, however, is a broader and more holistic concept than procedure. It incorporates procedure but it is not limited by it.

CFL is a process. Unlike adjudication, the procedure is not pre-determined by rules or statutes. Rather, it is up to the parties and their lawyers to decide how they will proceed. One of the key roles of CFL lawyers is to help the parties design a process that fosters the clearest decision making and most effective problem solving for *them*.

The CFL process is organic. It evolves over time, in response to the unique perspectives and priorities of the parties. The parties, guided by their lawyers, make decisions about their process as they proceed. Together, the lawyers and the parties are the participants. Throughout the remainder of this book, we use the term *participants* to describe all of them and the term *parties* in reference to the clients only.

CFL is designed to enable the participants to act as effectively as possible to maximize the outcomes for both parties. An effective CFL lawyer is constantly mindful of how the process is working for her client *and* for the other party. The lawyers in a CFL case involve both clients in all aspects of the decision-making process, as well as in the substantive outcomes. With CFL, the process is as important as the outcome.

PRINCIPLES OF CFL

The principles of the CFL process are as follows:

- *Team approach* – The lawyers and the clients work together as a team of equals, all pulling together on the same side of the problem.

- *Court is not an option* – Neither lawyer can commence a legal proceeding or threaten to do so during the CFL process. This provides an incentive for the lawyers and their clients to keep working together to find acceptable solutions and unleashes creative, *out of the box* problem solving. The team may include neutral experts when needed.

- *Recognition of the interdependence of the parties* – There is a shared belief that the best possible outcome can only be achieved if the needs and interests of both parties are met. Clients are not expected to agree with each other, but to accept that the other, along with his or her perspective and belief system, is a necessary partner in creating a solution.

- *Focus on interests* – Collaborative negotiations are interest-based, rather than adversarial. The parties exchange information and consider all available options before choosing the best solution to meet their identified interests.

- *Law is not the only standard* – Although CFL lawyers inform their clients about their legal rights and obligations, they encourage the parties not to limit themselves to outcomes dictated by the law.

- *Process and outcome are of equal importance* – In collaborative negotiation, the parties seek to understand and to be understood. The lawyers, in consultation with the parties, bear responsibility for creating a respectful, effective negotiation process. The parties own the outcome.

ASSUMPTIONS OF CFL

While the adversarial approach assumes that people in conflict do not have the capacity to make their own decisions, CFL assumes that most people in conflict can, with proper support, make decisions for themselves. They do not need either their lawyers or a judge to decide matters of importance for them. It is recognized that conflict, particularly about important personal issues, usually causes people to feel weak and self-focused and diminishes their capacity to make good decisions. However, CFL lawyers provide the parties with support and guidance to enable them to regain the capacity to think for and beyond themselves.

The nature and degree of support provided by a CFL lawyer to her client will depend upon a variety of factors, including the client's personality type, emotional state, cognitive abilities, education, and expertise, as well as the nature and complexity of the issues and the level of conflict between the parties. Clients may need help to voice opinions and concerns, to understand complex information, to deal with feelings of guilt, hurt or anger, and to appreciate the legal landscape.

Individual meetings may be necessary to allow the clients to vent strong emotions and to allow lawyers to *reality check* the clients' stated objectives when they diverge widely from accepted legal options and the objectives of the other spouse. For example, a client who appears angry about the obligation to pay spousal support in a long-term relationship needs to clearly understand that indefinite support is customary after lengthy, traditional marriages, where there is a need by the other spouse. In this situation, the dependant spouse's interest in her future financial well-being and clear legal entitlement to ongoing appropriate support are congruent. A CFL lawyer may convene an individual meeting with her client or take a break from the settlement meeting to have a brief discussion of this kind of issue. It provides the client with an opportunity to express strong feelings without harming the working relationship between the parties, and to negotiate realistically around the issue in question.

Whether client support is provided in the settlement meetings in the presence of all participants or by way of an individual meeting with the client is a question of judgment. While lawyers work together as a team in an atmosphere of transparency, it is also critically important that the lawyer maintains the client's dignity, allows her to *save face*, and maintains her trust and confidence. Such is the art and balance of collaborative negotiation.

Traditional negotiations conducted in the adversarial arena, cooperative as they may be, assume that the law dictates the outcomes available to the parties. Some lawyers and clients have tremendous difficulty letting go of the notion that results must comply with a statute and legal custom. The CFL process gives the parties, not their lawyers or the law, the right and responsibility to create their own outcomes. CFL lawyers encourage their clients to treat an outcome based solely upon statutory or case law as one option among many, to be assessed in terms of its ability to meet the interests of the parties in the best way possible.

THE STAGES

In general terms, the CFL process involves a progression through a series of stages. While they are sequential, there is nothing to prevent the participants from *looping back* to an earlier phase if they reach an impasse. However, it is extremely important that all stages take place and that none are skipped or glossed over. For example, for the CFL process to work well, it is essential that the client be properly prepared prior to participating in the first settlement meeting. Similarly, one cannot omit a discussion of the parties' individual and common interests before looking at settlement options.

We offer a summary overview of the stages in the remainder of this chapter with a more detailed analysis in the chapters that follow.

Stage One: The First Client Meeting

The process begins with an initial meeting between the client and her lawyer. The lawyer listens to the client's concerns and reviews process options. If the client has not yet made any decisions as to process, CFL is presented as one option for the client to consider, along with mediation and the traditional legal approach including litigation. The purpose of this discussion is to screen for appropriateness for CFL, and to help the client make an informed choice as to the most appropriate dispute resolution process for her.

If the client has already chosen CFL, the process may be discussed, questions answered and the Retainer Agreement signed. Afterwards, the lawyer may inquire of the client's interests and objectives and provide an overview of her legal position. The scope and duration of this discussion is subject to time considerations as well as avoidance of *information overload*. A comprehensive review of process may be all that a client can absorb during this first meeting.

Stage Two: First Contact with the Other Lawyer

Once both parties commit to the CFL process, one of the lawyers initiates contact with the other, preferably by telephone or a meeting as opposed to the traditional exchange of letters. At this early stage, the lawyers begin the team approach. They identify any urgent concerns for both parties and agree to exchange whatever preliminary disclosure is necessary to deal with those issues. The lawyers then arrange the first settlement meeting. They might conduct a *run-through* of that meeting to ensure that it will proceed smoothly.

Stage Three: Client Preparation

Before the first meeting, each lawyer has an in-depth, client-centred discussion with her client, to understand not only the facts of the case but also to learn what the client really wants. The lawyer explains the client's legal rights and obligations as one of many settlement options.

The lawyer prepares her client to participate effectively in the CFL process. They review the principles and assumptions of CFL. They discuss the respective roles of the lawyers and the clients and how they contrast with a more traditional, lawyer-dominated approach. They consider the protocol for effective participation and communication in the settlement meetings. Finally, the lawyer explains the various stages of the CFL process and, in particular, the settlement meetings at which they rely upon interest-based negotiation to resolve the issues.

Stage Four: The First Settlement Meeting

The lawyers welcome and introduce the participants. One of the lawyers reviews the highlights of the Participation Agreement and all of the participants commit to the CFL process orally and in writing. With the lawyers facilitating their discussion, the clients agree to the behavioural guidelines that will govern them in the process. The participants then turn their attention to any immediate concerns. An agreement on urgent matters at this stage contributes to the momentum of their problem-solving efforts.

An important task at the first settlement meeting is the identification and prioritization of the issues that each party would like to resolve. The lawyers begin to elicit the interests, concerns, and objectives of each party. The participants determine the information and documents that they require. They agree upon the time frames for the exchange of this information, assign homework tasks, and schedule dates for the next settlement meeting and those that are to follow.

Following the first settlement meeting, the lawyers debrief with their respective clients and with each other. They should continue these practices before and after each subsequent settlement meeting to flag and resolve problems and keep the process moving smoothly.

Stage Five: Subsequent Settlement Meetings

During the meetings that follow, the parties work together to resolve each of the issues. They identify their interests and objectives; analyze the information; develop as wide a range of possible options for settlement as possible; and move incrementally toward a comprehensive settlement agreement. An outcome that maximizes the satisfaction of the parties' common and individual interests is their goal. Toward that end, the participants may choose to involve third party experts or a neutral mediator to help them overcome impasses.

Stage Six: Settlement and Closure

The CFL lawyers prepare a written settlement document collaboratively, using language chosen by the clients wherever possible, and reciting the principles, assumptions, and rationale upon which their agreement is based. Ideally, all of the participants convene at a final meeting to review and sign the Separation Agreement and bring closure to the CFL process.

A Process Overview

CFL is a process determined by the parties, with the assistance of their lawyers, rather than by rules of procedure, which process evolves over time.

Principles

The parties and their lawyers take a team approach.
Court proceedings may not be commenced.
The parties are interdependent.
The focus is on interests and not positions.
The law is only one option.
Process and outcome are of equal importance.

Assumptions

Divorce is a normal life process for many people.
Most people in conflict have the capacity
to make decisions for themselves.
Lawyers can best assist their clients by providing them
with the support to enable them to do so.
Interest-based negotiation can produce better
outcomes than court connected negotiation or litigation.

Stages

The First Client Meeting
First Contact with the Other Lawyer
Client Preparation
The First Settlement Meeting
Subsequent Settlement Meetings
Settlement and Closure

ENDNOTES

1 Tesler, P.H. (2001). *Collaborative Law: Achieving Effective Resolution in Divorce without Litigation*. Chicago, IL: ABA Publications. p. 24.

5

The First Client Meeting

- *The Adversarial Way*
- *A Client-Centred Approach*
- *The Collaborative Way*
- *Screening*

THE ADVERSARIAL WAY

Lawyers and their clients are accustomed to a particular approach in the conduct of family law proceedings. Typically, the client initiates the contact by telephoning the lawyer's office at a time of marital crisis, to make an appointment. There is a shared expectation as to the nature of their first meeting. They meet to discuss the client's problems, facing each other across the lawyer's desk.

Following the courtesies that typically accompany introductions, the lawyer asks the client to describe the problem. As the client tells his story, the lawyer seeks details of a particular kind in order to place the information received into a legal compartment. He requests a history of the marriage and the reason for the marital breakdown in anticipation of a divorce proceeding. In matters involving children, the lawyer seeks particulars of the care provided by the parents and the responsibilities assumed by each of them. Support claims require information about the education, employment history, and income of each spouse. Details relating to the acquisition and valuation of the assets and liabilities of the parties are necessary to determine property issues.

Rather than *open-ended* questions, which allow the client to chart the course of the meeting, the lawyer asks *closed* questions that are narrow and focused. At this early moment in their professional relationship, the lawyer is already beginning to identify the critical components of a legal claim. He has no doubt experienced many similar such cases over the course of his practice and he may already have some preconceived notion as to how this new matter will unfold. The lawyer's perspective is almost exclusively legal.

At the end of the first meeting, the lawyer may offer a preliminary legal opinion with respect to the client's legal rights and obligations. He will probably initiate the process of data collection by informing the client of the documents required for the support and property claims. If there is any discussion of process options to resolve the marital dispute, it may not be held until the end of the initial interview by which time the client may be experiencing information overload. In most cases, the lawyer will offer to initiate contact with the other spouse or his lawyer if known. It is common to write a formal letter requesting the exchange of sworn Financial Statements and supporting documentation. In cases of perceived urgency, it is not uncommon for a lawyer to commence legal proceedings.

A process discussion of this kind might proceed as follows:

LAWYER: I suggest that I write to your wife telling her that I have been retained by you and asking her to meet with a lawyer who will then contact me. Usually, we then exchange letters in which we request Financial Statements and other documents.

CLIENT: What happens while we're putting all of that together?

LAWYER: Your wife's lawyer will likely propose that she have possession of the house while you continue to pay all of the household bills. You don't have to agree – in fact, you should stay in the house until we have resolved the children's issues.

CLIENT: Sounds pretty tense. After we get all of the papers together, do we meet with them?

LAWYER: Possibly. If the other lawyer and I feel that there is a reasonable chance of reaching agreement, we may decide to have a meeting. If so, I will call you.

CLIENT: What happens then?

LAWYER: We may have a four-way meeting. Generally, we set aside a half-day or more and the meeting will be held in one of our boardrooms.

CLIENT: What happens if we don't settle things there?

LAWYER: Either you or your wife can start a court proceeding. Even then, you will probably settle somewhere along the line. Few cases actually go all the way to trial

CLIENT: So, if we don't agree at the four-way meeting, how long do you think that it will be before she takes me to court?

LAWYER: You could be served with court documents within two or three weeks. Once served, we will have twenty days to prepare your response. If your wife tells her lawyer that she needs an order for custody and support immediately, she may bring a motion for an interim order. The motion would probably be heard in about one to three months. After this, several more months will pass before we appear before a judge on a settlement conference. If it doesn't settle there, a trial date will be set. You shouldn't expect a trial date any earlier than one year from when the court proceeding was started.

CLIENT: From what you've said, it sounds like you're going to have to do a lot of work for me. What will this cost?

LAWYER: I can't project your total legal expenses at this stage. It's far too early. My hourly rate is $280 and I bill my clients for all services including meetings, correspondence, telephone conversations, preparation of documents, pre-trial examinations, legal research, and, of course, time spent at court.

CLIENT: What is the worst I can expect?

LAWYER: It's impossible to predict the cost of litigation, but if there were to be a trial extending over three days, which is what I would expect in your case, the total could be more than $40,000.

CLIENT: You're scaring me. I don't have that kind of money. I have to think all of this over. What do I have to do now?

LAWYER: You should start to work on the Financial Statement and gather the other documents we need. I also require that you sign my standard Retainer Agreement and provide me with a cheque in the amount of $5,000 before I start to work on your file. Call my secretary within a week to schedule an appointment.

A client consults a lawyer for the express purpose of obtaining a legal opinion and advice as to what he should do. While information may be provided as to the applicable substantive law and the adjudicative procedure, there are no doubt other interests that may not be addressed if the initial consultation is conducted this way. Moreover, at the end of this first interview, the client may well feel shell-shocked by all that the lawyer has said. He receives a substantial amount of information, quite likely more than he could reasonably absorb. The lawyer asks him to obtain several documents and to prepare a legal form. Finally, the client must provide a great deal of money before the lawyer can start to work for him. Neither the process nor the outcome seems to offer him much hope. Is there another way to conduct a first meeting with a client? The CFL process begins here.

A CLIENT-CENTRED APPROACH

David Binder, Paul Bergman, and Susan Price offer an alternative that preceded and yet seemed to anticipate the arrival of CFL.[1] They begin by distinguishing the *legal* from the *nonlegal* dimensions of a client's problem. They identify four clusters of nonlegal consequences that may result from the resolution of the legal issues.

First, there are the *economic* ramifications. The potential costs of legal representation may adversely affect the quality of life of a person long after the issues are resolved. Second, the *social* impact of contentious proceedings alerts the disputing parties to the damage both the process and the outcome may have upon their relationship. Third, the *psychological* effects of unresolved conflict can be determinative of whether a party will continue with the pursuit of his cause. For some, negotiation and litigation can be extremely stressful while others are quite accustomed to these processes. Finally, there are the *moral*, *political*, and *religious* values that may be challenged. Parties may be asked to make choices that they are unable to reconcile with who they really are.

Every solution to a legal problem produces nonlegal consequences. Binder, Bergman, and Price describe the prominence of the nonlegal dimensions of problem solving. They begin with the proposition that even the most beneficial outcome will attract nonlegal costs along the way. In a contested custody proceeding, for example, a mother may be successful in her claim but, as a result, the father feels resentful. He may become less reliable both in terms of assuming his share of the parenting responsibilities and also contributing to the support of the children beyond what he is ordered to pay.

The choice of one set of positive consequences over another, inherent in choosing from among the available courses to follow, requires that the client make a difficult decision. The opinion of the lawyer as to the likelihood of success at trial will not necessarily be persuasive. An outcome obtained at trial has consequences for the client. He must ask whether these are more positive than what he might have attained through some other process. The problem is compounded if the choice is not between outcomes with positive nonlegal consequences, but, rather, alternatives with only negative nonlegal consequences. Either is capable of causing some damage; the client must choose that which will produce the least amount of harm.

As difficult as it is for a lawyer to predict the outcome of a trial, it is often even more problematic for the client to project upon these other nonlegal consequences. They may be the primary factors in determining the choice to be made by the client. It is paradoxical that the opinion of the lawyer on those matters for which he is best able to offer an opinion and make a recommendation are often secondary in the mind of the client who must make the decision. The lawyer may not be the most qualified person to assist the client with a problem where the nonlegal consequences are predominant.

Binder, Bergman, and Price recommend a *client-centred* approach as an alternative to the traditional interview. Rather than attempting to fit the client's problem within a familiar legal doctrine with an accompanying process to obtain a predictable outcome, the lawyer seeks an understanding of the problem as experienced by the client. An underlying assumption of a client-centred approach is that the client is the expert as to his economic, social, and psychological needs. The lawyer recognizes that every client problem is a composite of both legal and nonlegal concerns. Furthermore, there is the *affective* impact as well as the *cognitive* data to be ascertained. It is not just the *facts* that are important. How this client *feels* about what has happened is also significant. Together, the lawyer and the client diagnose the problem, formulate the solution, and prescribe the process that will achieve that outcome. This client-centred approach has its advantages. Binder, Bergman, and Price identify six attributes that distinguish it from the traditional approach.

First, the lawyer helps identify problems from a client's perspective. Considerable variance prevails among individuals as to their prioritization of the nonlegal dimensions previously discussed. For some, the economic are the most persuasive while, for others, moral, political, or religious values are paramount.

Second, the lawyer actively involves the client in the process of exploring potential solutions. This attribute is a necessary corollary to the first. Any prospective solution must respond to what the client indicates is of primary importance to him. Furthermore, there will no doubt be several options available. The client will want to select options that satisfy as many of his concerns as possible.

Third, the lawyer encourages the client to make decisions that are likely to have a substantial legal or nonlegal impact. The client is the best judge of what is best for him. The client-centred approach recognizes that he must remain the primary decision maker. The lawyer facilitates the solution-selection process; he does not own it – the client does.

Fourth, the lawyer provides advice based on a client's values. The client comes to the lawyer for advice and the client-centred approach does not minimize the importance of this service. Rather, it expands upon it. The advice-giving aspect of a lawyer's work should incorporate reference to the actual needs of the client he is seeing at that moment and not others previously seen with their own unique circumstances.

Fifth, the lawyer acknowledges the client's feelings and recognizes their importance. As with values, any client's emotions represent his or her response to the problem not that of some hypothetical or objectively determined other person. Emotional reactions are most often more significant than the events that precipitated the dispute. A solution that does not respond to the feelings of the client will not find ready acceptance no matter how consistently and logically it applies the law to the facts.

Sixth, the lawyer repeatedly conveys a desire to help. By making this client, with all of his needs, concerns, values, and emotions, the centre of attention, the lawyer invariably sends a clear message: *I am here to help you find the solution to your problem.*

THE COLLABORATIVE WAY

CFL endorses and adopts the client-centred approach. Indeed, it is a core element of the CFL process. With this approach, the lawyer broadens his perspective beyond the legal problems faced by the client to incorporate the nonlegal dimensions of his problems as well. The lawyer and the client together prescribe the process to be followed to arrive at solutions that take into account both the facts and the feelings of the client. With this approach, the client is the primary decision-maker, not the lawyer. The lawyer facilitates the client's decision making process.

During the first client meeting, a CFL lawyer explains the various dispute resolution process choices available to the client: litigation, traditional lawyer-to-lawyer negotiation, mediation, and CFL. The client will no doubt have many questions. Some of the anticipated questions concerning CFL are found in Appendix "A".

How is this collaborative approach applied in practice during that crucial first meeting? We envisage three scenarios:

Scenario One: The client consults the lawyer without any clear idea of the process which he wishes to adopt in order to resolve the issues, or even any idea that there are process options available;

Scenario Two: The client consults a CFL lawyer in response to a request from his spouse who wishes to pursue this option;

Scenario Three: The client would like to use a CFL lawyer, but his spouse has consulted a litigation lawyer who does not practise CFL.

Scenario One: Neither Spouse Has Yet Retained a Lawyer

In this situation, the focus of the first meeting with the client is upon process alternatives available to resolve the matrimonial dispute. In contrast to the traditional first meeting, where a discussion of process comes at the end of the consultation, process options are explained early in the meeting, before the lawyer embarks upon any extensive fact-finding or gives any advice with respect to the client's legal entitlements and obligations.

The lawyer first obtains a sense of the client's major concerns and objectives, immediate and long term, and his current situation. While so doing, he attempts to respond to the client's emotional state through *active listening*, a communication skill we consider in chapter 10. The lawyer then informs the client that he has a choice of several process options to resolve the issues: mediation with a neutral third party; traditional legal negotiation between lawyers with the possibility of litigation in the event of impasse; and CFL. Each option is described in terms of the overall structure of the process, the roles of the participants, the basis of decision making, the anticipated costs, and the prospective time frame for completion. The lawyer gives the client sufficient information to allow him to select the process that best meets his needs. At the same time, the lawyer obtains sufficient information to determine whether this client and this case are appropriate for CFL.

If the client expresses an interest in the CFL process, the lawyer provides him with an information package, which should include a brochure on CFL, a list of other CFL lawyers in the area and their contact numbers, articles on the CFL process, and websites which can be accessed for additional information. To inform the client's spouse of the CFL option, an information package can be mailed or delivered by the client to the other spouse along with a covering letter inviting her to participate in the process.

The following dialogue is an example of how a CFL lawyer might conduct a first meeting with a client who has not yet made any decisions about process.

LAWYER: You are at an important juncture, at the beginning of your separation. You have three choices as to process – the way that you want to resolve your separation issues.

CLIENT: I didn't realize I had choices about process. What are they?

LAWYER: One process option is mediation. In mediation you and your wife meet with the mediator, a neutral third party who will assist you with your negotiations. If you reach agreement in mediation, you bring the terms of the proposed agreement back to me for independent legal advice before any agreement is finalized.

CLIENT: Won't you be with me at mediation?

LAWYER: During the mediation process, I serve as your consultant and provide you with legal advice, as you need it. I don't usually attend the mediation sessions.

CLIENT: I'm not sure that I'm comfortable with that.

LAWYER: Another option is traditional negotiation between lawyers acting on behalf of you and your wife. If negotiations break down, either of you could commence a court proceeding to have the matters resolved by a judge. The results achieved in this process usually reflect what the law provides.

CLIENT: I don't want to go to court. Is there any other way?

LAWYER: Yes, there is. It is called Collaborative Family Law or CFL. If you and your wife choose this process, you, your wife, and your lawyers will sign a Participation Agreement. Under this agreement, neither of you can go to court while we are negotiating. If the negotiations break down and either you or your wife decides to go to court, both CFL lawyers are disqualified from acting.

CLIENT: Why can't we use the same lawyers? What's the point behind that?

LAWYER: We lawyers tend to go to court when we don't agree. In CFL, there is a total commitment to finding a settlement acceptable to you and your wife. Everyone's focus is on reaching agreement, not preparing for court.

CLIENT: I thought you said earlier most cases don't go to trial. What's the difference here other than I might have to hire two lawyers instead of just one?

LAWYER: The negotiations that we have in mind are entirely different. First, we do everything together in meetings of the four of us. At those meetings, you and your wife make the decisions about what it is you want to talk about and what information you need to make decisions. Your lawyers are there to help you but we do not take over the process. Second, we don't negotiate as two separate forces on opposite sides of the table. The four of us work together as a team. Finally, at the end of the day, you and your wife make the final settlement decisions. Again, your lawyers are there to provide you with legal advice and help you negotiate effectively, but we don't try to talk you out of something that you believe will work for you.

CLIENT: What's the down side of this way?

LAWYER: The greatest risk is that CFL may not succeed and you would then have to find another lawyer. That would involve additional expense and delay. It's important to be sure that you and your wife are both committed to finding solutions that work for both of you.

CLIENT: What's the up side?

LAWYER: This process takes far less time to initiate and complete. We should be able to do all of our work within a matter of months. Most cases take about three to five joint meetings, although there can be more if the issues are complex or communication between you is challenging. You and your wife make the important decisions. Your relationship is more likely to be preserved and perhaps even improved through your participation in a collaborative as opposed to an adversarial process. You'll keep control over the costs and results.

CLIENT: It sounds like a great approach. What's it going to cost me?

LAWYER: My hourly rate is $280. I bill my clients for the actual time devoted to the work. You will be with me on most occasions when I am working for you. In a court proceeding, there is often a great deal of wasted time preparing court documents that may never be read and dead time waiting to be heard by the judge. With CFL, there is no wasted time. While the costs vary depending on the complexity of the issues and the emotional dynamics between the parties, in most cases, legal expenses are generally in the range of $3,000 to $12,000 with the average being about $6,000 for each person.

CLIENT: If I choose CFL, what do I do next?

LAWYER: Here is my letter explaining the process, our local CFL association brochure, and my Retainer Agreement and Participation Agreement. You might also want to check out the website mentioned in the brochure. It has more information and a list of lawyers here who are trained in the practice of CFL.

CLIENT: I'm really interested in this process. I guess my wife has to agree.

LAWYER: Yes, she does. Feel free to share these materials with her. She can call me or a CFL lawyer for more information about the process. If both of you want to go ahead, let me know and I'll contact your wife's lawyer to arrange a meeting right away.

A suggested information letter to be provided to the client at the end of the first meeting is found in Appendix "B".

Scenario Two: Client's Spouse Wishes to use CFL

The client who decides to proceed with CFL may instruct the lawyer to write a letter to his spouse. Sample letters are found in Appendix "C". If the client has been asked to consider CFL by his spouse, the collaborative process should be reviewed with the client and the client's questions answered. If the client confirms an interest in pursuing CFL, the lawyer asks the client whether there are issues that need to be addressed without delay. He obtains enough information, with open-ended questions, to ascertain the client's immediate circumstances and needs, both substantive and psychological. The lawyer provides the client with a legal framework for the negotiation. While he explains to the client that the parties may choose outcomes different from or in addition to those provided by the law, the client must be informed as to his legal rights and obligations.

The lawyer agrees to initiate contact immediately with the other lawyer, to set a date, time, and place for the first settlement meeting and begin the CFL process. If the client indicates his willingness to commit to the CFL process, they may begin their preparation for the first settlement meeting. We discuss this aspect of the process in chapter 8. If there is insufficient time remaining in their first meeting for preparation, the lawyer schedules another appointment for this purpose. Throughout all of these meetings with the client, the lawyer follows the client-centred approach.

Scenario Three: Client Wants CFL but the Spouse has already retained a Lawyer who is not a CFL Lawyer

In our view, the CFL process cannot be followed unless both lawyers are qualified to conduct the process. The lawyer should refuse to enter into a Participation Agreement with another lawyer who has not been trained in CFL. As we discussed earlier, collaboration means something more than being cooperative. An untrained lawyer will not have the required knowledge of the process and may lack the mindset and skills to engage effectively and successfully in CFL.

In this situation, we recommend that the CFL lawyer work cooperatively with the other lawyer, use a client-centred approach, consider the interests and needs of both parties in formulating settlement proposals, and participate in four-party settlement meetings communicating and negotiating in a collaborative way. While this will not be a CFL case, it may be the next best thing to it.

SCREENING

Obviously, it takes two to collaborate. If one party is not willing to participate in a cooperative, problem-solving way, then the other must either capitulate to his demands, adopt a similar competitive, *win-lose* approach, or abandon the process. A collaborative client who discloses sensitive information may be prejudiced if the other side does not make reciprocal disclosure. A collaborative client may experience a profound sense of failure if the CFL process does not result in an agreement. He is then put to the delay and additional cost of retaining another lawyer to act in the adversarial arena.

To protect against these risks, it is essential to screen clients to assess whether they are suitable for the CFL process. Lawyers must determine whether the prospective client has, or can develop, the capacity to participate effectively in the CFL process. Clients must share a similar commitment to work *with* rather than *against* the other for mutually acceptable results. They must demonstrate an acceptance of the fact of their separation, the willingness to manage or learn to manage their emotions, an interest in the well-being of the other side, and a commitment to an honourable divorce process. They must value the benefits of maintaining their relationship, of taking a long-term view of the issues, and of retaining control over their own solutions.

Clients who wish to prove a point, punish or control the other spouse, enforce legal rights, or establish legal precedent are not suitable for this process. A client who refuses to make temporary arrangements to support a dependant spouse pending negotiations, equivocates on providing full disclosure, or unreasonably delays in starting the process is likewise not appropriate. A client who does not believe that the other spouse will ever provide honest disclosure or negotiate in good faith is not suitable for the process.

Individuals who suffer from serious drug or alcohol abuse, who have clinical issues, who are unwilling to take responsibility for their own choices, or who have difficulty following through with commitments made must be scrutinized carefully at the outset to determine whether sufficient support can be put in place to allow effective participation. If a lawyer is in doubt about any of these matters, he may wish to enlist the services of a therapist or experienced CFL lawyer to help screen for appropriateness or decline to recommend CFL.

Some CFL lawyers have a thorough understanding of the dynamics of domestic abuse and sufficient experience with this issue to enable them to manage the process effectively where spousal abuse has occurred and the abused spouse wishes to pursue CFL. Such a lawyer can ensure that the abused spouse is capable of asserting her needs and that appropriate protocols and ground rules are in place to create a safe environment for negotiation, both at and away from the table. He understands the psychodynamics of the abuser and the abused spouse and can ensure balanced negotiations. With a properly skilled lawyer, CFL may provide the best option for resolution for an abused spouse in cases where mediation and adjudication are not appropriate. However, lawyers who do not have sufficient experience with domestic violence may wish to refer that client to another CFL counsel or recommend traditional lawyer-to-lawyer negotiation.

There is likely to be a wide divergence of views as to which clients may be appropriate for CFL. Some lawyers believe that any properly informed client has the right to choose the process. Other lawyers assume an obligation for thorough screening and determination of appropriateness for CFL on behalf of the client. We recommend that CFL lawyers only enter into collaborative cases with clients and counsel with whom they feel confident. As the skill level of the lawyer increases, he may take on clients who present greater challenges in terms of their capacity.

CFL lawyers chosen by the parties must also assess whether they have the capacity to collaborate together. They may have a poor track record of working together and there may be a low level of trust between them. If a lawyer believes that he will have difficulty working with the CFL lawyer selected by the other client's spouse or partner, he should address this issue directly with the other lawyer. They should talk about their working relationship. They might consider retaining a mediator or CFL consultant to be paid by them.

Alternatively, a lawyer could refer a client to another CFL lawyer who might feel a greater level of comfort working with the other spouse's lawyer. Also, CFL is not the only process choice available to lawyers who would like to work together and avoid litigation. They could agree to follow the CFL model of collaborative behaviour but decline to enter into a CFL Participation Agreement.

Participation in the CFL process does not preclude the clients from later pursuing arbitration or litigation if negotiations break down. Even if they should so proceed, they may still have derived some benefits from their CFL experience. It may have improved their ability to communicate, streamlined the exchange of documents and information, and achieved a resolution of some of the issues, leaving only unresolved matters for adjudication or arbitration.

The First Client Meeting

A Client-Centred Approach

The lawyer elicits the client's legal and nonlegal concerns. The nonlegal dimensions of a client's problem include economic, social, psychological, moral, political, and religious concerns.

The Collaborative Way

Use a client-centred approach during the first client meeting.
Recognize that the client is the final decision maker on process and outcome.
Inform the client of the available process choices and the relative advantages and disadvantages of each.
Assist the client in making the decision as to the process that is most appropriate to meet his or her needs.
Screen for cases and clients appropriate for CFL; clients and lawyers must have process capability and commitment.

ENDNOTES

1 Binder, D.A., Bergman, P., & Price, S.C. (1991). *Lawyers As Counselors: A Client-Centered Approach* (2nd ed.). St. Paul, MN: West Publishing Co.

6

The Agreements

- *CFL Agreements*
- *The Retainer Agreement*
- *The Participation Agreement*

CFL AGREEMENTS

As indicated in the preceding chapters, there are two agreements prepared and signed to initiate the CFL process: the Retainer Agreement and the Participation Agreement. The first is a contract between the lawyer and her client alone while both lawyers and their clients sign the second as the participants. Over the course of the process, the participants may enter into other agreements with third parties and, at the conclusion, the parties may sign either or both of a Parenting Plan and Separation Agreement.

We limit our consideration to the Retainer Agreement and the Participation Agreement. Sample agreements are found in Appendices "D" and "E". In this chapter, we focus our discussion on those provisions of these agreements that represent a significant departure from traditional family law practice.

THE RETAINER AGREEMENT

While it is wise for lawyers to require clients to execute retainer agreements in all matters, it is essential in the collaborative process. All retainer agreements set out the lawyer's duties and responsibilities to the client and her fees and financial policies. The CFL Retainer Agreement differs from the traditional in some significant ways.

The CFL Retainer Agreement acknowledges that the client and lawyer agree to the terms and conditions set forth in the CFL Participation Agreement to be signed by the participants at the first settlement meeting. An executed copy of that agreement will be attached to the Retainer Agreement. At an earlier point in their relationship, the lawyer will have provided a copy of the Participation Agreement to the client for her review and responded to any questions concerning it. By attaching this agreement as a schedule and incorporating it as part of the Retainer Agreement, the lawyer does not have to provide a detailed description of the CFL process.

Questions arise in respect of a lawyer's obligations under the rules of professional conduct and the restrictions voluntarily imposed under the Participation Agreement. Foremost among these are her undertaking not to commence a court proceeding while a CFL process is ongoing and her disqualification as legal counsel in the event that the process is terminated. The rules require that the lawyer, as advocate, represent the client resolutely and honourably within the limits of the law. While the rule does impose a duty to pursue all appropriate remedies zealously and vigorously, it does not preclude a lawyer and her client from agreeing upon some limitation on such proceedings as will be undertaken.

The choice of CFL by a client is only made after her lawyer has sufficiently informed her of the process alternatives. The rules of professional conduct require that the lawyer encourage her client to compromise or settle a dispute whenever it is possible to do so on a reasonable basis. She is also to consider the use of alternative dispute resolution for every dispute. A decision to proceed with CFL is consistent with both of these professional obligations.

The Retainer Agreement provides that the lawyer will withdraw in the event that litigation is commenced, irrespective of who institutes proceedings or for whatever reason an action is begun. Many lawyers limit the scope of their work on behalf of their clients in disputed matters to negotiation. With the knowledge and consent of their clients, they refer files to litigation counsel once it becomes necessary to commence or defend an action in court. This practice does not contravene the rules of professional conduct and, in fact, it continues a traditional dichotomy of practice between the work performed respectively by solicitors and barristers. To that extent, CFL does not represent a departure from convention.

Beyond the litigation restriction, the Retainer Agreement must also clearly express how collaborative representation and negotiation is different. The CFL process requires that the lawyer and client undertake to negotiate in good faith and make full, voluntary disclosure of information that is relevant and important. The Retainer Agreement acknowledges that the lawyer, as well as the client, is bound by these undertakings and that she must withdraw in the event of a breach by the client. The Retainer Agreement further provides that, if withdrawal is required, the lawyer will ensure that her file is transferred to new counsel in an orderly fashion.

The Retainer Agreement should state the grounds upon which a lawyer may exercise her right of withdrawal. These may include misrepresentations by the client as to any matter relevant to the issues in dispute, the refusal of the client to disclose material information or documents, and client behaviour that is contrary to or inconsistent with her obligations under the Participation Agreement. The rules of professional conduct address the issue of withdrawal. A lawyer shall not withdraw her representation of a client except for good cause and upon notice to the client that is appropriate in the circumstances. If the client deceives her lawyer as to her willingness to abide by the terms of the Participation Agreement or there is a serious loss of confidence between the lawyer and the client as a result of the lawyer's requirement that she observe those terms, the lawyer may withdraw consistent with the rules of professional conduct.

THE PARTICIPATION AGREEMENT

Place in the Process

The Participation Agreement is the most important document in CFL. It describes in clear, straightforward language the collaborative law process and the undertakings that the lawyers and the clients assume when they make their commitments. A lawyer provides a copy of the Participation Agreement to her client when CFL is first discussed as a process option. They review it again during preparation as a preliminary to participation. The participants go over the Participation Agreement at the outset of their first settlement meeting to ensure that both clients fully understand what they are agreeing to do. All participants should publicly commit to the observation of its provisions. The Participation Agreement may be attached to the Separation Agreement to clarify the process used in arriving at the agreement.

Commitments

Participation Agreements generally contain the following commitments:

1. To settle the outstanding issues in a non adversarial manner using interest-based negotiation;
2. To rely upon their lawyers solely to assist them in reaching a mutually agreeable settlement;
3. To act in their children's best interests, to promote a positive, caring

relationship between the children and both parents, to use their best efforts to minimize any emotional damage to the children as a result of the separation, to avoid discussion of the separation issues in the presence of the children unless both agree, and to refrain from making any unilateral changes to the residence of the children;

4.   To ensure that all written and verbal communications are respectful and constructive during the settlement meetings, and elsewhere, and to agree not to take advantage of any errors made by the other side;

5.   To make full, voluntary disclosure;

6.   To retain neutral experts if they are needed;

7.   To reduce any temporary agreements to writing and execute them, which agreements may be converted into court orders in the event of withdrawal from or termination of the CFL process;

8.   To the grounds and procedure for withdrawal from or termination of the CFL process; and

9.   To not dispose of assets, alter life or health insurance coverage, or make any other unilateral changes during the process without the consent of the other.

The Participation Agreement concludes with an acknowledgment that the CFL process may not be successful, that each lawyer has a professional duty to represent his or her own client, and that he or she is not a lawyer for the other party.

Withdrawal or Termination

If a client behaves dishonestly or in bad faith, a lawyer's withdrawal from or termination of the CFL process is required. Bad faith behaviour includes refusals to provide full disclosure, unreasonable delays, breaches of temporary agreements, unilateral action to the detriment of the other party, persistent disrespect toward the other participants, and withholding of necessary funds to the dependant party required to meet living expenses or to pay legal fees during the process.

Some lawyers express the concern that withdrawal or termination for bad faith compromises the obligation to the client and that it may constitute a breach of the lawyer and client privilege. A notice of withdrawal or termination implicitly suggests that the client may have done or intends to do something contrary to the provisions of the Participation Agreement. This ethical dilemma is really no different than when a trial lawyer seeks to be removed from the record on the basis that she is unable to obtain instructions from her client. Neither the trial judge nor opposing counsel may ask for an explanation. The same logic applies to CFL.

A question arises as to when withdrawal as opposed to termination is appropriate. All CFL associations do not necessarily address this practice issue in the same way. It is imperative that their members resolve this matter so that it is clear as to what is expected from practitioners in these circumstances. Withdrawal is not an adequate remedy if the client simply retains another lawyer who sanctions the client's behaviour. In our view, the Participation Agreement should provide clearly that negotiating in bad faith or dishonestly requires that party's lawyer to terminate the CFL process. Withdrawal is appropriate in the event that the client fails to pay legal fees under the terms of the Retainer Agreement, the working relationship between the client and lawyer is not effective, or the client wishes to retain a new CFL lawyer.

Confidentiality

The Participation Agreement must also clearly deal with confidentiality, an issue paramount to CFL. The parties agree that all communications made and all information exchanged within the process are confidential and made without prejudice. If subsequent litigation occurs, the following conditions apply:

1. Neither party will introduce as evidence in court information disclosed during the CFL process, except documents otherwise compellable by law including any sworn statements as to financial status made by either party;
2. Neither party will introduce as evidence in court information disclosed during the CFL process with respect to either party's behaviour or legal position with respect to settlement;
3. Neither party will request or compel either lawyer to attend court to testify in any court proceedings or request or compel either lawyer to attend for an examination under oath with regard to matters disclosed during the CFL process;
4. Neither party will require the production in any court proceedings of any notes, records, or documents in the lawyer's possession; and
5. Neither party will introduce as evidence any report or notes or documents prepared by a neutral expert retained by the parties in the CFL process unless the parties accept the expert's report and recommendations.

These provisions raise other evidentiary and professional conduct issues. The distinction between privilege and confidentiality must be clearly
understood. Privilege pertains to the admissibility in evidence of certain
communications. Communications that are in the nature of settlement proposals are privileged and neither party is at liberty to give evidence of offers
made in the course of negotiations. The courts have also long recognized a
privilege in respect of lawyer and client communications. It is fundamental
to the adversarial process that a lawyer not be compelled to repeat what her
client said to her. Lawyers are further constrained by the rules of professional
conduct from revealing the information provided by their clients in the
course of their professional relationships.

The lawyer and client communication privilege and the confidentiality
provision found in the rules of professional conduct may only be waived in
certain circumstances. The client can always repeat what she said to her
lawyer and she implicitly foregoes the prohibition if she makes the communication in the presence of a third party. Furthermore, the privilege does
not apply if there is an imminent risk of death or serious bodily or psychological harm to others, as for example, children.

In the absence of protection from disclosure by virtue of either of the
foregoing evidentiary privileges, the parties to a process or service, in which
sensitive and compromising communications might be made, may rely upon
the *Wigmore Test* to prevent their repetition in a court proceeding. For that
test to apply, the court must conduct a four-part inquiry in which the following questions are asked:

1. Was the communication imparted in confidence that it would not
    be disclosed to others?
2. Is the preservation of secrecy essential to the success of the process
    or service relationship?
3. Is that relationship one that society wishes to foster and protect?
4. Will any injury to the relationship caused by disclosure outweigh
    the expected benefit to be derived from compelling disclosure?

The problem with relying upon the *Wigmore Test* is that lawyers are
unable to advise their clients in advance of their participation in a process
or service setting whether a court will apply it to their case. An inhibition
to disclose may remain.The limits of evidentiary privilege and the vagaries
of the application of the *Wigmore Test* make it incumbent upon lawyers to
ensure that there is an adequate confidentiality provision in the Participation
Agreement. Mediators insert similar clauses in their agreements. As the
courts encourage parties to negotiate settlements of their disputes, it is
anticipated that they will enforce these provisions. However, there has not
been sufficient jurisprudence to assert unequivocally that a court will do so

in a given case. CFL lawyers are well advised to educate the judiciary in their locale with respect to the CFL process and enlist their support.

Collaborative lawyers struggle with their professional and contractual obligations in respect of sensitive or personal information that clients instruct them not to share, which may not be strictly relevant from a legal perspective but would likely be important on a financial or psychological level to the other party. If a client requests that such information not be revealed, the lawyer must not disclose it by virtue of the confidentiality provisions found in the rules of professional conduct. However, if she considers that the withheld information could reasonably affect the other party's decision making, for any reason whatsoever, she should remind her client of the undertaking under the Participation Agreement to share all important information. It is often helpful to discuss how and when the information might be shared so as to minimize the anticipated reaction of the other party, as well as the consequences to the client if the CFL process ends. If the client refuses to permit the disclosure, the lawyer may have no alternative but to withdraw from or terminate the CFL process.

The Agreements

The Retainer Agreement

Introduction

Fees and Disbursements

The CFL Process

Termination

Withdrawal

The Participation Agreement

Introduction

Purpose

Children's Issues

Principles

Experts

Cautions and Limitations

Court Intervention

Withdrawal

Termination

Confidentiality

Rights and Obligations

Enforceability

7

First Contact with the Other Lawyer

- *The Adversarial Way*
- *The Collaborative Way*

THE ADVERSARIAL WAY

After being retained, a lawyer usually dictates a letter to the other spouse advising that he is now *acting for* or *representing* the client. It is an accustomed practice for a lawyer, even in this initial correspondence, to request extensive financial disclosure as a preliminary to anticipated negotiations. Typically, he will ask for the production of a sworn financial statement that discloses income from all sources, expenses, assets, debts and liabilities. The lawyer may also request documents to support this disclosure, including personal income returns, business statements, valuations, appraisals, and bank records. A deadline for delivery by some arbitrary and unilaterally determined date, with an ultimatum of a pending court proceeding in the event of default, often concludes such correspondence. In this first contact with the other side, the structure of the relationship and the communication is established; the lawyer is now the gateway to and the exclusive spokesperson for his client.

The first letter sets the tone for what will follow. The letter frames the issues generically and entirely within a legal framework. It is often demanding and confrontational. The message is clear; the lawyers determine the process, the clients do not. From the outset, the parties appear as adversaries. The request for production and conduct do not appear open for negotiation. A legal process, the commencement of a court proceeding, is usually the consequence of a failure to comply. Even a more conciliatory letter that does not mention court usually has an edge that sends a clear adversarial message.

What might be the anticipated reaction of the recipient to this standard form letter? Following a separation, spouses experience a variety of emotions. They may be angry; they may be hurt. They may deny what has happened; they may be ready to move on. Most will be afraid. Many aspects of their lives seem now to be beyond their control. They no longer know what their former partners are thinking or planning and they fear the worst. A letter of this kind may exacerbate this anxiety and fear. Rather than encourage cooperation, it may sow the seeds of confrontation.

The letter from the first lawyer announces the positions taken in a way that can only be interpreted as entirely favourable to his client alone. Upon receiving a letter of this kind, the other spouse may well take offence at what he is being asked to do. He may take it as a personal attack. He may decide to retain an equally forceful lawyer to protect himself and to make counter-demands.

If the lawyer is aware that the other spouse has already retained a lawyer, the initial letter will be addressed to the lawyer, who will send it on to his client. This letter will likely contain similar demands and evoke a similar reaction. While lawyers may be accustomed to this type of correspondence, most clients are not. They expect their representatives to respond in kind.

Whether the initiating process was a letter written directly to the other spouse or to his lawyer, the impact is the same. The parties have taken the first steps towards escalation of conflict and entrenchment. This early negotiation impasse is directly attributable to the manner in which the first lawyer to act initiated contact with the other side. It was an implicit invitation either to capitulate or to contest. The downward spiral of reaction, counter-reaction, counter-counter-reaction, and so on, in which the parties are already enmeshed, is perpetuated by their lawyers' initial involvement.

THE COLLABORATIVE WAY

The parties to a family dispute are not abstract constructs but real people experiencing something for which they were not prepared. They have emotions, deeply held values, and unique perspectives. People in conflict are usually angry and fearful, offended and defensive. The approach taken early by a lawyer may confirm the other party's belief that he is under attack. This reaction is not conducive to effective problem solving. If our goal as CFL lawyers is to establish a good working relationship with our client's spouse and his lawyer, then we must adopt another way to communicate with the other side. What are the messages that we want to send and how do we transmit those messages to serve our larger purpose?

Previously, we considered how a CFL lawyer might approach the other spouse. Here, we contemplate how that first contact with another CFL lawyer might be initiated and what they may attempt to accomplish. The lawyers' preliminary exchange offers an opportunity to break the reaction, counter-reaction loop and to set the tone for the creative resolution of the issues through joint problem solving rather than attacking from entrenched positions.

The initial contact with the other CFL lawyer may be in the form of a telephone conversation or a personal meeting. Telephones calls are quicker, cheaper for the clients, and easier to arrange. However, some lawyers prefer to meet with their counterparts. This approach is preferable if the lawyers have not previously worked together in a CFL case. We recommend a call or meeting in preference to a letter. A CFL lawyer should never send a letter that the other party may perceive to be adversarial. If a letter must be sent concerning a sensitive issue, the letter may be sent out in a draft form to the other lawyer. He may edit the draft and remove any wording or modify the tone that might inadvertently offend the other party. The final, edited version may be signed and sent.[1]

The first contact between CFL lawyers has a fairly limited purpose, although this limitation should not be seen to minimize its importance. This contact sets the tone for future collaboration and teamwork.

The goals of the first contact between CFL lawyers are as follows:

1. To exchange preliminary information about clients, advising of their concerns, priorities, and goals, if known;

2. To arrange the first settlement meeting and consider when and where it should take place to maximize the comfort and convenience of the parties;

3. To identify immediate issues to be resolved at the first meeting, such as a temporary parenting schedule and arrangements for paying bills;

4. To discuss any areas of possible agreement and potential; and

5. To walk through the matters to be covered at the first meeting and to divide responsibilities between the two lawyers in a balanced manner.

As a contrast to the confrontational overture featured in the adversarial approach, we offer this transcript of a telephone conversation between two CFL lawyers, Mary and John.

MARY: Hi John. I've just been retained by Joan Brown and I understand that you act for her husband, Mike. I think they've both agreed to pursue the CFL process.

JOHN: Yes, I'm so pleased that they have. Mike wants to get started as soon as possible. Let's discuss their immediate concerns.

MARY: As you know, Joan continues to live in the house with the three kids. However, she's short of cash and she needs Mike's financial help. Joan knows that Mike is feeling pressed right now with having to get his own apartment. She needs assurance that there'll be money to cover the household expenses while we negotiate.

JOHN: Sounds like we'll need to discuss that up front. Mike needs to re-establish contact with the kids right away. They call him every night and tell him how much they miss him.

MARY: Both of these issues are important and will need to be discussed early on in the first meeting. When do you think that we can get together?

JOHN: My client and I can set aside a half day at the end of next week – say Friday at 10:00 a.m. Does that work for you and Joan?

MARY: Yes, we could meet then. My office is convenient for both of our clients. Would it be alright to have the first meeting here at my office and decide the location of further meetings from there? I'll provide muffins, coffee and tea.

JOHN: That's great. What materials do you think we need for the first meeting?

MARY: We certainly don't need completed Financial Statements. For now, Joan would just like to see Mike's pay stub. Perhaps he could also list the current household bills that need to be paid.

JOHN: Mike doesn't need any information from Joan right now. During the meeting, the four of us can turn our minds to what else they are going to need. How do you want to run the meeting?

MARY: Why don't you welcome and introduce everyone? I can go over the Participation Agreement and ensure that everyone commits to the process. Perhaps, you can discuss the behavioural guidelines.

JOHN: That sounds fine. I think that covers everything that we need to discuss in advance of the meeting. I'll call if anything else comes up. I look forward to seeing you next week.

The first contact with the other lawyer should be respectful and productive. The lawyers share the immediate concerns of their clients. They neither make demands nor do they try to decide any of the issues for the parties. An exception to this rule may arise when one spouse has all the financial resources and will need to pay the dependant spouse's legal fees. That spouse's lawyer may call the other in advance to obtain his client's agreement to be responsible for the costs of the process or, at least for the first meeting, at which fee arrangements can be discussed.

This initial contact accomplishes only what is necessary to set up a successful first settlement meeting. The clients remain at the forefront of decision making.

First Contact with the Other Lawyer
The Collaborative Way
Telephone conversation or personal meeting.
Exchange preliminary information.
Set date, time, and place for
first settlement meeting.
Identify immediate issues.
Discuss areas of possible agreement and difficuty.
Review matters to be covered at
first settlement meeting.
Divide responsibilities for
first settlement meeting.

ENDNOTES

1 Tesler, P.H. (2001). *Collaborative Law: Achieving Effective Resolution in Divorce without Litigation*. Chicago, IL: ABA Publications. p. 112.

8

Client Preparation

- *The Adversarial Way*
- *The Collaborative Way*

THE ADVERSARIAL WAY

After a traditional lawyer has the disclosure she deems necessary, she provides her opinion as to the likely outcome, should the matter proceed to court. Instructions are sought as to the client's bargaining demands. Following the *distributive negotiation* model, the lawyer may recommend that her client ask for something even greater than where the client wants to end up, to allow for room to maneuver. She may also ask the client to allow her to make minor concessions to guide the settlement negotiations toward the desired outcome. They prepare to engage in a kind of *negotiation dance* – two steps forward, one step back – as they make their way around the bargaining floor.

At some point, the lawyers may decide to hold a settlement meeting to attempt to resolve or narrow the issues. The lawyers may prepare briefs for the settlement meeting that include copies of the materials exchanged, summaries of the issues in dispute, their positions in respect of them, and supportive precedents. This preparation activity suggests that the clients will be playing passive roles in a process dominated by their lawyers and the law. As the process does not anticipate any spontaneous interactions among the parties, there is no reason to prepare the clients to participate. The lawyers are in control and their clients are there primarily to observe and instruct.

THE COLLABORATIVE WAY

Once the parties have committed to CFL, the first settlement meeting will usually be arranged to take place within a week or two. The success of that session will be measured by the degree to which it instills in the parties a sense of comfort and trust in the process and with the other participants. The effectiveness of all meetings will depend, in large part, on the commitment of the parties to settlement and the level of skill of the lawyers and the parties themselves.

As we discussed earlier, the parties in the CFL process are equal members of a four-participant negotiation team. The role of their lawyers is to be facilitative and supportive, to create a safe environment for client-centered dialogue. It is the clients who have primary responsibility for decision making and problem solving. They lead the way in setting the agenda, sharing their perspectives and needs, developing options, and crafting a settlement that works for *them.*

In this environment, the preparation of the clients for the first settlement meeting is crucial to establish an effective process. A lawyer helps her client to acquire an understanding of and commitment to the principles and assumptions that govern CFL and their respective roles in that process. She identifies the client's process and substantive needs, both short-term and long-term. She guides the client in the development of the communication and negotiation skills required for effective participation.

We offer the following summary and discussion of preparation topics.

The Process

Client preparation begins with a thorough explanation of the CFL process, the philosophy upon which it is based, and the roles and tasks of the lawyers and clients. Clients must understand how collaborative negotiation differs from adversarial negotiation, and embrace the underlying principles and assumptions of CFL. It may be necessary to remind the parties of these basic principles if problems arise as the process unfolds.

The Role of the Lawyer

Collaborative lawyers maintain their advocacy role by providing legal advice, opinions, and protection. Although they ensure that their clients are negotiating with their *eyes open,* they seek an outcome that satisfies the interests of their clients as opposed to only what they may be entitled to obtain in accordance with the law. As they work together with their colleagues, they become advocates of mutual gain. Each lawyer assumes a supporting role as facilitator and coach. In essence, the lawyers are guardians of an effective process; the parties are responsible for the outcome.

What do we mean when we say that *the lawyers work with each other and the parties as a team of equals?* We imagine the participants together on one side of the table, or at a round table, as one team confronting a problem placed before them. This image stands in contrast to separate teams seated at opposite sides of the table in confrontation with each other rather than the problem. In practice, CFL involves cooperation on many levels. The intended teamwork should be explained to the clients in advance. They must be prepared to engage interactively in a way that might otherwise seem foreign to them.

Each lawyer will ask his or her own client what is important to him or her in the immediate and long term, and what he or she needs in place to feel comfortable with the negotiations. The parties will also need to know the circumstances, needs, fears, goals, and wishes of each party in order to be in the best possible position to assist in developing options that will satisfy both. A client should expect her lawyer to get to know the other party, to take the other *at face value*, and to show equal respect for the concerns and issues expressed by that person. All participants should be encouraged to listen carefully and thoughtfully to what every other person is saying without judgment, criticism, or innuendo. The lawyers should remind their clients that working together provides each of them with an opportunity to learn how to satisfy the needs and interests of the other, which will allow the development of options and mutually beneficial trades.

When clients are considering their legal options, the lawyers working as a team may provide a shared opinion as to the likely results at trial, assuming the court accepts the facts as understood by each side. If the lawyers do not agree as to the prospective legal outcome, the range of opinions they offer may underline the uncertainty and risk involved in proceeding to court. Lawyers can jointly estimate the projected costs and time associated with litigation, if their clients wish that information as they consider their alternatives to a negotiated settlement.

Lawyers working as a team do not take advantage of mistakes made by the other lawyer or party. To do so would undermine or destroy trust among the group members and risk the future durability of any agreement reached.

How does the role of lawyer as *facilitator* differ from the traditional role as *advocate?* The lawyers' primary task in the CFL process is to empower the parties to make their own best decisions. Toward that end, the lawyers establish a safe, positive environment for negotiation. A careful and thorough explanation of the process, the respective roles of the participants, the projected costs and time frame for its conduct and completion should all serve to give the clients a sense of regaining control over their lives. To learn that each of them is experiencing similar preparation will reduce some of their anxiety. The lawyers help their clients articulate their process needs and keep their process agreements. They ensure that communication is respectful and balanced. They want each person to trust the process and to feel comfortable working within it and with the other participants.

The lawyers emphasize to both parties the importance of complete disclosure of all relevant information. They encourage each person to inform the other of what he or she really wants to achieve and the importance attached to the various issues and factors. Lawyers help the parties appreciate the value of each giving the other any available information the other needs to assess the choices available to him or her. They broaden the definition of *relevance* well beyond its narrow legal definition to embrace all matters of *importance*.

At the first settlement meeting, the lawyers will facilitate a discussion as to effective communication and help the parties establish their communication protocols. They will help the parties define achievable and realistic goals, analyze their options, and provide *reality checking*. Collaborative lawyers note and celebrate success as mini-agreements are reached. They congratulate the parties on progress made.

Collaborative lawyers remain as advocates for their clients in the CFL process. However, they do not, as they might advocate otherwise when they perceive themselves as adversaries. In CFL, the lawyers redefine advocacy in two ways. First, they recognize that to achieve what is in the best interests of their clients, they must likewise satisfy the interests of their spouses. Second, they are not only advocates for the parties, but advocates of the process as well. To achieve the best outcome for both clients requires that lawyers maintain the integrity of the process.

The Role of the Client

Clients who choose CFL make a serious commitment to adhere to collaborative principles. What does this mean in practice? In concrete terms, what can clients do to function as effectively as possible to secure the best possible result for them?

Perhaps, the most significant thing that the clients can do is to demonstrate their willingness to respect the perspectives, interests, and values of one another. Each party possesses his or her own viewpoint on the issues and history of the relationship; each has distinct and overlapping interests; and each holds beliefs and values that devolve from life experience. When people are in conflict, they often cling to their unique versions of the *facts*. To question them on their assumptions may upset their sense of themselves and their worldviews at a time when they already feel insecure and unstable. Both parties may be quite reluctant to let go of the way that they frame the conflict. To do so might imply error or fault on their part.

It helps parties enormously to hear that collaborative negotiation does not require a determination of which version of the facts is true. When each accepts the validity of the other's story along with the feelings and values associated with it, they can begin the search for solutions acceptable to both, without the pre-condition that either must necessarily change his or her point of view or belief system.

The clients have other tasks and responsibilities: to communicate respectfully with all participants; to undertake to provide full financial disclosure of all important information; to put the children first at all times; to follow the *suggested guidelines*; to refrain from taking positions and focus instead on interests; to generate creative options; and to accept responsibility for creating their own best outcome. As clients may find it difficult to recall all of this information, we suggest that CFL lawyers provide a preparation handout package that may be similar in form and content to the insertions found in Appendix "F".

The Agreements

The lawyer provides a review and analysis of the Retainer Agreement and the Participation Agreement. It is unlikely that the discussion will be as in-depth as ours, although the lawyer ought not to overlook any of the essential aspects of the CFL process. The time devoted by each lawyer to this necessary task during client preparation reduces what might otherwise have to be spent at the first settlement meeting. All of the participants must sign the Participation Agreement before moving on with the process itself. Once this review and analysis has been completed, the lawyer will have her client sign the Retainer Agreement if she has not previously done so.

Information Exchange

CFL lawyers emphasize the necessity of each party providing all important information to the other. They do not limit disclosure to what is legally relevant. Information is important if it may influence the decision making of either party.

The lawyer opens a discussion with her client about information that will carry over into the first settlement meeting. *What information and documentation do you have already? What information do you need to obtain? Who can most easily obtain it? Is there anything you are worried about sharing with your spouse?* The lawyer should discuss with the client how vital an unfettered information exchange is to the integrity of the process and how withholding may jeopardize it. The lawyer also asks the client to consider the information that might be known only to the spouse. *What information does your spouse have that may be of importance to you? Is there any information that your spouse may not want to share with you?* The client may begin to prepare a financial statement and gather financial information.

Effective Communication

To participate effectively, each of the parties must share his or her own perspectives, interests, and values, while listening carefully to those of the other. For effective negotiation there must be effective communication.

Each of the participants, including the lawyers, must be vigilant in their efforts to avoid accusations, blame, and sarcasm. They must withhold argument or judgment. They must not interrupt each other. While a degree of emotional venting is to be expected, the parties should refrain from angry outbursts that might sabotage or slow down the process. Their lawyers should advise their clients during preparation that, at the settlement meetings, they may suggest that the parties take a break to regain their composure and refocus.

In chapter 10, we review in more detail the specific skills that promote effective communication in a CFL process.

The Client's Interests

Many marital partners facing separation feel distanced – emotionally, financially, and physically – from their spouses. They may express some difficulty with the notion that they have much in common. At this stage, competitive, positional bargaining may feel more natural. A helpful way to engage clients in the CFL process early on is to validate and normalize those feelings about the separation and the other spouse. Let the clients know that it is critical to their success in CFL to focus on their own self-interest – to give deep consideration to their own concerns, needs, wishes, goals, and priorities – and later those of their spouse. These interests are the building blocks of their agreement.

Some lawyers provide the parties with a detailed list of the issues normally covered in a Separation Agreement. This practice serves to make the discussions concrete and to help the client prepare for the negotiations. To ascertain the client's interests, lawyers should ask *open-ended questions* about the issues. *What are your major concerns? What are your goals? Why do you want that result? What interests would that proposal satisfy? What do you think your spouse will think about that idea? Are there any other ways that goal could be accomplished? What do you think that your spouse wants to achieve in this negotiation?*

Lawyers introduce their clients to the notion that solutions can be found within and beyond what the law dictates. Settlement alternatives also devolve from what real world circumstances offer or require, and, most importantly, what the parties themselves decide.

Realistic Expectations

The goals for the first settlement meeting are limited. The participants commit to the process and they sign the Participation Agreement. The parties share their immediate concerns and, possibly, their long-term goals. They resolve any urgent matters. The participants agree as to the information and documents required for subsequent meetings and they assign tasks. The first settlement meeting is an opportunity for each lawyer to meet the other party. There are four parties to this collaborative enterprise and it is important for them to establish rapport if they are to have an effective relationship.

Some clients may express frustration after the first meeting if they perceive the results to be modest given the cost and effort incurred up to and including that stage. The lawyers may pre-empt this feeling that little has been accomplished. They can explain beforehand that for this process to work successfully, it is necessary to set the tone for an effective process. The pace accelerates once the proper groundwork is laid.

Despite the best efforts of all participants, they may encounter problems and disappointments along the way. Lawyers prepare their clients for the unexpected. Either lawyer may intervene to offset a crisis or modify inappropriate behavior. A lawyer may validate the perspective of the other client. When a party says something that evokes a strong emotional response from the other, one of the lawyers may diffuse tension by reminding the affected party that such a statement offers an opportunity to learn more about the speaker and a mere statement will only result in action if they agree.

CONCLUSION

The clients may be anxious to skip over or truncate the preparation stage of the collaborative process to save costs and seemingly expedite settlement. It is usually necessary to go slow at first, to go fast later. This investment in time and effort up front will pay dividends as the collaborative negotiation process gets under way.

Client Preparation

The Collaborative Way

Process and Agreements

Review the process, principles, and assumptions of CFL.
Review the Retainer Agreement and Participation Agreement.

Roles of Lawyers and Clients

Explain the role of the lawyer:
to create an effective environment for negotiation
as a member of a negotiating team,
as a facilitator, and
as a negotiation and communication coach.
Explain the role of the client:
to commit to the process,
to express his or subjective experiences,
to listen to and respect the subjective experiences of the other, and
to assume responsibility for creating the outcome.

Disclosure of Information

Explain the importance of full disclosure
of all important information:
what does the client have and need?
what does the client's spouse need and have?

Communication and Negotiation

Discuss appropriate communication skills:
to speak without blame, sarcasm or judgment,
to ask questions and to listen to the responses, and
to avoid interruptions.
Review interests, needs, wishes, goals of the client and
the client's spouse - immediate and long term.

Expectations

Encourage the client to maintain
realistic expectations of process and outcome.

9

The Settlement Meetings

- *The Adversarial Way*
- *The Collaborative Way*
- *Setting the Table*
- *The First Settlement Meeting*
- *Subsequent Settlement Meetings*
- *Settlement and Closure*

THE ADVERSARIAL WAY

We have no precise model for the adversarial approach to settlement meetings. While *four-way meetings* have become familiar to most family law practitioners, there is no extant literature describing the way in which they are typically conducted. They are strictly voluntary; there is no provision for them in either our procedural rules or family law rules. Some practitioners make effective use of them; others dread and avoid them.

The course a traditional four-way meeting takes depends primarily upon the lawyers. These meetings tend to be lawyer-driven rather than client-centred. Generally, the expectation is that there will be only one such meeting and that the goal of that meeting will be to reach a settlement on all issues. The climate of a traditional four-way meeting depends upon the personalities of the participants, particularly the lawyers, and their respective negotiation styles, strategies, and tactics. These usually reflect the adversarial system in which the lawyers operate. A traditional meeting often extends over several hours, long past the exhaustion point of both lawyers and clients alike. Four-way meetings can be as tactical as examinations for discovery and trials.

As the lawyers do most of the talking, the course the negotiation typically takes at a four-way meeting is an attempt to reconcile incompatible bargaining positions or *to bridge the gap* between them. The lawyers maintain control over the flow of information. They do not want to reveal more than what is needed in the event that the case ultimately proceeds to court. Some lawyers prefer their clients to remain silent or seek a private meeting before speaking to avoid potential damage to their cases. Often, lawyers and their clients break off into private meetings, moving to a form of shuttle negotiation similar to what is characteristic of the collective bargaining process. If settlement is reached, it is frequently achieved by splitting the difference between the positions of the two parties. There may be little or no examination of the clients' interests or option generation to meet those interests. If the meeting fails to result in a settlement, the parties return to the litigation track.

THE COLLABORATIVE WAY

Four-way meetings need not resemble the combative minefield that we associate with traditional competitive negotiations. With a greater understanding of the *process* character of these meetings, the use of interest-based negotiation rather than positional bargaining, and the skills necessary to control and manage conflict, lawyers will find four-party settlement meetings to be extremely effective as a means of resolving family disputes.[1] The settlement meetings comprise the heart of the CFL process. Everything done beforehand is in anticipation of them. In large measure, success or failure is determined by what occurs at them.

SETTING THE TABLE

Prior to the first settlement meeting, the lawyers consider how to *set the table*. The dinner metaphor is appropriate, as we are all familiar with the impact that thoughtful presentation has upon the enjoyment of a meal. There are several matters to consider for a CFL meeting to be as successful as possible.

The room setting says to the participants how this negotiation is going to proceed. The long rectangular boardroom table is not ideal for collaboration. If each lawyer and client sit across from the other, the message is that they are on opposite sides. We want them to feel that they are working together. A small, square or rectangular table will suffice. A round table is preferable, with comfortable chairs. Snacks and beverages should be available to nourish the participants as needed.

The lawyers encourage their clients to give these settlement meetings significant priority in their lives. Together, they select a day of the week and a time of the day that will best assure them of maximum concentration on this work.

The lawyers must assure each other and their clients that their attention will not be broken by interruption. As the settlement meetings are likely to be held at the office of one or the other of the lawyers, staff members should be instructed that neither lawyer is to be called away to take a call or respond to some other matter. Cellular telephones are turned off. Appointments to follow should not be set too close to a settlement meeting. Lawyers should allow about two hours for the first settlement meeting, although they may finish before the allotted time.

THE FIRST SETTLEMENT MEETING

Introductions

At the outset of the meeting, the lawyers and clients must settle upon how each will address the others. Using first names promotes informality and friendliness. Offering beverages and light food can relax the parties and give them time to settle into the meeting.

Creating a Safe Process

Divorce lawyers are familiar with clients who are angry, hurt, afraid, and difficult. Does this mean that the CFL process works only for those rare cases where the parties are amicable and have their emotions in check? The answer is no. Most separating spouses experience strong feelings about the separation. The CFL process allows them to express their feelings in a controlled and safe environment.

With the breakdown of a marriage, communication between spouses often becomes dysfunctional. The character of their interpersonal interactions may have contributed to the marital breakdown itself. Poor communication between them induces a lack of knowledge and understanding as to their intentions. Each wonders and worries about what the other is thinking or planning. Feelings of betrayal and mistrust accompany these anxieties and fears. The more fearful and anxious the parties, the greater is the potential for them to be non-communicative and to rely upon their lawyers to obtain legal outcomes.

In order for the clients to resume control over their lives and to develop the capacity to solve problems effectively, they must feel that the process in which they are to participate and to which they are being asked to commit, is *safe*. To create a climate for success, the CFL process must respond to the psychological as well as the substantive needs of the parties. The lawyers work together to create in the clients a sense of trust in the process, if not in each other, and to build a safe negotiating environment for both of them.

To accomplish this task requires that the lawyers spend considerable time at the outset of the process clarifying the nature and purpose of collaboration. A substantial part of the first meeting is spent dealing with the CFL process and guidelines for effective participation in that process, despite pressure from their clients, who may be anxious to proceed immediately with the negotiation of the substantive issues.

The CFL process does not seek to repair damaged or destroyed interpersonal trust between the parties. This task is better assigned to a marriage or separation counsellor. In order to create a safe place, personal trust is replaced with process trust. Keeping promises, honouring deadlines, and respecting the process needs of the other are all important. They serve to establish and maintain process integrity. The clients learn that their failure to observe and follow the general principles and assumptions of CFL and to honour their agreements, commitments, and undertakings may sabotage the process.

To create a safe process on a practical level, the lawyers ensure that neither party is compromised by their participation in the CFL process. They consider the agreements that should be made by their clients to preserve the status quo in respect of their property, to maintain existing life and health insurance benefits, to provide for the retroactivity of support agreements to the date of separation, and to suspend the running of any legal limitation periods. The parties also undertake not to take any unilateral action that may have an impact on the other during the negotiations.

The Participation Agreement

The lawyers begin by welcoming the parties to the meeting and extending credit to them for their choice of process. One or both lawyers may review the highlights of the Participation Agreement. The clients are asked if they have any questions. Alternatively, the clients may be asked to take turns reading the entire agreement and questions are addressed as they proceed.

A *signing ceremony* may be helpful. The formal signing of the agreement in the presence of all participants serves to reinforce their commitment. They are reminded of their respective roles and the requirements of the process. The parties agree to act in the best interests of the children, to communicate respectfully, to make a voluntary exchange of information, and to use neutral experts. They acknowledge the consequences for them should they not observe the terms and conditions of their agreement, and the termination of the process in the event that it does not work for them. Lawyers and clients declare their commitment not to resort to litigation or the threat of litigation and to work toward mutually beneficial agreements.

Behavioural Guidelines

The participants are not quite ready to proceed. They must yet consider how they are going to conduct themselves in the process. We do not favour the term *ground rules* which sounds rather heavy-handed and punitive. Still, there are some suggested *behavioural guidelines* that facilitate effective negotiations.

Each participant undertakes that he or she will not interrupt another while he or she is speaking. We cannot process what a speaker is saying if two attempt to talk at the same time. Most people are aware of what can occur in a negotiation once a person perceives that he is under attack by another. That person defends himself and, often, unleashes a counter-attack. The negotiation can rapidly deteriorate into an exchange of accusations. The parties ought to be aware of this propensity and to be watchful of language that may lead them in this direction. *Speak to all others as you would have everyone else to speak to you.* We might call this the *Golden Guideline of CFL Communication.*

Before concluding this stage in the process, the lawyers should ask their clients if they have suggestions as to any other appropriate behavioural guidelines. The clients know their own *hot buttons.* They are more qualified than their lawyers to develop a comprehensive and effective communication protocol.

Immediate Concerns

At the first settlement meeting, the clients are asked if there are any immediate matters to be resolved. The problem solving begins here with an understanding of the necessary facts, an exploration of the underlying interests of each party, the validation and acknowledgment of their feelings and concerns, and the creation of options to meet the identified needs. The goal is to develop a sufficient response to answer the immediate concern *without foreclosing other long-term options for settlement.*

The short-term solution crafted may require some direct action by the other party. The principal provider may be asked to support the party in need during the negotiation process either by maintaining existing arrangements for the discharge of household and other expenses or by providing periodic payments to him. On child-related concerns, the parties may agree to meet with their children together, to obtain family counselling, or to a short-term parenting schedule. Whatever the response to an immediate concern, it is effective if it eases the mind of the party who voiced it, if it enables him to engage in the process without distraction and worry, and if it leaves as many future possibilities for settlement open as possible.

Opening the Discussion

The lawyers then invite the parties to speak about what each of them would like to accomplish in the CFL process. After each party has spoken, any of the participants may ask clarifying questions. This step is important. It offers each of the parties an opportunity to participate early in the process and to talk about what is really important to him or her. A deeper exploration of their underlying interests comes later.

As the parties speak, their emotions and sensitivities may surface. Every communication provides information both as to the subject of the dispute and the relationship of the disputing parties. Family matters are never solely about the facts; they are also about feelings. Through the use of active listening, an effective CFL lawyer expresses his empathy with both clients and not just his own. The recognition of the emotional and relational content of the communications of both parties is central to accurate issue identification and ultimate resolution.

Issue Development

After each party has had the opportunity to speak, the lawyers attempt to identify and summarize the issues that emerged. One may facilitate the discussion while the other acts as recorder. Whichever of them performs the task of drawing out the issues, he or she seeks confirmation from the parties of what is in dispute. The facilitator frames each item in neutral language and the recorder adds it to the *agenda* that the participants create together. Initially, numbers are not placed beside the issues. Once all of the issues have been recorded, the lawyers ask the parties which they would like to discuss first. They organize the issues on the agenda in the order that the parties prioritize them.

Recording the agenda on a flip chart serves several purposes. First, it provides an example of what the parties can produce through their collaborative efforts. They have proven to themselves that they can at least agree upon what it is that they need to resolve. Second, the agenda requires that each party focus on the problem as they have stated it rather than upon the other person, whom he or she may feel is responsible. It enables them to separate the problem from the people, the first phase of the negotiation model to which we have previously alluded and which remains to be discussed. Finally, the agenda stands before the parties at all times as a guide to the work that they have yet to do. As they resolve issue by issue, the agenda records the progress they make and encourages them to continue.

Information Exchange

At this point in the process, the parties decide what information and documents they require in order to move forward with the negotiations. We suggest the parties agree to share any information which may affect the choices available to them on any of the issues.

In addition to sharing existing financial records, they may require an appraisal or an evaluation of certain of their assets such as real property, a business, or a pension. Other documents may need to be obtained and produced. Rather than exchanging a standard *shopping list*, the parties negotiate what information and documents *they* need to resolve their issues and what they do not require. If it is necessary to obtain other documents or to instruct some other person to produce or prepare a report, the participants must agree as to which of them is to assume responsibility for these assignments and how the costs are to be paid. Usually experts will be jointly retained by the parties and provided with an agreed mandate in writing.

Wrap-up

The participants schedule a mutually convenient date and time for their next meeting. They are aware of the time necessary to complete their production and disclosure *homework* assignments. As there are always the schedules of four persons to consider, it may be prudent to set dates for two or three meetings in advance. They can always be canceled if not needed.

At this point in the meeting, one of the lawyers provides a summary of what the participants accomplished, the homework to be completed by each of them, and the intended topics for discussion at the next meeting. The host lawyer may dictate or prepare the minutes of the meeting in the presence of the others or immediately after the meeting. The minutes are e-mailed or faxed to all others. If all discussions have been summarized on a flip chart, a legal assistant may reduce the notes to writing and forward to all parties. After receiving any supplementary or closing comments, the participants adjourn their first meeting. It is always helpful to conclude on a high note, with one or two preliminary agreements in place. If either party raises a particularly contentious issue towards the end of the meeting, any discussion should be deferred to a subsequent meeting.

Debriefing

As soon after the first meeting as possible, each lawyer should make brief contact with his or her own client to get feedback with respect to his experience with the process. The lawyer and client may need to coordinate the completion of homework assignments. Additional individual meetings with the client may be needed on occasion to help him complete his work or to discuss other concerns.

The CFL lawyers should touch base with each other by telephone for a few minutes to debrief the settlement meeting. Any concerns about their or the clients' working relationship should be identified and discussed early, before they escalate. Relevant feedback from the clients with respect to the process should be shared.

These post-meeting discussions between CFL lawyers provide them with an opportunity for reflection and skill development. They can address specific concerns with respect to their relative effectiveness in a collaborative process.

SUBSEQUENT SETTLEMENT MEETINGS

Prior to the second settlement meeting, the CFL lawyers should again speak by telephone to ensure that the homework assignments are being completed as anticipated and to determine whether any issues have arisen since the previous meeting. If so, they can discuss how these should be handled when they resume. At the opening of the second meeting, either of the lawyers may ask whether there have been any intervening events that the parties wish to discuss before they continue. Once they have dealt with any new matters raised, the lawyers review the minutes of the previous meeting. The parties discuss their homework assignments, provide the requested information, exchange their documents, and, with the assistance of their lawyers, formulate their agenda for this meeting.

With each of the issues on the agenda, the lawyers ensure that the parties have sufficient information to make good decisions. The discussion that ensues is more focused than in the first settlement meeting. The lawyers endeavour to discover and give voice to the underlying interests of the parties. When their interests have been revealed and analyzed, they direct themselves toward the generation of as many creative options for settlement as possible. The lawyers solicit and record ideas and contribute suggestions. After they have compiled a sufficient list of such options, each is assessed to ascertain the extent to which it satisfies the interests of the parties and meets the criteria of acceptability set by them.

The parties should decide whether or not an agreement on any issue represents a final settlement of that particular matter. It is more likely that they intend that there be no final agreement on anything until there is a final agreement on everything. However, they should still record their tentative resolution on agenda issues as they proceed. This practice contributes to the perception of momentum in the settlement process.

During the settlement meetings, the parties deal with as many of the issues as time permits. They conclude each settlement meeting as they did the first and adjourn until their next meeting.

SETTLEMENT AND CLOSURE

When the parties have resolved all of their issues, their lawyers begin to reduce the terms of their settlement into a written Separation Agreement. As with all other aspects of this process, the work should be undertaken collaboratively and not by one lawyer alone. They can draft it together on a computer in the presence of the parties or one lawyer can prepare an initial draft for review and amendment by all participants.

The agreement, which documents the understandings reached in the collaborative process, will be different in form and content than an agreement prepared after a traditional lawyer-to-lawyer negotiation. We suggest that the following aspects be considered:

1. Use plain language:
   Given that the CFL process is client-centred and client-driven, we propose using plain, non-technical language, and words used by the parties themselves, whenever possible. The parties may be referred to using their names as opposed to *the husband and the wife*. Use words such as *afterwards* or *from now on* rather than as *hereinafter* or *henceforth*. Lengthy, repetitive releases and standard clauses may be revised to achieve the desired legal effect and protection, without unnecessary words. The agreement should be clear, binding and enforceable, but also easily accessible and user-friendly.

2. Expand preamble:
   The preamble to the agreement should confirm that the parties have participated in a CFL process and that they have reached an agreement which may not represent what they might have obtained if they had followed the applicable statutory and case law. We offer a sample of suggested clauses that might be considered.

   • The parties believe the agreements reached satisfy their legal and non-legal, financial and psychological interests of them and their children.

- The agreements reached are based in part on the regard the parties have for each other, the well-being of their restructured family unit and the importance each places on their future relationship.
- The parties have received independent legal advice from their respective lawyers and understand the legal effect of this agreement. They understand that the issues may have been resolved in a way that is entirely different from what a court might have awarded or from what a negotiated agreement based entirely upon the applicable statutory and case law might have provided.
- Each party has provided all information the other party deemed relevant or important to the issues.
- Each party has relied on the following disclosure (insert the documents provided, as for example sworn Financial Statements, actuarial valuation of pension, estimate of value of business prepared by jointly retained valuator, etc. as appropriate); each party is satisfied with the extent and accuracy of the disclosure; and neither party seeks any further disclosure.
- The parties themselves have created this agreement and they believe it provides the best possible outcome for them.

3. Set out principles, intentions and objectives:
   For each of the parenting, support, and property sections of the agreement, we recommend the insertion of a statement of the principles that the parties adopted or created to govern and guide their decision making, the intentions of the parties in reaching their agreement, and the objectives the agreement is expected to achieve for the parties and children. These statements may be referred to at the time of any variation or review, they may assist in understanding and interpreting the agreement in the event of a misunderstanding or breach; and they serve as a reminder to the parties of their shared values and interests.

4. Clarify follow up and task completion:
   The agreement should clearly outline what remains to be done to put the agreement into practice; who is responsible for what task (what each client will handle, what each lawyer will do and not do); and a timetable for task completion.

5. Provide an adequate and appropriate variation and dispute resolution mechanism:

Parties to a CFL process will appreciate that agreements about families are not carved in stone and may need adjustment from time to time. Most agreements will contain provisions for review for enumerated reasons or at certain times. Support arrangements may be reviewed when each child completes high school, daycare is no longer required, or a stay-at-home spouse completes retraining. Parenting arrangements may be reviewed periodically, in the event either party wishes to relocate, or on the request of either parent. Whatever agreement they negotiate regarding changes as a result of the occurrence of one or more of these circumstances, the review process should be clear and precise.

As well, the agreement should provide a mechanism or process for resolution of future disputes, which may well arise. The parents may agree to resolve parenting issues by allocating decision-making authority in specified areas to one or the other parent. Alternatively, they may agree to pursue mediation, mediation-arbitration, or some other appropriate dispute resolution process, in respect of parenting or support issues. Parties who experienced success with CFL will often choose to return to that process.

A Separation Agreement negotiated in a CFL case in which Victoria Smith and Sharon Cohen were the lawyers, modified to remove any information that might identify the parties, can be found in Appendix "G".

The Settlement Meetings

Setting the Table

Select a mutually acceptable date, time, and place.
Arrange for room and table conducive to
collaborative communication and negotiation.
Provide refreshments.
Ensure that there will be no interruptions.

The First Settlement Meeting

Welcome and introduce the participants.
Review and sign the Participation Agreement.
Create a safe environment, process trust.
Develop and commit to behavioural guidelines.
Identify and resolve immediate concerns
Invite the parties to open the discussion.
Prepare agenda of issues to be resolved.
Determine information and documents needed.
Decide upon use of experts.

Assign homework.
Schedule next meeting.
Prepare summary/minutes of meeting.
Debrief.

Subsequent Settlement Meetings

Check on homework assignments before next meeting.
Inquire of intervening events.
Review summary/minutes of previous meeting.
Provide information, exchange documents.
Formulate agenda.
Negotiate issue by issue.

Settlement and Closure

Prepare Separation Agreement.
Use plain language.
Expand preamble.
Set out principles, intentions, and objectives.
Clarify follow-up and task-completion.
Resolve variation and dispute resolution mechanism.
Meet for signing ceremony.

ENDNOTES

1 Ryan, J.P. (1992). Mediator strategies for lawyers: the four-party settlement conference. *Family and Conciliation Courts Review*. 30: 364-372. Palo Alto, CA: Sage Publications, Inc.

Part Four:

CFL Skills

- *Communication*
- *Negotiation*
- *Intervention*

10

Communication

THE ROLE OF COMMUNICATION

The heart and soul of the CFL process is good communication. Good communication among the lawyers and other participants in the four-party settlement meetings is essential in order for effective problem solving to take place. The lawyers model good communication themselves and they facilitate good communication between the disputing spouses. In this way, they endeavour to maintain the conflict at a low level and prevent escalation.

EFFECTIVE COMMUNICATION

Communication is more than just *talking*. It is a complex interaction of the thoughts and feelings of two or more persons that involves at least three steps:

Step One

The speaker decides what she wants to communicate and puts the message into words. The choice of words is highly personalized and reflects the speaker's own personal style, education, social class, status, language, ethnic, and cultural background, as well as the particular setting in which the communication takes place. Along with the words, the speaker communicates her feelings about what she is saying through nonverbal cues, as for example, with smiles or gestures. The speaker may avoid eye contact or other direct engagement, which is another form of nonverbal communication.

Step Two

The speaker receives the communication, which does not mean that the listener interprets the message in the same way the speaker intended. The listener, like the speaker, has her own subjective experience that acts as a filter for the information that is being communicated. The listener responds by acknowledging verbally what he has understood and his subjective reaction to the communication of the speaker.

Step Three

The final step in the communication process involves an acknowledgment by the speaker that the listener received the speaker's original message as intended. If not, the speaker attempts to clarify and the communication process continues.

Communication is challenging enough when it occurs between only two people. However, when four persons are involved in a CFL meeting, communication is significantly more complex. Unlike in an adversarial setting where communication tends to be highly structured and *one-on-one*, in CFL communication occurs informally and in many combinations. For example, there are six dyadic conversation possibilities:

1. between the lawyers;
2. between the clients;
3. between lawyer one and his or her client;
4. between lawyer two and his or her client;
5. between lawyer one and the other client; and
6. between lawyer two and the other client.

In addition, conversations can take place among three or even all four participants at once.

This form of communication is direct and dynamic. It can promote greater understanding between the parties and the development of creative ideas. However, with informality and spontaneity come potential pitfalls.

Communications may not always be completed and participants may not always know whether their messages have been received and understood.

For effective communication, we recommend adopting the following principles:

1. **Direct (not indirect)**

   The communication should be made directly to the person for whom it is intended. When the message is not given directly, it is quite likely that it will not be received and acted upon, or else ignored altogether.

   Indirect – *It would be nice if people came prepared for the meeting.*

   Direct – *Joan and Mike, we need to have Mike's sworn Financial Statement if our meetings are to be productive.*

2. **Clear (not masked)**

   Communications can be clear and open or vague and masked. When messages are not clear, there is a strong possibility that they will be misunderstood or misinterpreted.

   Masked – *Things have a habit of disappearing around the house.*

   Clear – *Mike, have you taken the video camcorder from the house?*

3. **Congruent (not incongruent)**

   When communications are incongruent, the verbal and nonverbal messages do not match. The listener therefore does not know as to which message to respond.

   Incongruent – (*while smiling and not looking directly at the other*) *Joan, I'm really sorry if my comments offended you.*

   Congruent – (*while sincere and looking directly at the other*) *Mike, I'm really sorry if what I said offended you.*

4. **Accurate (not inaccurate)**

   The information communicated may be correct or incorrect. Incorrect data lead to misunderstandings and escalate conflict.

   Mike is advised that the meeting is set to begin at 2:30 rather than 2:00 and everyone is annoyed with him for arriving late.

5. **Constructive (not destructive)**

The way that the message is framed may affect how and even whether it is received or denied by the recipient. Even critical comments may be communicated in a constructive manner so that the listener can take them in and respond to them appropriately, rather than simply defensively.

Destructive – *Mary, your client has had more than enough time to provide better financial disclosure than this!*

Constructive – *Mary, we're having problems understanding why it is taking so long for you and your client to prepare the financial disclosure we need to resolve these issues. What can we do to make this happen?*

6. **Intentional (not unintentional)**

Effective communications are intended. However, some communications are made and received inadvertently, when they are not intended as communications.

Joan and Mike overhear their lawyers referring to a case as a dog's breakfast and they assume, mistakenly, that it is theirs.

7. **Empathetic (not unfeeling)**

Communications contain both verbal and nonverbal components. When the parties are deliberate as to the emotional and relational aspects of their communication, it becomes more effective. The speaker identifies the feeling and connects it to a reason that the listener feels the way she does about that matter.

Mike, you seem upset that Joan didn't consult you before making decisions about the children's activities on your free time.

As communicators, we send both non-verbal and verbal messages. Each form is important and, together they comprise the totality of the communication.

BARRIERS

Word Barriers

The words used by speakers do not themselves have an unequivocal meaning. Rather, it is the interpretation that the listeners apply to them that provides the understanding of what was said. Listeners rely upon their experience, knowledge, education, beliefs, and personal history to filter and supplement the communications of the speaker. If a speaker uses the term *orthodox* to describe how she resolves problems, one listener might draw the conclusion that she is a very conservative and unimaginative person, while another may conclude that she acts in accordance with some particular religious conviction.

Word choice likewise affects the interpretation of a speaker's spoken message. The use of slang or unfamiliar technical words to impress a listener can easily lead to misunderstandings. On the other hand, using words and phrases that are colourful, possess human interest, or contain personal references may sustain her interest. In a conversation between a lawyer and her client, the use of words like examinations for discovery, motions, and settlement conferences, without an explanation of their meanings, may serve to confuse rather than enlighten.

Incorrect grammar and syntax can also affect the interpretation of the message. A poorly constructed sentence requires that the listener decode the message, leaving it open to a multiplicity of meanings.

Emotional Barriers

The experiences, beliefs, and values, or the *biases*, of a listener affect her interpretation of a message to the extent that she deems what is said to be acceptable or unacceptable. In general, the ability to listen effectively diminishes in direct response to statements that are contrary to these biases. If Mike reacts to a message from Joan with, *That's typical of you, Joan,* their communication could easily degenerate into an argument, with neither side listening to the other. Mike's bias against whatever it was that Joan conveyed in her previous statement causes him to dismiss it without effectively listening to what it was she was about to say.

A similar problem arises when the listener *prejudges* what is being communicated. She tunes out, stops listening, and either waits for the conversation to end or interrupts the speaker. If Joan believes that the only worthwhile suggestions are those conveyed by her or her lawyer, she may not hear an otherwise good idea from Mike or his lawyer. She prejudges their contributions to be of no assistance in the resolution of their problem.

As a result of these factors, communicators often make assumptions about what is being said or hear only what they want or expect. Once again, they block out all or part of the messages that do not conform to their expectations. This communication habit may occur automatically and it is more likely unconscious rather than deliberate. It can lead to a speaker framing her remarks or questions in such a way as to generate a particular response. To communicate in this fashion is effective if it is done for the purpose of articulating from the perspective of the other although it can be ineffective if considered to be manipulative.

Physical Barriers

In this context, we consider the physical capacities, limitations, practices, and habits of the parties as speakers; how they use their voices. A person who shouts, whispers, talks too quickly or slowly, speaks in a monotone, emphasizes in an exaggerated manner, or talks with an unfamiliar accent affects the communication by the way she physically speaks the words. Furthermore, speech or reading impediments such as dyslexia may be problematic for effective listening, as are actual physical hearing problems.

The above factors may be unavoidable. However, there are inhibitors of this kind that can be addressed. A speaker's habits, such as foot tapping, winking, twitching, along with her physical appearance may be equally or more distracting for the listener. External distractions such as traffic, telephones, and temperature can also affect the quality of listening. Frequent interruptions are likewise disruptive. The communicators can eliminate or at least minimize the impact of these forces. A closed door sends a message.

NON-VERBAL COMMUNICATION

People communicate without using any words whatsoever, by their facial expressions, body positions and movements, gestures, tone of voice, use of distance, and choice of clothing and jewelry. In fact, these non-verbal communications may be even more important than the actual words that are said in terms of the meaning intended by the speaker. Lawyers often communicate with each other by letter or by telephone. As each of these is verbal and the lawyers are not together during the communication, they are losing access to a great deal of what is being communicated by each of them to the other.

To be able to observe the facial expressions and body language of the person the speaker is addressing enables her to interpret the impact of the verbal communications upon that other person. The effect is reciprocal.

Each of the participants to the communication acquires an understanding of what was actually intended by their respective communications.

The following expressions of non-verbal communication demonstrate how people communicate with one another without using words:

1. **Body Orientation**

   The degree to which a speaker faces toward or away from the listener through the positioning of the body, feet, and head can indicate her attitudes toward and involvement with the communication process.

2. **Body Posture**

   The way in which a speaker stands or sits can indicate dominance, submission, self-esteem, interest, or tension. These messages may not be obvious, so that the listener should be aware of subtle changes.

3. **Gestures**

   Speakers use their hands, arms, and feet in ways that often reveal their underlying emotions. If angry or frustrated, a speaker might tap her fingers rapidly; if anxious or tense, she might shift position constantly; if open to the ideas of others, she might lean forward and relax her arms; or, if rigid or controlling, she might maintain her legs and arms firmly crossed. An effective communicator watches for subtle changes in the other.

4. **The Face and Eyes**

   Facial expressions are the most noticed parts of the body but they are not necessarily the easiest to read. They can be so fleeting; sometimes, they last for only a fraction of a second. Eye movements can be particularly revealing. Rapid blinking indicates nervousness, staring suggests hostility, eyes wide open express fear, rolling of the eyes shouts disgust, and moist eyes say sadness. Similarly, the lips and mouth reveal friendliness with a smile, discomfort with the licking of the lips, and anger or tension with a sneer or pursed lips. Even the setting of the jaw or the flaring of the nostrils proclaim underlying feelings.

5. **The Voice**

    Tone, emphasis, speed, pitch, use of pauses, and volume are all important indicators of the meanings behind the words speakers use.

6. **Clothing and Other Appearance Accessories**

    People use clothing and other appearance accessories to communicate information about themselves. They can be used to intimidate others or, at least, to influence their perception of them. The *power suit* and gold Rolex watch are examples of communication instruments that may or may not be effective depending upon the way they are received by others. Certain clothing or hairstyles may be deemed inappropriate in particular settings. Some religious or ethnic communities may regard the appearance of others offensive as being either too formal or too informal.

7. **Environment and Furnishings**

    The physical setting, architecture, interior design, and furnishings can all affect the communication that takes place within. Two people speaking to each other across the typical large boardroom table interact in a more formal and perhaps hierarchical manner than they would if seated casually in a room without any table. Chairs at different heights place the person who is looking up at the other at a disadvantage. Cozy or stark décor can also set the tone for communications.

8. **Use of Space**

    The distances between people may communicate strong messages about their relationships. People who sit far apart may be communicating the gap they perceive between their interests, whereas those who sit close together may be indicating a belief in their capacity to work together.

    Keeping that distance can serve to maintain superiority or provide protection. Reducing this distance can either escalate a conflict or promote cooperation. The more dominant a person is, the more space she can keep around her and the more freedom she has to invade the personal space of others.

    Some typical North American distances are as follows:

    > Intimate distance – 18 inches and less;

Personal distance – 18 inches to 4 feet;
Social distance – 4 to 12 feet; and
Public distance – 12 feet and outward.

Both the amount of space and its location are important. The head of the table or central seat may be an indication of actual or claimed dominance.

9. **Culture**

Generalizations are difficult as a result of person-to-person, culture to culture variances. Nonverbal communication is subject to egocentric and ethnocentric differentiation. An aboriginal person may not make direct eye contact with another out of a sign of respect, rather than because he or she is avoiding that other. In some cultures, it is not appropriate for an unrelated male to shake hands with a female. Rather than putting her at ease, this may cause her great discomfort.

VERBAL COMMUNICATION

We classify the skills deemed essential for effective practice within a CFL setting into categories that correspond with the form of expression and the circumstances in which they are used. In summary, they are *questioning*, *stating*, *listening*, and a final cluster that we call *other communication skills*.

QUESTIONING

Generally, the first words spoken at the first settlement meeting following introductions are addressed in the form of a question. Questions are one of the most important tools of the skilled communicator. By her choice of the form and content of her questions, a speaker elicits the subject areas of discussion, exerts some control or at least guidance over the direction that the communication process will take, and obtains disclosure of the underlying needs and interests of the parties. Good questioning achieves many purposes. It encourages self-exploration; it generates an exchange of information; it brings to the surface facts, opinions, and attitudes; and it facilitates effective communication in the process as a whole. The skilled questioner knows when to ask a question, what question to ask, and how to ask the question.

Although there are other forms of questions, they are most often of either the *open-ended* or *closed* type. Each of these forms possesses advantages and disadvantages. The effective questioner chooses judiciously between them during the communication process.

Open-ended Questions

Investigative journalists use open-ended questions to draw out a wide range of responses on a broadly stated topic. They usually begin with *who, why, when, where, what, or how. How do you plan to handle this problem? What do you like most about the children's present school? On what basis did you make the decision to quit your job? When did you begin to realize there was a problem?*

Questions that are preceded with a *why* can sometimes intimidate respondents. They may be perceived as judgmental or evaluative in nature. As a result, a party may respond defensively or negatively. However, *why* questions can frequently be framed in alternative language. *What led you to make that decision?*

Open-ended questions do not restrict or circumscribe the range of possible answers. Rather, they encourage the respondent to answer in a free and comprehensive manner. They cannot be answered by a simple *yes* or *no*; they are non-directive and they do not suggest answers. Open-ended questions are effective in stimulating discussion by asking for the respondent's knowledge or opinion about a topic. They can be also be used to help the respondent to elaborate upon her needs, fears, desires, and concerns.

Open-ended questions engage the parties to respond. They are empowering; they invite active participation. These questions solicit complete information that might not otherwise be forthcoming if the questioner restricts herself to closed questions.

Closed Questions

Closed questions narrow the focus of the inquiry to specific subject areas. Usually, they follow an open-ended question to clarify information provided or to obtain more specific details. *What is the value of your home? Did you earn $65,000 last year? I understand that your children all play soccer. Is that correct?* Closed questions can be located on a spectrum extending from those that invite the listener to provide information to questions that ask the respondent simply to confirm or deny something said earlier. Trial lawyers use leading questions during the cross-examination of adverse witnesses, a practice that should not be followed in CFL.

A closed question may call for a specific response, which may be suggested by the questioner, in which event the response is limited to a *yes* or *no* answer. Closed questions are used to obtain very specific information, confirm statements, and to focus or direct the communication process when necessary. They also allow the questioner to check out agreements and to obtain commitment to a specific course of action. However, they are not very helpful for exploring or drawing out general information.

Closed questions elicit details. They provide signals to the responding party as to facts that are important. They may even motivate a person who experiences difficulty getting started. If the questioner relies exclusively on closed questions, she may harm the rapport with the respondent. That other person may feel a sense of denial of an opportunity to inform the questioner of everything that she deems significant. As a result, important information may not be disclosed. Also, lawyers and others often betray a tendency to diagnose problems prematurely. They attempt to fit every problem into a familiar framework and they ask closed questions with that pursuit in mind.

Probing or Follow-up Questions

A questioner who receives a response should not assume that she obtained the answer simply by virtue of the other responding. A vague response to an open-ended question will generally not be sufficient, especially when the question concerns a highly sensitive area. In these situations, it is essential to follow up with probing questions that encourage the respondent to go further and provide more details, to expand upon an earlier answer, to clarify, or to explain the initial response. *Can you tell me more about that? Could you please explain what you meant by your last answer? In what way is that especially important to you? Could you put that another way so that I can understand better?*

On occasion, it may be necessary to rephrase the original question or ask it over again in several different ways, once, twice, or even more times, with each further probing question narrower and more specific than the previous questions.

Failure to Answer

A question may not be answered for one or more reasons: the question was not heard; the question was not understood; the question was too complex or contained more than just one query; the question was perceived as insulting, intrusive, aggressive, or biased; or the listener does not wish to reveal the information for her own reasons. If this happens, it is important to understand the reason for the respondent's failure to answer appropriately.

The questioner should:

1. repeat, rephrase, or simplify the question;

2. acknowledge that the question may be perceived as intrusive and inquire as to what information the respondent feels comfortable revealing; or
3. or explore why the respondent does not wish to disclose the information, whether it is a lack of trust, a concern about confidentiality, or some other reason.

When the basis for the lack of a response is understood, the questioner can address those issues with the respondent.

The Purposes of Questioning

Questioning fulfills a variety of purposes as follows:

1. To Verify Information

Use primarily closed questions to verify or check facts and determine whether your information is correct. *Did you call the real estate agent to ask him to come over on Thursday?*

2. To Gather Information

To get the facts, your questions can be open-ended or closed. Open-ended questions, especially those that include key words and phrases such as *Could you explain. . .*or *Can you tell me more about. . .* will result in more details, whereas closed questions such as *Does your appraisal support your valuation of. . .* will generate more limited responses.

To uncover factual information, start with broad, open-ended questions, which *open the door,* and give the respondent the freedom to answer in any way she wishes. Later, zero in upon specific areas raised in the answer by using closed questions.

3. To Explore

Questions are useful to develop new ideas, to change the course of the discussion, and to encourage the listener to reflect. *Suppose you tried it this way, what do you think might happen?*

They are also helpful in exploring a person's opinions, reactions, attitudes, and values. When exploring personally sensitive areas, avoid the use of the word *why,* which may imply criticism. Instead, choose phrases such as *How do you feel about. . . What's your reaction to. . . Could you explain your reason for. . . What are your thoughts about. . .*

4. **To Justify**

    Questions can be used to challenge rigid thinking and old ideas and to confront the listener. *What makes you so sure of that? Why is that so important now? How does your proposal meet the principles and goals you have agreed upon?*

5. **To Obtain Commitment**

    Use closed questions to get commitment, agreement, or acceptance of your proposals. *Are you ready to sign an agreement that. . . Do you agree that. . . Do you intend to. . .*

Before she frames a question, a speaker should ask herself questions. *Why am I asking this question? What am I looking for? How will I use the answer?*

STATING

When lawyers are talking, they are either asking questions or they are *making statements*. Several terms could be used to describe this second function including *affirming, asserting, declaring,* or *stating*. All of these terms describe a form of communication in which the speaker provides information, states a position, offers a proposal, or responds to statements made by the other party. However, with some of these, other intentions are associated with some purpose.

Some use the terms, *assertive* and *aggressive*, interchangeably. In fact, assertion properly understood connotes an equal measure of concern for the listener and the speaker, while aggression is the instrument of the self solely without any interest in the needs of the other. We prefer the term *stating*, as it is neutral of purpose. As with other skills, we can communicate in this way constructively or destructively.

If the speaker makes her statements with the interest of both parties to the dispute in mind, it will more likely be received positively by the listener. However, there is often a tendency to attribute fault or responsibility to the other. In the CFL process, the parties are both accountable for their actions and responsible for the problem-solving process. In preparing them to participate in CFL, their lawyers should coach them, prior to the first settlement meeting, how to speak for themselves. They should make their statements

using the first person, singular pronoun, *"I,"* and avoid making statements
with the second person pronoun, *"You."*

"I" statements demonstrate that the speaker accepts responsibility for
her actions and words and that she is not blaming the other person. *"You"
statements* generally precede accusations or attributions of fault. They tend
to elicit either outright denials or defensive responses. Defensiveness is not
conducive to effective communication. The listener focuses upon formulating a response and does not listen to the full message conveyed by the
speaker. An "I" statement precludes accusations and judgment as it describes the problematic behaviour. This form of statement allows the listener
to acknowledge that there is a problem, which requires her attention, without
admission that she is at fault or even the precipitate cause.

The "I" statement formula requires that the speaker follow three steps.

1. **Describe your feeling.** *I FEEL. . ..*

2. **Describe the specific behaviour that gives rise to your feeling.**
    WHEN. . .such and such happens.

3. **Describe the effect or consequences that the behaviour has on
    you.** *BECAUSE. . .* **"You" statement** – *Joan, you are so disorgan-
    ized that you never get anywhere on time.*

    "I" statement – *Joan, I get annoyed* (feeling) *when you are late to
    pick up the children* (behaviour) *because I have to work very hard
    to keep the children from getting upset* (consequence of behaviour).

In the second example, the speaker states the problem, identifies the
feeling, and describes the effect upon him without expressing any judgment
about the behaviour of Joan. The "I" statement ought not to be construed
as a weaker expression than a "You" statement. It is expressed with no less
conviction and force. However, an "I" statement allows a listener to understand the emotional content of the speaker's communication without feeling
defensive. "I" statements are more amenable to constructive problem solving than are "You" statements.

LISTENING

We experience listening as an act. Listening leads to either a statement
or a question. Listening is often performed in total silence as entirely a
mental act. It fills the void between the spoken words of communicators.
This apparent lack of visibility should not in any way minimize its importance for effective communication.The average person spends about 75%

of each working day engaged in verbal communications. Logically, about half of this time is or should be spent listening to what others have to say. Yet, most people do not know how to be effective listeners. They miss or misconstrue much of what is said and, consequently, they address the wrong problems and adopt inappropriate solutions. Moreover, a lack of good listening skills leads to tension and distrust, which contributes to conflict escalation.

Effective listening requires energy and concentration, patience and self-discipline. The average person speaks only about 125 words per minute and can listen to 400 words per minute. Instead of responding or reacting immediately, the effective listener remains patient and focused on the speaker and does not interrupt. This listener hears the speaker out, whether or not she is in agreement with what is said, in order to understand completely the message that is being sent.

In order for good communication to take place, the speaker must know that she has been heard and heard correctly. People need to be heard on two distinct levels, the *cognitive* and the *affective*. The cognitive level consists of the substantive content, the facts and information that are communicated, a level within which traditional lawyers are most comfortable. The affective level incorporates the emotions and feelings attached to the substantive content and the relative degree of importance which the speaker places upon those facts and that information. The collaborative approach requires that the lawyers attend to this level as well as the cognitive.

The listening skill most important in a CFL context is *active listening*. It is a very powerful skill and one that is essential for effective practitioners to master. Active listening is used to uncover the underlying interests of the disputing spouses, a necessary preliminary to the interest-based model of negotiation that we describe in chapter 11. It involves more than quietly paying attention to what is being said, maintaining eye contact with the speaker, and nodding occasionally. These behaviours are important *passive listening* skills. However, passive listening is not sufficient for effective communication to occur. The clients must know that they have been heard and heard correctly. This requires the listener to reflect back to the speaker, in her own words, what the listener has heard.

The essence of active listening is *paraphrasing* or *summarizing* what has been heard, followed by *repeating* or *restating* the main ideas and feelings back to the speaker, in the listener's own words. Active listening gives the speaker the sense that she has been fully heard and understood by the listener, on both the cognitive and affective levels. It does not convey that she agrees with the speaker's statement. Active listening offers the speaker the opportunity to correct any possible misunderstandings by the listener. At the same time, it builds rapport and a sense of trust, which in turn facilitates further effective communication.

Active listening should be used before reacting, responding, arguing, blaming, defending, criticizing; whenever people are expressing strong feelings or evidencing a strong need to talk; when people need to sort out their feelings or thoughts; or when a listener is unsure what the speaker is really trying to communicate.

Active listening requires four steps:

1. **Concentrate fully on what is being said** and the way in which it is being said, including the nonverbal indicators such as tone of voice, facial expressions, gestures, and bodily posture.

2. **Identify the major content of the speaker's message**, (the main message that the speaker is trying to communicate) and the accompanying affect (the emotions or feelings that accompany the main message).

3. **Paraphrase or restate in your own words** both the central ideas expressed by the speaker and the feelings which you have identified, using words of a comparable emotional intensity.

4. **Listen for the speaker's response**, confirming that you have heard and understood accurately, or correcting your misunderstanding.

MIKE: (*with emphasis*) I can't believe that you could just announce that our marriage was over without any explanation.

LAWYER: You sound shocked that Joan left without first talking things over with you. (*Identifying feelings and paraphrasing message in own words*)

MIKE: Yes, I sure am. She had no reason to walk out. I've always tried to make her happy. (*Confirming and continuing*)

LAWYER: So you must be feeling really confused because you don't understand the reasons behind her actions.

MIKE: That's for sure. Why wouldn't she say something about what led her to making a decision that would so drastically affect our family?

LAWYER: Have you any ideas about that yourself?

For effective active listening, we offer these guidelines and suggestions:

• Decide that you really want to listen and hear what the other person has to say. Anticipate that you are going to hear something interesting.

- Concentrate hard and listen to everything. Imagine that you have to repeat the information to someone else, so you don't want to miss anything. As the other person talks, try to summarize what she is saying to yourself.

- Try putting yourself in the shoes of the other person to understand how she might be feeling. Choose a word that matches that feeling.

- Do not argue, interrupt, finish the other person's sentence, offer advice, give suggestions, recount your own personal experiences, or become defensive.

- Remain neutral and nonjudgmental at all times. Accept and attempt to understand the speaker's message, whether or not you agree with it. Put aside your own personal views and opinions while you are listening.

- Be focused and give the other person your full attention. Use your own body language to convey interest and to encourage the speaker to continue. Avoid distractions, such as a ringing telephone.

- Remember that listening takes effort and be patient.

Active listening involves paraphrasing the emotions of others. It is closely linked with empathy or the ability to feel as others do when they encounter a particular experience. Many lawyers are unaccustomed to dealing with feelings in their work and will need to practise this skill.

OTHER COMMUNICATION SKILLS

Many of the skills that CFL practitioners use are the same skills relied upon by effective mediators. We offer a summary review of some mediation practices that are applicable in a CFL context.

Responding to Intense Emotions

Communications are generally impeded when either or both parties are experiencing and exhibiting particularly high levels of emotion. These feelings extend across a continuum. Anger moves from irritation to annoyance to anger to fury to rage. Anxiety begins with concern that becomes worry, anxiety, fear, and then terror. Sad people may feel lost, then sad, then depressed, and, at some point, even suicidal.

To facilitate communication, it is necessary first to defuse these high intensity emotions. The technique used is a version of active listening. The initial response is made solely to the affective or emotional level of the message previously communicated. The listener attempts to summarize in a single word the feeling message expressed and to reflect this back to the speaker. It is important not to overstate the feeling but, rather, to try to find a word that approximates or only slightly understates the emotional intensity of the speaker. Only after the feeling has been acknowledged, does the listener begin to respond to the cognitive or substantive level of the message. At this point, the speaker's emotional state may be less intense and she may be in a more receptive mood for communicating. The lawyer acknowledges the high emotion first before they proceed.

> JOAN: (*with voice raised*) He's got to stop being so insensitive to my needs.
>
> LAWYER: You sound like you are very upset.
>
> JOAN: Yes. You're darn right I am. I am extremely upset and I have every right to be!
>
> LAWYER: It's very upsetting when you don't feel that you are being heard.
>
> JOAN: (*subsiding*) Yes, it sure is. I'm simply trying to improve myself and it's frustrating when Mike doesn't acknowledge that.

Responding to Denial and Resistance

In many cases, an active listening response appears to fall on deaf ears. The speaker denies the feeling attributed to them, sometimes quite vigorously. Denial is a psychological defence mechanism that a person uses to protect their ego. This type of response inhibits effective communication and the practitioner must attend to it. First, the practitioner must respond to the affective or emotional level only, using another, less intense word to describe the person's feeling. If this effort is likewise met with a denial, the practitioner should reflect back the person's nonverbal behaviour that indicates their feelings.

The lawyer attempts active listening and the party denies the attribution. At that point, it becomes necessary to identify the behaviour and turn it back to the party to describe what they are feeling in their own words.

> MIKE: (*with voice raised, face flushed*) Joan has got to recognize

how trapped I feel in my work. She refuses to think of my situation.

LAWYER: You sound like you're really upset about this.

MIKE: Who me? Upset? I don't get upset. Not me.

LAWYER: Well, it seemed to me from your agitated tone of voice that you were upset about something. How would you describe the way her behaviour has affected you then?

Confronting

Confronting is another useful skill, which can be used to facilitate blocked communications. Confrontation is not synonymous with accusation. *You must be crazy to think that way.* Rather, the skill involves holding up to the person, in a completely neutral and nonjudgmental way, her inconsistent behaviours and responses. The purpose is to have the other person reflect upon these inconsistencies. It is this dissonance and not the person that is confronted.

LAWYER: Joan, you say that you want Mike to be able to have a place of his own where he can live comfortably with the children when they are with him, but you want to have possession of the matrimonial home for an indefinite period. How is he going to acquire another place for himself if he does not get his share of the house equity?

Reframing

Reframing, a potent variation of active listening, is a skill which involves restating an emotionally charged, negative statement, and turning it into a neutral or even positive statement, without losing the essential content of the speaker's message. It is used to de-escalate and manage conflict, to facilitate positive communications and constructive problem solving, to identify interests underlying stated positions, to moderate demands, and to eliminate negative, value-laden language which serves to impede effective communications.

Reframing emphasizes positive goals and needs, and eliminates blaming and accusations. The reworded or reframed statement is put in terms that can be heard and understood. It is not simply a reaction. The exasperation of the party cannot be overlooked. However, it would not be effective for the participants to reaffirm the initial sentiment expressed by the party.

Reframing allows them the means to acknowledge the feeling while moving ahead in the process.

> JOAN: I'm not going to sit here and listen to Mike whine about his life.

> LAWYER: You would like to take a more constructive approach to resolving your problems. Is that correct, Joan?

Reframing is a challenging technique. A reframe must not minimize the feelings of the speaker nor patronize her.

Pre-empting

Pre-empting is a technique used to head off, prevent or soften undesirable behaviour by predicting its occurrence in advance. For example, where the parties have not seen each other for some time, the lawyers might comment at the outset of the first settlement meeting on how difficult it must be for each of them under the circumstances. They should commend them for taking this first step towards resolution and offer to take a break whenever they find it difficult to continue.

Focusing

Focusing is a skill used to bring a party back on track whenever she wanders off on an irrelevant tangent or is *all over the map*. It requires a polite interruption, *parking* the newly introduced topic for discussion at a later time, and focusing the discussion back to the previous topic. The concern expressed must be acknowledged and validated. However, the parties remain focused upon one task at a time.

> MIKE: (*when discussing the division of property*) I don't know how I am going to return to my writing career. We have no money.

> LAWYER: You sound worried about your future happiness, Mike. We have to look at the life goals for all members of your family. Right now let's concentrate on how you will divide your property and come back to that concern later.

Summarizing

Periodic summarizing of the information disclosed through the settlement process is an extremely effective technique. It is often useful to summarize the collective issues to be discussed prior to moving on to uncover the interests underlying the issues. It may be helpful to summarize the interests of each party as well as their mutual interests before beginning the option generation phase.

> LAWYER: So you are both here today to find a solution that maximizes each of your time with your children and continues your role as an involved parent.

Good communication skills on the part of both lawyers and clients are necessary for effective collaboration.

Communication

The Steps in Effective Communication
Decide upon the message.
Sending the message.
Receive the message.
Respond to the message.
Acknowledge receipt of the message.

Non-verbal Communication
Communication through body orientation, body posture, gestures, facial expressions and eye movements, voice, clothing and accessories, environment and furnishings, use of space, and culture.

Verbal Communication
Questioning, stating, listening, and other skills.

Questioning
Open-ended questions invite narrative accounts;
they provide a great deal of information.
Closed questions narrow the focus of the inquiry;
they provide more details.

Stating
Use "I" statements; they inform the listener
of the speaker's feelings and the reasons.
Avoid "you" statements; they attribute fault or responsibility.

Listening

Passive listening involves quietly paying attention,
maintaining eye contact, and nodding.
Active listening involves paraphrasing and restating
what the speaker said and felt when speaking.

Other Verbal Communication Skills

Responding to intense emotions, responding to denial and resistance,
confronting, reframing, pre-empting, focusing, and summarizing.

11

Negotiation

INTEREST-BASED NEGOTIATION

Along with communication, interest-based negotiation is a core skill for collaborative practice. We devote this chapter to a discussion of the interest-based negotiation model developed by Fisher, Ury, and Patton and the Harvard Negotiation Project. Following this discussion, we offer a variation for CFL.

As originally presented in *Getting to Yes*, the interest-based negotiation model is comprised of *four basic points* entitled, *people*, *interests*, *options*, and *criteria*. In a subsequent version, the Harvard Negotiation Project expanded the *four basic points* to the *seven elements*.[1]

Interests

Have the parties explicitly understood their own interests?
Do the parties understand each other's priorities and constraints?

Options

Are sufficient options being generated?

Is the process of inventing separated from the process of making commitments?

Legitimacy

Have relevant precedents and other outside standards of fairness been considered?
Can principles be found that are persuasive to the other side? To us?

Relationship

What is the ability of the parties to work together?
Is there a working relationship between their negotiators?
Are the parties paying attention to the kind of relationship they want in the future?

Communication

Is the way the parties communicate helping or interfering with their abilityto deal constructively with the conflict?
Are mechanisms in place to confirm that what is understood is in fact whatwas intended?

Commitment

Are potential commitments well-crafted?
Does each party know what it would like the other party to agree to?
If the other side said yes, is it clear who would do what tomorrow morning?

Alternatives

Does each side understand its Best Alternative To a Negotiated Agreement – its BATNA?
Are the negative consequences of not settling being used to bring the partiestogether?[2]

In this synopsis of the interest-based negotiation model, we integrate the four basic points and the seven elements.

INTERESTS

"The basic problem in a negotiation lies not in conflicting positions, but in the conflict between each side's needs, desires, concerns, and fears."[3] The needs, desires, concerns, and fears that underlie a negotiator's bargaining position constitute his interests. Interests motivate people. "Your position is something you have decided upon. Your interests are what caused you to so decide."[4] The disclosure of interests may reveal more areas of compatibility between two parties to a negotiation than would be evident from merely looking at their bargaining positions. The interests of the parties are the keys to successful negotiations for two reasons. First, for every interest there are likely several possible ways to satisfy it. Second, many more compatible than conflicting interests lie behind opposed positions.

The identification of interests is a challenge for interest-based negotiators. While the benefits of looking behind positions for interests may be obvious, how to accomplish the task is not so apparent. "A position is likely to be concrete and explicit; the interests underlying it may well be unexpressed, intangible, and perhaps inconsistent."[5] A negotiator should first ask "Why?" He must be clear that he is not seeking justification of a position of the other but an understanding of the needs, desires, concerns, and fears that position addresses. To grasp why the other negotiator will not make the decision a negotiator seeks, he should ask "Why not?" Does he have an interest that stands in the way of making that decision?

Each side to a negotiation likely has multiple interests motivating him or her to take a position. It is unlikely that they have identical interests. Furthermore, a negotiator may be subject to the influences of others – an employer, a new partner, a business partner, a family member – to whose interests he is sensitive. The most powerful interests are basic human needs: security, economic well being, a sense of belonging, recognition, and control over one's life. These needs are often overlooked as the emphasis in a negotiation is usually given to monetary considerations. A helpful practice tip is for a negotiator to write down his interests and the interests of the other as those interests occur to him and certainly before the actual negotiation.

Interests may relate to one or more of the *substantive, procedural, and psychological* concerns of the parties or either of them.[6] Substantive interests relate to the tangible issues, the matters of substance at the core of the dispute; what it is that has to be decided. Procedural interests concern the process for interacting, communicating, or decision-making; how it is that the decision will be made and, once made, implemented. Psychological interests pertain to how a party is treated, respected, or acknowledged; what or how he feels prior to, during the course of, and at the conclusion of the process.

An example of the distinction between positions and interests in a family context is found in a dispute over spousal support. The dependant spouse asserts a claim for support. Her position is that she be paid the sum of $1,000 per month for the remainder of her life. Her husband's position is that he is willing to pay her $350 per month for three years. The principal substantive interests of the wife are her financial needs, her ability to maintain her lifestyle. Her procedural interests may include her need for punctuality and regularity with the payments. Her psychological interests may be a fear of poverty, a desire for retribution, and the recognition of her contributions to the marriage.

The husband has substantive interests, primarily his own financial needs, particularly if he is to maintain a relationship with his children. His procedural interests may include aligning the support obligation with the receipt of his salary. He too has psychological interests, perhaps a need to absolve his sense of guilt, while at the same time a desire to get on with his new life. Together, the husband and wife share common interests, their children and financial security.

Fisher, Ury, and Patton discuss *interests advocacy* in practice as well as in preparation. They recommend that negotiators make their interests come alive. It is important that the other feels the importance and legitimacy of a negotiator's interests. A negotiator should acknowledge openly that the interests of the other are also important. "(I)f you want the other side to appreciate *your* interests, begin by demonstrating that you appreciate *theirs*."[7]

Negotiators should put the problem before the answer; they should give their interests and reasoning first and their conclusions later. The other side may never listen if they believe that the speaker already has the solution to the problem. A negotiator must look forward, not back. "You will satisfy your interests better if you talk about where you would like to go rather than about where you have come from."[8] The principled negotiator is concrete but flexible; he remains open for fresh ideas. Interest-based negotiators are hard on the problem, soft on the people. They should be just as hard about interests as positional bargainers are about positions.

OPTIONS

The story of two children dividing an orange is a tale familiar to students of interest-based negotiation.

> Yet all too often negotiators end up like the proverbial children who quarreled over an orange. After they finally agreed to divide the orange in half, the first child took one half, ate the fruit, and threw away the peel, while the other threw away the fruit and used the peel from the second half in baking a cake. All too often negotiators "leave money on the table" – they fail to reach agreement when they might have, or the agreement they do reach could have been better for each side. Too many negotiations end up with half an orange for each side

instead of the whole fruit for one and the whole peel for the other. Why?[9]

The solution was determined before the interests were developed. If the interests had been identified, other options for the resolution of this dispute might have been considered.

According to the interest-based negotiation model, negotiators must separate the act of inventing options from the act of judging them. "Since judgment hinders imagination, separate the creative act from the critical one; separate the process of thinking up possible decisions from the process of selecting among them. Invent first, decide later."[10]

Brainstorming is one method often used by negotiators to generate creative options. The lawyers ask the parties to suggest as many ideas as they can to resolve a particular issue. While one of the lawyers facilitates this process, the other records the proposals made on a flip chart or white board. The parties are not to criticize any of the options during brainstorming. They defer their evaluation until they have exhausted their collective capacity to contribute. After the brainstorming session is over, the parties review the options, single out the most promising ideas, eliminate those that are unacceptable, and weigh the relative advantages and disadvantages of those that remain. As an alternative to conducting the entire brainstorming process at a single settlement meeting, the parties may develop their options between sessions, provided that they are careful not to become committed to particular problem solutions.

Notwithstanding the value in having a variety of options from which to choose, negotiators seldom take the time to generate them. Their positions appear at opposite ends of a linear spectrum and the only other option considered is *splitting the difference.* There are four major obstacles to inventing an array of options. First, negotiators often exercise premature judgment as to the appropriate course to take which in turn hinders the imagination. Second, they frequently search for a single answer rather than a variety of answers. Third, negotiators assume a fixed pie; they think in zero-sum terms. Fourth, each of them concerns him or herself with only his or her interests, whereas to satisfy self-interest requires equal regard for other-interest.

Other processes besides brainstorming are available to assist the parties with the development of creative settlement possibilities. They could adopt a *building block* approach in which they construct a settlement incrementally, one block at a time. Alternatively, they could *image* a final agreement: what does it look like; what are its principles; and how can those principles be used to guide the parties in their negotiations. They might opt for the *one-text* or *single-text* procedure described by Fisher, Ury, and Patton.[11] The lawyers prepare a text of a possible settlement scenario drawing upon the interests of the parties. The parties respond to this draft with suggestions, following which the lawyers prepare a second version. This process repeats itself until all that remains is what the parties themselves created.

Tessler offers another method to negotiate collaboratively: *Propose, Explain, Upgrade*.

In collaborative practice, try eliminating the concept of "counterproposal." It implies positional bargaining and opposition. Words matter; words shape thought. Instead of counterproposals, think of the steps in negotiating this way:

- PROPOSE: Put together a concept for settling one, many, or all issues, and present it at a four-way meeting. The idea is to develop a concept that meets all legitimate needs of both parties to the maximum extent possible, or that allocates deficiencies equitably if that is not possible. But do not become attached to the proposal.
- EXPLAIN: At the same or the next meeting, the agenda is limited to answering all questions from the other client and other lawyer that they may have about the proposal. No attacks, critiques, or defences; no alternatives. The agenda consists solely of continuing to ask and explain until the shape and content of the proposal are fully understood by all.
- UPGRADE: At the next four-way meeting, the lawyer and client who did not make the initial proposal respond by offering their improvements, or upgrades. The upgrades consist of ideas that will make the original proposal work better in meeting the legitimate needs of both clients and/or allocating deficiencies equitably.
- The process continues with explanations and upgrades, until agreement is reached or a new proposal is offered.[12]

This model resembles the one-text or single-text instrument with a single, significant difference: one of the parties develops and presents the initial proposal rather than the lawyers or a neutral.

In the support dispute previously discussed, a number of options are conceivable. The parties could suggest several different amounts for the support to be paid. The payments could be indefinite or time-limited or subject to review upon the occurrence of certain events, such as the remarriage of the wife or the last of the children ceasing to be dependant. Support could be tied to specific purposes such as retraining or the purchase of a vehicle to enable the wife to obtain employment.

Options will be more or less appealing to the parties to the extent that they maximize the satisfaction of their common and individual interests. If the wife does obtain and maintain secure employment with the assistance of her husband, the parties will more likely be able to preserve comparable lifestyles in accordance with the standard enjoyed prior to their separation. She may still require some *top-up* support. However, the wife is moving toward economic self-sufficiency and the husband acquires a sense that he too can move ahead with his new life. Each of them should then be better able to contribute toward the support of their children in satisfaction of that common interest.

Interest-based negotiators look for options that realize mutual gains. The goal is to find those that will leave each party equally satisfied. "We tend to think of 'our' options designed to meet our interests and 'their' options designed to meet their interests. Yet the shared goal is to find an option that meets the interests of both sides at least well enough to be acceptable to them."[13] Invariably, there are some common interests. Negotiators must search for them. A variation of the theme of searching for shared interests is to consider ways that differing interests may be complementary or dovetail. An interest-based negotiator must do whatever he can to make the decision to accept easier for the other party, to step into his shoes and ask if this idea is something that he would find acceptable.

LEGITIMACY

An external standard of legitimacy, such as precedent or the law, may convince one or the other of the parties that an outcome is acceptable. The terms, *objective criteria* and *standards of legitimacy*, can be used interchangeably. The development of appropriate criteria is another challenge for interest-based negotiators. For any dispute, there may be more than one standard available: market value, precedent, professional standards, costs, what a court would do, moral standards, equal treatment, tradition, and reciprocity. The criteria must be independent of the will of either party and they must be legitimate and practical. The development of acceptable procedures for determining appropriate standards is an alternative to listing them. Methods include taking turns, drawing lots, and letting someone else decide.

In determining standards and procedures, interest-based negotiators should observe three practices. First, they should frame each issue as a *joint search*. It may be helpful to begin by identifying their *principles*. Second, they should reason and be open to reason as to which standards are most appropriate and how they should be applied. Third, negotiators should never yield to pressure, only to principle. They invite their negotiation partners to state their reasons; they suggest the objective criteria or standards of legitimacy they think should apply, although they remain open to other suggestions; and, they do not give in to pressure.

Among the concerns expressed about the principled negotiation model is that voiced by Deborah Kolb and Gloria Coolidge.[14] They observe that "advice to separate people from problems and focus on objective criteria, gives a rationalized and objective cast to negotiation that may be quite different from the subjective and embedded forms of feminine understanding."[15] The interest-based negotiation model does not preclude the parties from creating their own *subjective* criteria to assess the options they generate. As with objective standards of legitimacy, they may identify principles that will guide them in making their critical decisions.

RELATIONSHIP

In *Getting to Yes*, Fisher, Ury, and Patton recommend that negotiators separate the people from the problem. "A basic fact about negotiation, easy to forget in corporate and international transactions, is that you are dealing not with abstract representatives of the 'other side,' but with human beings. They have emotions, deeply held values, and different backgrounds and viewpoints; and they are unpredictable. So are you."[16] This observation is all the more applicable to family disputes.

When considering the parties to a negotiation as human beings, it is important to consider how they interact and interrelate. "In diagnosing a conflict we will want to look at the state of the relationship. What relationship did the parties have prior to this conflict? Are they likely to have future dealings? What is the level of confidence each party has in the reliability of the other? Each negotiator?"[17] Negotiators must not overlook relationship issues in the negotiation of substantive issues; they may account for a part of the problem. Attending to them will likely be necessary in the process, and their resolution may be an essential component of the solution.

A negotiation proceeds at two levels simultaneously. Negotiators endeavour to obtain results that satisfy their substantive interests. However, they also have an interest in their relationship. Most people want to avoid doing anything that might imperil a mutually beneficial ongoing relationship. At the very least, negotiators generally want to maintain an effective working relationship while they attempt to negotiate an agreement, as Roger Fisher and Scott Brown suggest in their sequel to *Getting to Yes*.[18] They offer their unconditionally constructive strategy: a negotiator should do only those things that are both good for the relationship and good for him, whether or not the other reciprocates.[19]

Another dimension of this element is the entanglement of the substantive and relationship issues. People misinterpret statements made in the course of a negotiation on substance as comments about them personally and about their relationship with the other person. This is particularly true in the divorce context. Interest-based negotiators must be able to deal with substantive issues while maintaining a good working relationship.

COMMUNICATION

"Without communication there is no negotiation. Negotiation is a process of communicating back and forth for the purpose of reaching a joint decision."[20] There are three major communication problems that impede progress in a negotiation. First, there may be no communication; the negotiators may have given up on talking to one another or at least in a meaningful and productive fashion. Second, even if the negotiators are talking, they may not be listening to one another. Third, negotiators may misinterpret what others are saying.

To improve communication negotiators should consider the following four suggestions. First, they should listen and acknowledge what is being said. Second, they must speak to be understood. Third, they should speak for a purpose, ensuring they deliver their intended message. In short, negotiators adopt the communication practices and protocols outlined in chapter 10. They ask open-ended and closed questions as appropriate, they use "I" statements and not "You" statements, they actively listen, and they paraphrase, reframe, and summarize.

COMMITMENT

Commitment refers to the mutual intent of both parties to commit to the implementation of their agreement. "Parties are often asked to commit early and publicly to what they will and will not do. If they do so, each subsequent move in the negotiation is likely to be seen as a strategically difficult and politically costly concession."[21] If commitment is sought prematurely, the parties are often unable to appreciate interests or to explore options. For this reason, immediate temporary parenting and financial arrangements should not foreclose any final settlement possibilities.

At some point in their negotiation, the parties find the option that maximizes their interest satisfaction and meets the criteria they set for themselves. It is appropriate that each then ask the other a question. *Are you willing to commit yourself to this agreement?*

ALTERNATIVES

BATNA is an acronym for *Best Alternative to a Negotiated Agreement.* It first appears in *Getting to Yes* in answer to a question. "What if they are

more powerful?" It might well be asked whether the interest-based negotiation model is appropriate if one of the parties has more power than the
other party.

Negotiators ought to avoid the *bottom line* approach. A bottom line is
a position and it prevents a party from deriving the maximum benefit from
the negotiation. In particular, it inhibits the imagination. While a bottom
line may protect a negotiator from accepting an agreement that should be
rejected, it may also result in the rejection of an agreement that should be
accepted.

> The reason you negotiate is to produce something better than the results you
> can obtain without negotiating. What are those results? What is the alterna-
> tive? What is your BATNA – your Best Alternative to a Negotiated Agree-
> ment? That is the standard against which any proposed agreement should be
> measured. That is the only standard which can protect you both from accepting
> terms that are too unfavourable and from rejecting terms it would be in your
> interest to accept.[22]

BATNA provides both security and flexibility. A better BATNA adds to
the power of a negotiator. Negotiators should develop their BATNAs and
consider the BATNAs of the others with whom they negotiate.

A party to a family dispute should identify his BATNA in respect of
each substantive issue. As an example, he may wish to remain in the matrimonial home. Before he enters into the negotiation, he must be aware of
his alternatives in the event he is unable to negotiate that agreement with
his spouse. His BATNA might be to acquire another accommodation or it
might be to proceed to court where he can seek an order for possession of
the home. An awareness of his BATNA enables him to express himself
more forcefully and persuasively in the negotiation. He has a sense of the
direction he will take if he is unable to negotiate the desired outcome. It is
preferable to appearing so deeply committed to a goal that he is unable to
consider anything else.

In the language of interest-based negotiation, *options* and *alternatives*
are separate constructs. Options are what the parties create together in
negotiation. Alternatives are not shared. They may be the same or they may
be different. What tends to be consistent among negotiators is a tendency
"to underestimate the costs to themselves of not reaching agreement and to
overestimate the costs to the other side."[23]

Each party has alternatives to a negotiated agreement. One possible
alternative is to commence litigation. He or she must consider the consequences associated with that alternative including the likelihood of the
desired outcome, the degree of risk, and the cost and delay involved. Another
alternative is to preserve the status quo. A reminder of party BATNAs may

help the parties to overcome negotiation barriers. They recognize that failure to move beyond impasse condemns them to their alternatives. The alternatives also provide a litmus test for the acceptability of a negotiated outcome. They are held up in comparison with the options created in negotiation and their relative advantages and disadvantages are revealed.

NEGOTIATION AND CFL

If we integrate the seven elements of interest-based negotiation with the CFL process, a collaborative negotiation model emerges with its own *seven steps*.

1. **Issues**

    In their opening statements, the parties explain what they hope to achieve in the CFL process. The lawyers assist them in identifying the issues that will comprise their agenda. When necessary, the lawyers reframe the issues into a list of problems, which require a joint solution.

2. **Information**

    The lawyers explain the legal context and act as information resources. The parties collect all information related to the problems to be solved. They decide what information they require to consider the issues. They assign the production tasks, jointly retain required experts, and estimate the time frame for delivery. Negotiation of any final agreement is deferred pending full information exchange.

3. **Interests**

    As they discuss each of the issues on their agenda, the parties explore for underlying interests – their needs, desires, fears, and concerns. The lawyers give those interests voice through active listening. Some practitioners record interests on a flip chart or white board and/or in the minutes of the meeting.

4. **Principles**

    The parties agree upon principles to guide them in the assessment of their options. The parties may choose standards derived from the law or developed by them. These principles should then be noted on a flip chart or white board and/or in the minutes of the meeting and later in the Separation Agreement.

5. **Options**

    Aware of their underlying interests and with their principles before them, the parties then engage in option generation. Options come from three sources: the law, the real world, and the parties themselves. Brainstorming is effective here although there are other methods to develop an array of options. Initially, the ideas should be sought from the parties. If they are unable to put forward anything other than their pre-negotiation points of view or they have exhausted their ideas, the lawyers may intervene to assist while avoiding taking over this part of the negotiation process.

6. **Alternatives**

    The clients' respective BATNAs may be self-evident or they may explicitly describe them at some point in the process. During the negotiation, a reminder of them can be an effective intervention to move beyond impasse.

7. **Agreement**

    The parties select the options that maximize their interest satisfaction, comply with their principles, and are preferable to their alternatives. The lawyers draft a Separation Agreement using clear, plain language, setting out the parties' principles, intentions, and goals, and generally confirming the basis upon which the Agreement was reached.

Although the seven steps are presented sequentially, the participants need not follow them in the above order with the exception that they should not proceed to options prematurely. They may find it necessary to loop back to a previous step, should they encounter a barrier or impasse, which we discuss in greater detail in chapter 12.

FACILITATION

Throughout this book, we refer to CFL lawyers as facilitators or as facilitating a negotiation. The noun, *facilitator*, and the verb, *facilitate*, derive from the Latin word, *facilitas*, which means to make easy or less difficult. Facilitation is an activity familiar to a diverse population of professional consultants and intervenors in a variety of contexts that includes adult education,[24] organization development,[25] and mediation.[26]

Moore offers a sample explanation of the role of the mediator that may be offered to parties prior to the commencement of mediation.

> My role as mediator will be to help you identify problems or issues that you want to talk about, help you clarify needs that must be met, assist you in developing a problem-solving process that will enable you to reach your goals, keep you focused and on the right track, and generally help you define a new relationship that each of you will find more comfortable and acceptable.[27]

He submits that a main task of the mediator is to *facilitate communication* and *information exchange*.

Mediators and CFL lawyers are negotiation facilitators within their respective processes. However, there is a critical distinction in the relationship that each has with the parties to the dispute. A mediator does not act for either of the parties; he is neutral and he must not provide any form of professional advice to either of them. A lawyer is the legal representative for one of the parties. Throughout the process, he provides legal advice and support to him.

Lawyers as advocates are accustomed to conducting negotiations as spokespersons for their clients. In CFL, the principals to the negotiation are the parties themselves. It is their process. Their lawyers are there to assist them. This facilitative role ought not to be construed as passive. On the contrary, the lawyer as facilitator is active. Rather than asserting positions, making demands, reciting precedents, and bargaining on behalf of the client, he asks questions, actively listens, reframes and summarizes. His goal is to help the parties reveal their underlying interests, generate creative options, and ultimately negotiate mutually acceptable settlement agreements. Effective facilitation requires a different skill set than advocacy.

The role of the CFL lawyer as facilitator changes over the course of the negotiation. During the preliminary stages, the parties are still acclimatizing themselves to the process and it is usually necessary for the lawyers to play a more *directing* or *guiding* role. They set the climate, establish the process, clarify the roles of the participants, help the parties define their goals, and overall enable them to acquire a sense of identity as a distinct group with a purpose.

As the negotiation unfolds, the lawyers assume a *coaching* role. They surface issues, legitimize concerns, facilitate communication, manage emotions, invite input and feedback, and keep the discussions focused and moving forward. Once the parties begin to engage directly with each other in problem solving the issues, their lawyers limit themselves to a *supporting* role. They offer their own resources and ideas to maintain momentum if the parties appear to be stuck or intervene if they encounter more formidable barriers.

A CASE STUDY

As an example of the CFL negotiation model in practice, we offer this brief case study. Joan and Mike met in 1982 and married in 1984. At the time of their marriage, Mike was a struggling author of science fiction short stories and novels. Joan was an elementary school teacher and she had been teaching for four years. They had little property other than the furnishings of their respective apartments and a car. They moved into Joan's two-bedroom apartment. Mike used the additional room as his study.

Their first child, Jillian, was born in 1987. Joan took the maximum maternity leave and afterwards returned to teach full time. Realizing that they needed more money each month, Mike went to teachers' college and secured a teaching position. He began to teach secondary school English. Mike continued with his writing although he had to move his desk from out of the spare bedroom, which had become the nursery, into the living room. He tried to work in the evenings although he found it difficult. There was simply not enough time or space.

Joan and Mike bought a house. They had two more children, June and Mickey. The children are now 14, 11, and 7. Joan taught part time for a few years but, eventually, they decided that it was too much for her to manage. They devoted themselves to their children. Joan looked after most of the day-to-day responsibilities. Mike participated fully in their extra-curricular activities. He taught summer school to fund family holidays and the children's summer camp. There was little time or energy left for the marital relationship.

After the youngest of their children was in full-time attendance at school, Joan developed a catering business that she operates out of the home. Mike supported Joan's endeavour; he helped her develop their promotional materials and website and took over more of the care of the children. Over time, Mike became envious. He had always dreamed of being an author. Teaching was his second choice. He found it impossible to teach during the day and write in the evening. Joan seemed to be realizing a latent desire to be an independent business person. His personal ambitions seemed thwarted and, furthermore, Joan seemed preoccupied and distant.

Mike became increasingly despondent. Joan became increasingly focused on her business. They began to argue. As their arguments became more frequent, they were less careful about avoiding this behaviour in front of the children. They sought marital counselling, which was ultimately unsuccessful. They decided to separate and they sought legal advice.

Joan and Mike consulted with CFL lawyers and agreed to participate in this process. At the first settlement meeting, they were successful in dealing with their immediate concerns and developing an agenda of the issues they needed to resolve. Each of them was required to obtain other information and documents in anticipation of the negotiation that was to begin at the next settlement meeting.

We offer an outline of their negotiation using the *seven steps* template.

1. **Issues**

    1.   Children
        (a)   Parenting Schedule
        (b)   Decision making
        (c)   Information exchange

    2.   Support
        (a)   Child support
        (b)   Child-related expenses
        (c)   Spousal support

    3.   Property
        (a)   Disposition of the home
        (b)   Division of other property and debts
        (c)   Equalization

2. **Information**

- Sworn Financial Statements
- Income tax returns
- Mike's pay stub from employer as to salary
- Joan's financial statements and tax returns for business
- Joint actuarial valuation of pensions
- Bank records

3. **Interests**

Mike
- Maximize quality time with the children
- Obtain home suitable for children
- Resume writing career

Joan
- Maintain standard of living
- Develop business
- Ensure financial security
- Keep children in neighbourhood

Shared
- Protect the children from negative impact of separation
- Avoid disruption in lives of the children
- Share parenting responsibilities meaningfully

- Establish effective co-parenting relationship
- Maintain children's lifestyle
- Resolve dispute early and inexpensively
- Avoid court

4. **Principles**

1. Parenting principles developed by the parties.
   (a) Share parenting time and responsibilities equitably
   (b) Mutual involvement in decision making for children
   (c) Maintain quality of life for children
   (d) Mimimize disruption in lives of children

2. Financial plans developed with input from financial advisors.
   (a) Maintain comparable standards of living
   (b) Help Joan achieve economic self-sufficiency
   (c) Plan for payment of post-secondary education for children
   (d) Ensure future financial security for both

3. The child support guidelines and property equalization legislation.

5. **Options**

1. Parenting
   (a) Primary residence with Joan, secondary residence with Mike, alternate weekends and one evening a week.
   (b) Share parenting, alternate weekends from Friday to Monday morning and two evenings with each parent overnight.
   (c) Share parenting with one week with each parent.
   (d) In all cases, share decision making

2. Child Support
   (a) Mike pays basic child support in accordance with the Child Support Guidelines and proportionate sharing of extraordinary expenses.
   (b) Mike pays Joan difference between table support payable by him and table support payable by her plus share extraordinary expenses proportionate to income.
   (c) Each parent contributes a proportionate amount into a bank account for the children to cover expenses such as clothing, tutoring, activities, school expenses, daycare, and payments to education fund.

3. Spousal Support
   (a) Periodic spousal support payable by Mike to Joan for

an indefinite period, subject to variation in the event of a material change in circumstances

(b) Periodic spousal support payable by Mike to Joan for five years

(c) Periodic spousal support payable by Mike to Joan to be reviewed after two years

(d) Lump sum spousal support payable by Mike to Joan equal to amount needed for Joan to buy out Mike's interest in the house

(e) No spousal support

4. Property
   (a) Exclusive possession of the matrimonial home in favour of Joan for two years until support review
   (b) Sale of home, pensions equalized out of proceeds and each to purchase new home in area
   (c) Joan to buy out Mike's interest in the home, taking into account equalization payment Mike owes Joan on account of pensions

The participants may choose to resolve each of the substantive issues separately or group them into integrated option packages.

6. **Alternatives**

Each party could retain new litigation lawyers to go to court. The additional costs will reduce the range of choices available to them. The resulting tension and uncertainty will have a negative impact upon their children and their ability to co-parent. Their lawyers are unable to predict the outcome.

7. **Agreement**

The parties agree to share parenting and decision making, have the children reside with each parent under a week-about parenting schedule. Joan will buy out Mike's interest in the home taking into account the equalization payment Mike owes Joan to equalize their pensions. Mike will pay table child support and spousal support to equalize their net disposable incomes. Extraordinary expenses for children and education fund to be shared proportionate to incomes. Child and spousal support will be reviewed in two years in CFL when Joan's business is established. The parties anticipate a reduction or elimination of spousal support at that time which will allow Mike to take summers off to write. The lawyers prepare an agreement that incorporates their settlement. The participants reconvene to review, amend and sign the agreement.

Negotiation

The Seven Elements of
Interest-based Negotiation
Interests
Options
Legitimacy
Relationship
Communication
Commitment
Alternatives

The Seven Steps of
CFL Negotiation
Issues
Information
Interests
Principles
Options
Alternatives
Agreement

The Lawyer as Facilitator
A Director or Guide
A Coach
A Supporter

ENDNOTES

1 Fisher, R., Kopelman, E., & Schneider, A.K. (1994). *Beyond Machiavelli: Tools for Coping with Conflict*. Cambridge, MA: Harvard University Press; Fisher, R. & Ertel, D. (1995). *Getting Ready to Negotiate: The Getting to Yes Workbook*. New York: Penguin Books USA Inc.

2 Fisher, R., Kopelman, E., & Schneider, A.K., *supra*, p. 75.

3 Fisher, R., Ury, W., & Patton, B. (1991). *Getting to Yes: Negotiating Agreement Without Giving In* (2nd ed.). New York: Penguin Books USA Inc., p. 40.

4 *Ibid.*, p. 41.

5 *Ibid.*, p. 44.

6 Moore, C.W. (1996). *The Mediation Process: Practical Strategies for Resolving Conflict* (2nd ed.). San Francisco, CA: Jossey-Bass Inc., Publishers.

7 Fisher, R., Ury, W., & Patton, B., *supra*, p. 51.

8 *Ibid.*, pp. 53.

9 *Ibid.*, pp. 56-57.

10 *Ibid.*, p. 60.

11 *Ibid.*, pp. 112-116.

12 Tessler, P. H. (2001). *Collaborative Law: Achieving Effective Resolution in Divorce without Litigation.* Chicago, IL: American Bar Association, p. 115.

13 Fisher, R., Kopelman, E., & Schneider, A.K., *supra*, p. 76.

14 Kolb, D.M. & Coolidge, G.G. (1993). Her place at the table: a consideration of gender issues in negotiation. In J.W. Breslin & J.Z. Rubin (Eds.) (1993). *Negotiation Theory and Practice* (2nd ed.) Cambridge, MA: The Program on Negotiation at Harvard Law School.

15 *Ibid.*, p. 263.

16 Fisher, Ury, and Patton, *supra*, pp. 18-19.

17 Fisher, R., Kopelman, E., & Schneider, A.K., *supra*, p. 80.

18 Fisher, R. & Brown, S. (1989). *Getting Together: Building Relationships As We Negotiate.* New York: Penguin Books USA Inc.

19 *Ibid.*, p. 38.

20 Fisher, R., Ury, W., & Patton, B., *supra*, p. 32.

21 Fisher, R., Kopelman, E., & Schneider, A.K., *supra*, p. 81.

22 Fisher, R., Ury, W., & Patton, B., *supra*, p. 100.

23 Fisher, R., Kopelman, E., & Schneider, A.K., *supra*, p. 78.

24 Knowles, M. S. (1975). *Self-Directed Learning: A Guide for Learners and Teachers.* Englewood Cliffs, NJ: Cambridge Adult Education Prentice Hall Regents; Knowles, M.S. (1980). *The Modern Practice of Adult Education: From Pedagogy to Andragogy.* Englewood Cliffs, NJ: Cambridge Adult Education Prentice Hall Regents; Knowles, M.S. (1998). *The Adult Learner* (5th ed.). Houston, TX: Gulf Publishing Company.

25 Schwarz, R.M. (1994). *The Skilled Facilitator: Practical Wisdom for Developing Effective Groups.* San Francisco, CA: Jossey-Bass Inc., Publishers.

26 Moore, C.W., *supra*.

27 *Ibid.*, p. 196.

12

Intervention

- *Barriers and Impasse*
- *The Nature of Impasse*
- *Barrier Categories*
- *Prevention*
- *Process Interventions*
- *Caucuses*
- *Third Party Interventions*

BARRIERS AND IMPASSE

The greatest challenge to CFL lawyers may arise when the parties encounter communication barriers or reach an impasse in their negotiations. We use these two terms interchangeably as synonyms for process obstacles. Ordinarily the parties would be able to withdraw from their settlement discussions and commence court proceedings. In CFL, this option is not so readily available to them. Under the Participation Agreement, they do not waive their rights to litigate. However, they must first terminate CFL and then retain other lawyers. The thrown-away expenses for the aborted process and the anticipated transaction costs to initiate a court proceeding with new lawyers may deter them. What can be done to revive CFL?

To overcome barriers and impasse typically requires some form of intervention by the lawyers. They must do something, but they ought not to assume control over the process. The lawyers may attempt to restore the process through the application of one or more of the communication and facilitation skills previously discussed. They may elect to take a break with each lawyer meeting with her client privately, a process similar to the *caucus* used in mediation. The lawyers, in consultation with the parties, may decide to involve a third party. What is needed is some form of intervention to get them unstuck, to move them beyond their impasse.

THE NATURE OF IMPASSE

Previously, we discussed *barriers* that affect the communications between the parties. While a barrier represents an impediment to progress along a pre-determined course, an *impasse* implies something of even greater significance. The word impasse suggests that the parties have arrived at a *dead end*. They have gone as far as they can go and they are unable to achieve any forward movement whatsoever. The obstacles seem insurmountable.

Typically, impasses are multi-layered phenomena with the elements occurring at three different levels: *external*, *interactional*, and *intrapsychic*. An impasse that originates outside the relationship of the parties is external; an impasse that relates to their interrelationship is interactional; and an impasse that lies solely within one or the other of the parties is intrapsychic. Impasses can occur at one or more of these levels contemporaneously.

With an external impasse, third parties, either intentionally or unwittingly, may say or do something that results in the parties resorting to and becoming entrenched in their pre-negotiation positions. Parents, siblings, friends, new life partners, and business associates are all potential candidates. As a result of their encroachment, the influenced party may distort her own views or those of the other party, take a rigid and inflexible stand on an issue, or make extreme demands and refuse to make reasonable concessions.

An interactional impasse may arise as a result of ineffective communications between the parties. They hold to false assumptions and misunderstandings. Alternatively, the impasse may be a manifestation of a dysfunctional marital relationship.

Intrapsychic impasses refer to particular psychological problems or mental illnesses affecting only one of the parties, thereby diminishing her capacity to participate meaningfully in collaborative negotiations.

Understanding the nature of an impasse enables the lawyers to determine who should be involved in the settlement discussions, the level at which the interventions are to be made, and what needs to be done to move forward.

BARRIER CATEGORIES

We distinguish between two categories of barriers: *psychological* and *process*. In this section, we identify them and we follow with a description of some of the intervention strategies found in the literature and others that are drawn from our own practice experience.

Psychological Barriers

Robert Mnookin and Lee Ross state that psychological barriers do not arise as a result of deliberate efforts to achieve an advantage in a negotiation or attempts at the promotion of self-interest over other-interest.[1] "Instead, they reflect cognitive and motivational processes, or more precisely, biases in the way that human beings interpret information, evaluate risks, set priorities, and experience feelings of gain or loss."[2]

Barriers of this kind render negotiators incapable of recognizing settlement offers beneficial to them. A negotiator may also misunderstand or misinterpret the cause or source of the problem. The other party is not simply being intransigent. Rather, cognitive and motivational forces are likely influencing both parties in the choices they make in the negotiation.

Mnookin and Ross describe six psychological barriers.

1. **Fairness or Equity**

   The parties bring with them into the process a sense of what is fair and equitable and they may reject anything that offends this principle.

2. **Biases**

   A bias represents the ways in which individuals see and make sense of the world. These worldviews of the participants affect their decision making.

3. **Reactive Devaluation**

   A party to a dispute rates a proposal made by the other party less favourably than if it were made by her or a neutral third party.

4. **Risk Aversion and Loss Aversion**

   Most persons prefer to avoid both risk and certain loss. They will reject anything that appears to be moving them in either of these directions.

5. **Judgmental Overconfidence**

   A party persuades herself of the strength of her position due primarily to the greater access to information supportive of that position.

6. **Cognitive Dissonance Reduction and Avoidance**
   The parties to a dispute rationalize or justify past failure to resolve a dispute and whatever they must do to achieve their objective.

Process Barriers

In a sequel to *Getting to Yes*, *Getting Past No*, William Ury provides his analysis of the potential process barriers to cooperation.[3]

1. **Reaction**

    When one party strikes, the other strikes back. This reaction serves only to perpetuate the "action-reaction" cycle of the conflict.

2. **Emotion**

    One party becomes angry or hostile. As a result, she becomes fearful or distrustful. She may withdraw and refuse to continue.

3. **Position**

    One party bargains positionally. She may become entrenched. Either that party or the other must give in. She may not know how to bargain otherwise.

4. **Dissatisfaction**

    Notwithstanding the goal of mutual gain, one party may have no interest in such an outcome.

5. **Power**

    If one party sees the conflict as a "win-lose" contest and she perceives that she has more power than the other, she will use this advantage to coerce.

PREVENTION

Before we consider process interventions, we first ask whether there is something that can be done to prevent impasse and barriers from arising. Whenever possible, the lawyers in a CFL process ought to do everything they can to avoid and prevent its occurrence.

The lawyers should begin by identifying the process and outcome expectations of their clients. All of the participants must have a clear understanding of their respective roles. As well, each party must articulate and understand his or her goals and objectives and those of the other party. Lawyers can offer reality checks when the intended pursuits of their clients seem unrealistic, extreme, or vague.

A client may profess that all she wants is what is fair. Her lawyer might ask her about fairness. *How do you define what is fair? How will you know when a result is fair? What needs to be present to feel fair to you? If we acknowledge that fairness is in the eye of the beholder, can you explain what fair means to you?*

PROCESS INTERVENTIONS

If barriers occur or an impasse arises, CFL lawyers intervene in one of three ways. First, they may intervene *within the course of the settlement meetings* with all of the participants present. Second, each lawyer may conduct a *private meeting* or *caucus* with her client. Third, the lawyers may enlist the services of a third party to assist them. Some suggestions of what to do when things go wrong is found in Appendix "H". We consider the general process interventions now and the more specific caucus and third party interventions later.

Breakthrough Negotiation

Ury offers his *Breakthrough Negotiation* model as a five-step strategy to break through the barriers to cooperation. If obstacles to principled negotiation are encountered, a negotiator should first *go to the balcony* and look at what is happening. Step back from the process and examine it objectively, from a distance. She should then *step to the side* of the other and listen to and acknowledge her arguments. A negotiator should *reframe* the positions of the other by accepting and restating what she says in the form of settlement alternatives. If there is a gap between their interests, *build a golden bridge* between them. Each party must save face and perceive the outcome as a victory. Finally, the parties should *use power to educate* rather than escalate a conflict. This may involve a fuller discussion of interests, options, and alternatives, or developing a greater understanding of complex issues.

Personal Power and Influence

Mediators frequently encounter impasses in their work. Christopher Moore identifies twelve forms of mediator power and influence in a *continuum of mediator intervention*.[4]

1. **Management of the Negotiation Process**

    The mediator manages the negotiation process. Some mediators are overt in exercising control over the process. They are directive as to party conduct and behaviour. Other mediators are more subtle.

They remind the parties of the agreed behavoural guidelines and their stated objectives for the mediation.

2. Communication

The mediator draws upon her skills to manage communication within the mediation. She uses active listening and reframing to clarify and define the problems. An alternative intervention is the modeling of effective communication and negotiation behaviours.

3. Physical Setting

The physical setting of the negotiation facility, as, for example, the seating arrangement, table shape, room size, and the availability of breakout rooms influence the conduct of the process. Any of these can be changed as an intervention to overcome impasse.

4. Timing

The dates and times selected for the sessions as well as their duration may constitute barriers to effective participation and, once again, a mediator may be more or less directive on these matters as another intervention.

5. Information Exchange

Mediators may limit themselves to asking questions and making suggestions to indicate the information that would be helpful. Alternatively, they may be more proactive and actually identify the information that needs to be exchanged.

6. Associates

The participation of certain associates of the parties, as for example, family members, may affect the parties' attitudes and behaviours. A new partner or parent affecting the negotiation from the sidelines may be brought into the negotiations by way of a private meeting with that parties' counsel or into a settlement meeting with the other spouse and lawyer.

7. Experts

A mediator can influence the course of a negotiation by suggesting the involvement of experts.

8. Authority

The recognition by the parties of the authority of the mediator is itself a form of influence that the mediator can use to intervene. The parties may be prepared to rely upon the mediator's expertise in matters of procedure and, on occasion, substance.

9. **Habits of Disputants**

The behaviours of the parties themselves may be influential. With parties who have long-standing relationships in which routine patterns have been established, mediators can appeal to those personal habits as an intervention.

10. **Parties' Doubts**

All parties express doubt about their bargaining positions and the appropriate settlement options. Mediators can use these doubts and the risk inherent in predicting the courthouse option to encourage parties to open their minds to other possibilities.

11. **Rewards and Benefits**

While only a party can offer rewards or benefits to persuade the other party to settle, a mediator may be able to offer some indirect rewards to induce settlement. The relationship of the mediator with each of the parties may be the only positive reward that she can offer. In addition, the mediator can point out the benefits of a particular settlement option.

12. **Coercive Influence**

The mediator may be able to exercise a measure of persuasion over the parties that Moore refers to as coercive influence. A subtle form of coercive influence is the reaction of the mediator, whether verbal or nonverbal, to the behaviours of the parties in the mediation.

The above mediator interventions can be adapted by lawyers in a CFL setting, subject to such modifications as are required in recognition of the different roles mediators and lawyers play in their respective processes. The intervention may be more powerful when exercised by lawyers, given that they do not have the duty of neutrality that mediators must honour.

Critical Questions

To move the parties through a real or perceived impasse, the collaborative lawyer can ask the parties one or more of the following questions:

*   Create uncertainty in rigid thinking to move parties away from their positions. *Do you believe that what you are proposing is a likely outcome? How will you convince your spouse of the reasonableness of your proposal?*

*   Recheck information and obtain further information as required.

Do you have all of the information that you require to deal with this particular issue?

- Address the relative importance of an issue. *How important is this issue to you in the overall scheme of things?*

- Address party fears directly. *What is it that you are most concerned about here?*

- Identify areas of progress to date. *What have the two of you accomplished to this point?*

- Construct a hypothetical scenario. *What if you were to do the following?*

- Experiment with possible options on a trial basis. *Why don't you try this arrangement over the course of the next week and we can talk about it when we get back together?*

- Refer one or both parties to counselling or therapy to deal with anger or other behavioural problems. *Do you think it would help you in this process if we were to refer you to someone for a private consultation before we continue?*

- Ask the parties to reflect upon what is happening in their process. *What do you think is happening in your settlement negotiations? Are you making forward progress? If not, what is in your way?*

- Identify the impasse and talk about it directly. *Do you think that (the perceived cause of the impasse) is making it difficult for us to continue with this process? How can we move beyond this impasse?*

- Be aware of what you as one of the lawyers may be doing that is contributing to the impasse. *Am I a part of the problem?*

- Invite consideration of the parties' BATNAs. *What is the best alternative for each of you if you are unable to reach an agreement through the CFL process?*

- Invite consideration of the transaction costs of an alternative to a negotiated agreement. *Should we discuss what your legal expenses might be if you withdrew from the CFL process and decided to proceed to court?*

Each of these interventions is introduced by a question. The CFL lawyer does not impose her opinion as to what the problem might be. Instead, she empowers the parties to figure it out for themselves by asking them critical questions.

An Apology

An apology is a powerful tool for changing the dynamics of a negoti-ation and creating a climate conducive to collaboration. To do so, the apology must be from the heart. It must be sincere and spontaneous it and must be offered at the right time. Lawyers are generally reticent to recom-mend that their clients offer apologies. Some view it as an admission of liability. To clients, an apology often represents an acceptance and acknow-ledgment of personal responsibility and regret for the problem.

If an apology is made at the first settlement meeting, it can generate a positive feeling and get the process started on the right foot. When circum-stances indicate that an apology might be appropriate, the lawyer canvasses the possibility during preparation. The lawyer should not exert pressure upon her client to do so. An insincere apology can be worse than none at all. Rather, she should instill in the client the goodwill potential it holds. An apology may also have a powerful impact on a negotiation that may have reached an impasse.

The form of the apology is important. *I am truly sorry if you were hurt by something that I said or did* is preferred over *I am sorry that you feel hurt by something I said or did.* Moreover, the apology should be uncon-ditional and unequivocal. It ought not to be followed by some defensive explanation of behaviour. There are many ways to apologize. The word apology need not appear at all; there are acceptable and appropriate alter-natives. *I understand how you feel. I agree that this is a real problem. I acknowledge that I have really inconvenienced you. I see what you mean. You have every right to be angry with me. Thank you for letting me know how you feel.* If the client wishes to make an apology, the CFL lawyer can coach her on the most effective way in which to make it.

An apology from one party may invite the other to reciprocate. If the other so responds, it creates a very positive climate for collaboration. How-ever, reciprocity is a bonus, not an expectation. It is implicit, not explicit. The most effective apologies are those offered without anticipation of an apology or concession made in return. While it may have the effect of reducing the demands of the other, it is not offered in lieu of something else. An apology is in addition to whatever a party should receive in respect of her substantive concerns.

Silence

Sometimes, the most powerful intervention is simply to allow the parties to sit with the problem, in silence. When an impasse arises, and other interventions are not appropriate or have not been helpful, the lawyers may summarize the progress made, restate the final, seemingly insurmountable problem, and permit the parties to contemplate the consequences of failure to achieve resolution. Both parties will come to the awareness that the end of the CFL process may be at hand, with all the thrown-away cost and effort that would entail. The investment in the process, the partial agreements reached, and the relationship building that has happened thus far, not to mention the substantial cost to retain new lawyers, get them up to speed, and litigate, are strong incentives to stay at the table.

Eventually, if the lawyers can resist the urge to keep talking and come to the rescue, one of the clients will usually break the silence with a tentative suggestion for moving forward. The other may respond with an idea or build upon the proposal of the party who broke the silence. Silence from the lawyers eloquently puts responsibility for resolution where it belongs – with the parties. When the process seems on the verge of failure, the most dynamic, creative thinking and problem solving can emerge.

Time-outs

A *time-out* or a *caucus* is another common mediator intervention that can be adapted for use in a CFL setting. While similar to a caucus, in that each represents a break from the four-party settlement meetings, they are distinct. A time-out is simply what its name implies; it need not represent anything more. The caucus is another matter. It is a private consultation between a lawyer and her client outside the settlement meeting.

Any of the participants could at any time request a time-out for a variety of reasons. If either of the parties appears to be experiencing real difficulty in the settlement meetings, it may be all that is required. A time-out allows her an opportunity to collect her thoughts, to reflect on what has been said, or to consider a settlement proposal. Resort to a time-out should not be relied upon every time emotions run high in a four-party meeting. Often, strong feelings need to be expressed and worked through. However, a time-out is sometimes needed to allow a person to cool down or regroup. Client preparation should include a discussion about the possibility of re-questing time-outs during the settlement meetings.

CAUCUSES

A client may feel the need to seek the advice of or simply discuss matters with her lawyer in private. In that event, the intervention takes on the character of a caucus. The lawyers may actually be the persons to suggest private lawyer-client meetings to review their progress in the negotiations to that point, to consider how they might overcome negotiation barriers and impasse, and to obtain instructions. We recommend that individual meetings with clients take place after calling a break in the discussions, thereby adjourning or ending a settlement meeting, or between sessions, rather than in the course of a meeting, which may break the connection between the participants.

The caucus intervention provides a lawyer with an opportunity to review the course of the settlement negotiations with her client, to clarify her underlying interests, to receive input as to how she may be feeling about the way matters are progressing, and to obtain suggestions as to how to improve or otherwise change the process. A party can vent her emotions and frustrations in a caucus without causing irreparable damage to the relationships among the participants.

During a caucus, a lawyer can reality-test a party's proposed solutions to the problems and offer some perspective on what might be done to further the interests of that party in the negotiation. The lawyer may also assist a party to formulate a more appropriate settlement offer that meets more of the parties' mutual interests. Finally, a client may wish to confide in the lawyer and reveal information in caucus that she does not yet want to share with the other participants. The lawyer will help the client assess whether this information is relevant to the resolution of the issues and, if so, coach her on how it might be disclosed.

The lawyers may decide that a caucus between the two of them during a settlement meeting might likewise be an effective intervention. However, this approach ought to be carefully considered before implementation. The parties may feel that they are being denied participation in the decision making. If so, the process may be transformed into the more traditional lawyer negotiation model that the participants were attempting to avoid. We recommend lawyer caucuses be used sparingly. It is preferable for the lawyers to discuss their concerns at a debriefing session after a settlement meeting.

If the lawyers decide to caucus with their respective clients during a settlement meeting, they must agree as to the extent to which they will disclose what is said in caucus to the other lawyer and her client. Their private solicitor and client communications are privileged and only the client can waive that privilege. Lawyers must be certain of their instructions concerning disclosure before they resume the settlement meeting.

In caucus, the lawyer and client should agree upon some course of action to propose that may restore a process that is at apparent impasse. Once the participants arrive at a consensus as to what they should do to overcome their process barriers, they should consciously implement their strategy. It may be helpful for them to review their progress once they resume. An impasse that was sufficiently serious to lead to party caucuses will likely require their concentrated attention. They do not want to slide back into their pre-intervention condition.

A caucus is a useful device. However, care must be taken that the participants do not set a precedent for how they will conduct their negotiations. The CFL process operates on the premise that the parties will arrive at the best solution to their problems if they work together.

THIRD PARTY INTERVENTIONS

As a supplement to the skills and expertise that the lawyers and parties themselves bring to the CFL process, the participants might consider an intervention by a qualified neutral third party. Included among such persons are psychologists, therapists, family counsellors, assessors, actuaries, business valuators, real estate appraisers, accountants, financial advisors, mediators, evaluators, and arbitrators. Some third parties are called upon to offer counsel or guidance to one or both parties. Others are engaged as experts to investigate and report their observations and recommendations. Still others are neutrals retained to provide some other form of dispute resolution service to the participants at impasse. Third parties may be used inside or outside of the settlement meetings.

The parties will need to consider and resolve the following questions as a preliminary step prior to an intervention by a third party:

1. What is the purpose for involving this person?
2. What is her mandate?
3. How will she be retained?
4. Who will be responsible for the payment of her account?
5. If the third party is an expert, will her opinion and recommendations bind the parties or be advisory?
6. If the expert's report is not binding, what use will be made of the information provided?
7. How will the expert provide her opinion or information to the parties and their lawyers?

8. Will the confidentiality provisions of the Participation Agreement cover the expert's opinion, report, and preparatory notes?

We consider these questions in our discussion of the various third parties that the clients may enlist as intervenors. We cluster these interventions into three categories: social psychological for counselling or assessment; financial intervention for valuation and advice; and neutral intervention for dispute resolution.

Social Psychological Interventions

CFL lawyers possess or strive to acquire a sophisticated understanding of the social and psychological impact that separation and divorce has upon adults and children. If the issues require therapeutic intervention, the children's input is desired, or the relationship between the parties is particularly challenging and emotionally charged, the parties may want to involve persons with special expertise in child development and family dynamics. These experts can either be brought into the CFL process or the parties can be referred out to them for assistance.

Referral to a Child Psychologist or Child Psychiatrist

A mental health professional can help the parties improve their ability to communicate about their children, acquire an understanding of their children's developmental needs and capabilities, and teach them how to minimize the impact of the separation and divorce process on their children, taking the age and stage of development of each child into account. The expert can also assist the parents with the development of their Parenting Plan, give them professional advice with respect to their decision-making options, and facilitate with the determination of an age-appropriate allocation of the time that the children spend with each parent.

Referral to Child, Marital, Family or Individual Therapists

A referral to a psychotherapist may be necessary to help one or both parties on an individual basis to deal with the loss, grief, and anger incidental to separation and divorce. This support may be invaluable in improving that party's capacity to communicate and negotiate effectively. Separation counselling with a therapist may be required to help the parties let go of the marital relationship and move forward with their separate lives. It can help family members work together to resolve behavioural problems with children that arise or become worse as a result of their parents' separation. The children may need to have their own therapist, especially those who are caught in the middle between their separating parents. Play therapists can help very young children deal with their conflicted feelings.

Support groups for separating spouses and the children of divorce are also very useful outlets for the expression of intense feelings and to learn coping strategies. The CFL lawyer should be familiar with such facilities and have brochures on hand outlining their services.

Referral to Child Advocate/Parenting Coach

A qualified person may be asked to intervene directly as a child advocate. She can meet with older children and, with their consent, present their views to the parents for consideration. Once parenting plans are negotiated, a parenting coach can help high conflict parents implement their agreement through further appropriate intervention.

Referral for an Assessment

The parties may decide to jointly engage an expert to conduct an assessment of the needs of the children and the respective capacities of the parents to meet them. The assessor may provide her information orally and informally by attending a settlement meeting or by meeting with the parties alone. Alternatively, the parties may find it beneficial for the assessor to prepare a written report to be submitted for consideration or presented by the assessor at their next settlement meeting.

The parents may ask the assessor to meet with older children so that they can make their concerns known. The views of the children can be shared with their parents only if the children consent to the disclosure. If the parents direct the assessor to prepare a report setting out her opinion on a variety of matters pertaining to the children, there are two important decisions that the parties must make and their agreement must be made in advance and reduced to writing. The parties must decide whether the recommendations of the assessor will bind them or be advisory only and whether the confidentiality provisions of the Participation Agreement will cover the report in the event the CFL process breaks down. Some practice groups permit the work of neutral third parties to escape confidentiality if both parties agree or if both parties accept the recommendations.

Responsibility for the Accounts of Social Psychological Intervenors

When an expert is retained to inform the parties about child development and family dynamics for the purpose of assisting them with the development of appropriate parenting arrangements, she will be retained jointly by the parties. Each parent may contribute an equal amount toward this expense or their contributions may be proportional to their incomes. Alternatively, they may decide to pay it out of the family joint account or one parent may pay the entire amount with the understanding that it will be factored in as an additional liability to be considered in their property distribution.

Therapy for one of the parties only is often thought to be the sole responsibility of the individual who sought it out. However, it may be appropriate that this expense be shared in view of the potential contribution that it can make to the success of the process. One of the parties may have an employee assistance plan available to her to cover the costs. In other cases, one spouse has the income or resources with which to absorb or share this expense. It is by no means a given that the party who is receiving the treatment should have to bear this burden alone.

Financial Interventions

Using Business Valuators and Financial Advisors

If a party is self-employed, a partner in a firm, or the controlling shareholder of a corporation, it is generally necessary to determine the nature and value of her interest in such business enterprise and the party's income for support purposes. As a business valuation can be an expensive proposition, the fiscally prudent course is for the parties to retain this expert jointly with the understanding that her opinion will be binding upon them. Otherwise, a displeased party may disregard the report and it will have served no useful purpose, particularly if the confidentiality provisions of the Participation Agreement apply.

Where the financial affairs are complex, the business assets substantial, and/or the level of trust between the parties low, the valuator may be asked to prepare a formal written report. To facilitate the valuation process, the valuator should be provided with direct access to any person within the business or associated with it, as for example the company accountant, to gather data and compile a history. The valuator may meet with the parties and their lawyers to present a draft report and allow them to provide feedback and ask questions. If a settlement is negotiated at this point, the parties can forego the preparation of the more formal report and reduce their fees.

If the financial affairs of the business are less complex, the parties are more trusting of one another, and/or the cost of retaining an expert is an issue, the parties may instruct the valuator to provide an informal estimate of value only and present it orally at a settlement meeting with a summary of her calculations and results. With a small family business, the opinion of the firm's accountant may suffice, provided that she enjoys the confidence of both parties.

The parties may choose to enlarge the mandate of the financial expert beyond valuation. Generally, these valuators are accountants who may provide advice as to the most beneficial way to dispose of or transfer property in order to minimize tax consequences to the parties. Financial advisors may be brought in at this stage to recommend investments that may enhance their incomes.

Using Appraisers and Actuaries

Appraisers and actuaries may be retained to provide neutral opinions as to the value of real property and pensions. Their reports provide the objective criteria recommended by Fisher, Ury, and Patton. Rather than each party obtaining individual expert opinions, they should settle upon an appropriately qualified person, engage this expert jointly, and accept her opinion as final and binding.

Responsibility for the Accounts of Financial Intervenors

The parties must agree in advance as to the responsibility for the payment of the account of the business valuator, appraiser, or actuary. A sole income earner may pay the cost in full, the fees may be allocated equally, or one of the parties might pay the account with the understanding that her assumption of this responsibility will be factored into the ultimate property settlement. Finally, the parties must clearly state whether the confidentiality provisions of the Participation Agreement are to apply to any of these reports. A misunderstanding on this matter could prove fatal to the process.

Neutral ADR Interventions

A mediator facilitates or assists disputing parties in their negotiations, an early neutral evaluator provides an expert opinion as to the probable outcome if the issues were litigated, and an arbitrator conducts a private hearing that concludes with a final and binding award. Each of these interventions helps the parties move forward through their impasse and continue their collaborative negotiations on a new footing.

Mediation

Mediators have strong communication and interest-based negotiation skills. Mediation will continue as a complement or supplement to the CFL process. Faced with complex parenting issues or challenging dynamics between the parties, the lawyers may refer their clients to a mediator. The understandings the parties reach in mediation may be incorporated into the Separation Agreement negotiated in the CFL process or a mediated Parenting Plan may be attached as a Schedule.

It is not uncommon for the Participation Agreement to anticipate mediation and make specific provision for it. The parties must agree as to the terms of reference, responsibility for the payment of the mediator's fees, the report, if any, to be prepared by the mediator, and the extent to which any materials prepared in the course of mediation, including any written Memorandum of Understanding or report, are to be covered by the confidentiality provisions of the Participation Agreement.

Facilitation

When the participants reach impasse in their four-party settlement meetings, they should consider inviting a mediator to facilitate their negotiations. This is a very powerful intervention, especially when the lawyers themselves may be contributing to the impasse. In a five-party meeting, the mediator helps the CFL participants to improve their communications, to understand the nature of the impasse, to uncover previously undisclosed interests, and to move beyond impasse. The four CFL participants then continue with their ongoing settlement meetings on a new basis of understanding.

Early Neutral/Case Evaluation

If the parties reach an impasse on a single issue, their lawyers may refer them to an evaluator to provide an advisory opinion. The evaluator can be a senior member of the family bar or a retired family judge. She will give her expert opinion of the applicable law and the likely disposition of the case if it were to proceed to court. Use of EN/CE may be appropriate when the lawyers themselves cannot agree with respect to the application of the law to the facts of the case, and the parties are consequently far apart in their expectations. The evaluator can prepare a formal written report for the lawyers and clients or she can attend a settlement meeting to discuss her opinion informally.

The value of EN/CE is that it helps the lawyers and their clients take a sober fresh look at their case and evaluate it more objectively in their subsequent negotiations. As a process, EN/CE occupies a position on the ADR spectrum between mediation and arbitration. It is similar to advisory or non-binding arbitration.

Arbitration

If all other attempts to resolve the impasse prove unsuccessful, the parties may consider binding issue arbitration. They cloak the arbitrator with the authority to make a final and binding decision in respect of a single issue. The broader process expectation of the parties remains as before. They will return to their CFL settlement meetings following the delivery of the arbitrator's award.

Unlike all of the other dispute resolution processes, arbitration is governed by statute law. It is imperative that the lawyers prepare an Agreement to Arbitrate that satisfies the statutory requirements. This agreement should address the issues to be determined, the procedure to be followed in the arbitration, the law or any other standard of decision making that will apply, whether or not the arbitration is to be binding upon the parties, and rights of appeal. As with the other third party interventions, there must be a consensus on responsibility for payment of the arbitrator's account and whether the arbitrator may award costs. The confidentiality provisions of the Participation Agreement will not likely cover the arbitration proceedings as the governing legislation in most jurisdictions provides that a party may apply to the court for judgment in accordance with the award.

Arbitration is the process of final recourse to overcome impasse. We suggest that its use in CFL be limited to the resolution of a single or very few issues when the facts are essentially agreed. In this situation, the lawyers may submit an agreed statement of facts and the issues to the arbitrator for a written decision, which will bind the parties and be incorporated into their settlement.

Many hold the view that a more extensive intervention essentially concludes the CFL process, as it is contrary to the principles of CFL. Where the facts are in dispute, it may be possible to permit the parties to take a break from the CFL process, retain new lawyers to represent them in the arbitration, and to bring the result back into the CFL process, which may then resume.

Each collaborative law association will need to make a protocol decision about the availability of arbitration to resolve impasses.

Interventions

Source of Impasse
External, Interactional, **or** *Intrapsychic*

Psychological Barriers
Fairness or Equity
Biases
Reactive Devaluation
Risk Aversion / Loss Aversion
Judgmental Overconfidence
Cognitive Dissonance Reduction and Avoidance

Process Barriers
Reaction
Emotion
Position
Dissatisfaction
Power

The Breakthrough Strategy
Go to the Balcony
Step to the Side
Reframe
Build a Golden Bridge
Use Power to Educate

Other Process Interventions
Mediator Interventions
Critical Questions
An Apologies
Silence
Time-outs

Caucuses
Private meetings of lawyers and their clients
Private meetings between the lawyers

Third Party Interventions
Social Psychological Interventions
Financial Interventions
Neutral ADR Interventions

ENDNOTES

1 Mnookin, R.H. & Ross, L. (1995). Introduction. In K. Arrow, R.H. Mnookin, L. Ross, A. Tversky, & R. Wilson (Eds.)(1995). *Barriers to Conflict Resolution*. New York: W.W. Norton & Company, Inc.

2 *Ibid.*, p. 6.

3 Ury, W. (1991). *Getting Past No: Negotiating Your Way from Confrontation to Cooperation*. New York: Bantam Books.

4 Moore, C.W. (1996). *The Mediation Process: Practical Strategies for Resolving Conflict* (2nd ed.). San Francisco, CA: Jossey-Bass Inc., Publishers.

Part Five:

CFL Outcomes

- *Parenting*
- *Child Support*
- *Spousal Support*
- *Property*

13

Parenting

- *Children and CFL*
- *Knowledge and Resources*
- *Law Talk*
- *CFL in Practice*

CHILDREN AND CFL

For divorcing spouses with children, parenting is usually the single most important issue between them. Many clients choose the CFL process in order to preserve or repair their ability to communicate and interact for the sake of their children. Most parents share the common goal of promoting and maximizing the welfare of their children and insulating them, as much as possible, from the effects of their separation.

The parties must move away from the adversarial language of *custody and access*; away from positional bargaining which sets one parent against the other in a fight for who will win custody of the children; away from an insistence on parental rights, towards a consideration of how they will fulfill their parental obligations to their children after separation. Parents must find a way to set aside the intense emotions engendered by their separation – anger, guilt, jealousy, and depression – and learn how to separate the spousal and the parental relationships. Parents want and need to find ways to relate in an amicable, or at least business-like, manner regarding their children.

Although the children themselves are not usually present in the CFL process, they are the constant focus of the participants. With the help of their lawyers, the parties learn how to work together as partners to put their children first. This does not mean that every CFL negotiation results in joint custody. It means that the parenting arrangements in each CFL case are designed to meet the individual needs and interests of these parents and their children. The outcome sought is *win-win-win*.

KNOWLEDGE AND RESOURCES

An effective CFL lawyer is knowledgeable about the emotional stages of the separation and divorce process, the needs of divorcing spouses, and the needs of children at different ages and stages of their growth and development. To deal appropriately with children's issues, lawyers require sufficient knowledge to help the parties design age-appropriate parenting schedules and workable decision-making procedures.

Some lawyers will be extremely comfortable dealing with parenting issues. Others may wish to refer complex, highly conflicted, or otherwise challenging parenting disputes to mediation.

CFL lawyers should be aware of the mental health professionals and resources available in their communities who can assist separating and divorcing families. These would include family and marital counsellors, individual and child therapists, and support groups for separating spouses and children. Participants can be informed about the availability of such resources and encouraged to make use of them as needed. CFL lawyers can arrange the referrals. They should also be able to recommend or lend reading materials to educate their clients about children's needs and possible parenting arrangements.

LAW TALK

Surprisingly, the language of the law that describes post-separation, parent-child relationships corresponds with that found in the criminal law and the law of property.[1] The term *custody,* for example, is a term commonly applied to incarcerated criminals. It is also used in relation to the conservation of property. *Law talk* in relation to children implies that they are prisoners or property. Parents divide their children in much the same way as their tangible assets.

Similarly, the word *access* derives from property law, where it is used to describe a right to enter and pass over adjoining land without hindrance. Applying this language to parent-child relationships undermines and disempowers the parent who does not have *custody*. The non-custodial parent is stripped of any meaningful input into the child's life; his status is reduced to that of a visitor. In fact, the term *visitation* is used in place of *access* in some jurisdictions in the United States. We *visit* the ill and the infirm; we do not generally *visit* our children.

Many custody disputes are essentially arguments over semantics, the name given to the particular parenting arrangement. There is a real danger in applying static labels to parenting, which is a dynamic process. The legal labels, *sole custody* and *access*, tend to reinforce the idea that one parent takes exclusive charge of the children, while the other is denied all parental status. If one parent loses authority over and input regarding his children, then he often begins to act as a non-parent or visitor. On the other hand, if the expectation is that both parents will continue to be responsible for the post-separation care of the children, it is much more likely that they will live up to this expectation and fulfill their parental obligations.

The words we use to describe post-separation, parent-child and parent-parent relationships are extremely important in legitimizing parental roles. The real challenge for CFL lawyers is to help parents work out the nuts and bolts of the substantive arrangements for the care and rearing of children, using language which is familiar and makes sense to them. We recommend that CFL lawyers avoid use of the terms *custody* and *access* and encourage the parties to create a *Parenting Agreement* or *Parenting Plan*. The Parenting Plan will set out the details and incidents of parenting, including the time the children will reside with each parent, how the parents will obtain and exchange information regarding their children, and the procedures for decision making and dispute resolution.

Lawyers may wonder if the courts will accept non-traditional language in domestic contracts submitted for incorporation into orders. Canadian courts are accepting Parenting Plans that do not use the terms custody and access, provided the agreement covers all of the *incidents of custody,* such as residence, time spent with each parent, and decision making. The use of the term, *shared parenting*, is also gaining ground, both in and out of court.[2]

The role of CFL lawyers is to help parents focus on the comprehensive details of their ongoing parenting arrangements, rather than simply fight over legal labels. All too often they encounter preliminary, positional bargaining. *I want full custody* or *I want the children no less than 50 per cent of the time.* The challenge for CFL lawyers is to guide the parents toward a consideration of the interests underlying each of their positions and child-centred solutions to parenting. *What does full custody mean to you? What kind of relationship do you really want to have with your children? How can this be worked out in your day-to-day living? What do your children need from each of their parents? What are your strengths as a parent? What are the strengths of your spouse? What are the children's schedules? What are each of your schedules and availability? Which of you will assume what responsibilities? How will you communicate and share information about your children? How will you make major decisions? What if you disagree about major issues – how will you resolve disputes?*

CFL IN PRACTICE

Opening

As in every settlement meeting, it is important to set the appropriate tone for collaboration in the lawyers' opening comments. It is useful to acknowledge that resolving issues around the children is the most important task the parties have. They share a common goal in wanting the very best for their children, both in the immediate term and in the long term. Parents share the goal of raising emotionally well-adjusted adults who will not be damaged by their parents' separation. The lawyers can also touch upon some normal fears and concerns of separating parents, such as the fear of losing their children or of having another person stand in his or her place. They may note that the greatest challenge for most separating parents may be to accept that they will never live with their children all of the time again. Their children experience this profound loss as well. They usually want and benefit from substantial involvement with both parents, without conflict.

It is often helpful to ask each parent to talk briefly about each of their children and to show a couple of pictures of them. These pictures can remain on the table in view of the parents. When conflict levels rise, the lawyers can return to the photographs and remind the parties of their shared goal to work out the best possible plan for their children.

Information

The Legal Options

At some point in the negotiations, the lawyers may review and describe the options available to the parties for describing their parenting arrangements. They include sole custody, joint custody, split custody, divided custody, and shared parenting. It may be necessary to explain the legal implications for each of these options.

Clients should also understand the legal presumptions and criteria applied by the courts in determining matters regarding children. In Canada, the sole legal test for the determination of all matters in respect of children is the *best interests* of the child. A court asks in each case, *what is in the best interests of this child or these children?* Any factors that the law may consider in determining parenting arrangements may also be referenced. The broad range of judicial discretion in determining best interests is obvious. Most parents agree that they know better than anyone else what is best for their particular children. The lawyers should explain that the parties are free to create their own parenting arrangements with as much detail and specificity as they wish, and to put any label or indeed no label at all on those arrangements.

The Parenting History

Early in the CFL process, the lawyers invite the parties to describe how they parented during cohabitation. *Which of them assumed the primary responsibilities for their health, education, and general well being? In what ways was the other involved? How did they apportion between them the tasks associated with the various activities in which the children participate?*

If the parties are already living separate and apart, other questions arise. *With which of their parents do the children maintain their primary residence? When do they see the other parent? What is the quality of the time that they spend with each of their parents? What are the roles assumed by the parents in respect of their parenting responsibilities?*

Principles

Each parent will then be asked to identify the guiding *principles* he or she would like to govern parenting of their children. *What goals do you have for your children? What goals do you have for yourselves? What principles do you want to govern the decisions you make for your children?* Most parents have no difficulty agreeing to principles that will guide them in making decisions and arrangements for their children. They should be recorded on a flip chart or whiteboard and those that are held in common noted. This step in the process is very important; it should not be overlooked. If the parties subsequently reach an impasse in their discussions, the lawyers can refer to the agreed principles and ask how the proposals being advanced accord with them. The principles can be set out in the Parenting Plan.

We offer the following list of sample parenting principles:

- It is the children's right to have unconflicted closeness to both parents;
- It is the responsibility of both parents to provide the children with unconflicted closeness to both of them as well as emotional, financial, social, academic and recreational support;
- The parenting plan should be adjusted to reflect the children's ages and stages of development and their wishes and schedules, where appropriate;
- The children will be free from having to take sides with, defend, or downgrade either parent;

- Each child will be guided, taught, supervised, disciplined, and nurtured by each parent without interference from the other parent;
- Each child will know both parents and spend time with both parents on a regular basis, for holidays, and for vacations;
- The children will develop and maintain relationships with other significant adults (i.e. grandparents, step-parents, and other relatives) as long as these relationships do not interfere with or replace each child's primary relationship with his parents;
- Both parents will be informed about medical, dental, educational, extra-curricular, and legal matters concerning their children;
- The parents will treat each other with mutual respect and courtesy at all times;
- The parents will not express differences of opinion in the presence of the children and will set up a private time to deal with these matters;
- The parents will speak directly and not use the children as go-betweens;
- The parents will encourage love and respect for each parent and each parent's extended family.

Issues

Once the parents have agreed upon their parenting principles, the participants then turn to the parenting issues. The lawyers elicit the issues and note them on a flip chart or white board. When needed, the lawyers reframe the issues in non-judgmental, neutral language. For example, if one of the parents complains, *She's got to stop using the children as spies,* either lawyer could reframe this statement, *It seems you're concerned about involving the children in your marital dispute. How can we address that issue?* If a father says, *She refuses to let me have the kids half the time*, it might be reframed as, *It is important that you have a substantial and meaningful involvement in the lives of your children. How can we structure a residential schedule to address this concern?*

After all of the issues have been identified and reframed positively, the parties prioritize them and decide the order for discussion.

Interests

In a parenting dispute, it is important to distinguish between the interests of the parents and the interests of the children. The law states that such disputes are to be determined in accordance with what is in the best interests of the children. However, it is often the interests of the parents, cloaked in the language of the best interests of the children, which drive the dispute. In CFL, the lawyers encourage each parent to reveal his or her concerns and to consider those of the other, as well as the needs and interests of the children.

A common parenting dispute involves the claim by one parent for sole custody and the other for joint custody. One or more underlying interests usually fuel this conflict. The parent who seeks sole custody may be willing to consult with the other parent but wants the authority to make final decisions. The parent who seeks joint custody wants meaningful input into the children's lives. The interests of both parents may be addressed with an agreement for shared parenting, an obligation to consult and share information, and vesting all final decision-making authority in one parent or allocating final decision-making authority in areas of health, education, activities, and religion between the parents. This arrangement affords both parents input into decision making and yet allows for a method for breaking a tie in the event of disagreement, which may be acceptable and consistent with the family history.

Other disputes reveal different concerns. A non-primary-residence parent seeks joint custody out of fear that the primary-residence parent may move the permanent residence of the children. An agreement for prior notice of any intended move and an obligation to return to the CFL process, or, alternatively, pursue mediation and/or arbitration to resolve mobility issues may satisfy this interest. A parent concerned about the amount of time that he will have with a young child under a proposed Parenting Plan may agree to annual review of the parenting arrangements. A schedule allowing increased time away from the primary-residence parent as the child gets older may represent a satisfactory response to this concern.

It is important to look at each child separately. Adolescents have different needs than pre-school age children. One of the parents may more readily respond to the interests of one child than can the other. The emotional bond between a child and one of his parents may be stronger than with the other. A child may be extremely sensitive about any move, whether from a parent, siblings, friends, the family home, the neighbourhood, or his school. Some form of neutral intervention, such as a mediator who interviews the child, may be necessary to have these interests voiced effectively.

The level of conflict between the parties must be addressed. Parents for whom communication is difficult may require more detailed arrangements. They need to minimize continuing interaction and negotiation.

At the end of a settlement meeting, the lawyers summarize all of the interests – those of the parents and those of the children. The parties may then be given homework. They may be asked to develop proposals for the next settlement meeting that reflect their agreed principles, and maximize the satisfaction of as many of the identified interests as possible. The parents may be given blank calendars and asked to create at least three possible parenting schedules and be prepared to explain which best meets their principles and interests.

Options

The range of options extends along a spectrum. At one extreme, the children reside primarily with one parent and the other is involved in their lives to a minimum degree only. On the other end, the children may live with each of their parents for approximately equal amounts of time and both of them participate in all of the decision making. Within this polarity lie a variety of other possibilities. In each instance, particular outcomes are differentiated on the basis of the residential arrangements and the level of participation of the parents in the day-to-day lives of the children.

Each option has its advantages and disadvantages. If the parents opt for a more traditional approach with the children residing predominantly with one parent who has exclusive decision-making authority on all matters, the parties avoid the difficulties associated with constant consultation on their parenting responsibilities. However, the less involved parent may feel cast outside the family. He may be less willing to take on other obligations and his children may not look upon him as a parent in the same way that they do with the parent with whom they spend most of their time. With shared parenting, each feels a sense of total involvement in the raising of their children and shares the obligations as well as the joys of parenting. However, these arrangements require more contact, communication, and negotiation between the parents.

With each of the options, the parties must consider acceptability with reference to the parenting principles earlier developed by them and the interests of themselves and their children previously disclosed. *Does this option fulfill our principles and maximize the interests of all affected by it?*

Alternatives

The alternative to a negotiated parenting agreement is adjudication or arbitration. In the event that the parties reach impasse, it may be helpful for their lawyers to remind them of their stated preference for a resolution developed by them as opposed to one imposed by the court or an arbitrator. The lawyers can also return to the language of the legislation. They may again inform their clients of the wide range of judicial discretion concerning children. The courts tend to resolve parenting issues in broad, standard terms in contrast to the customized, detailed arrangements that parents can negotiate for themselves.

The lawyers may find it helpful to remind the parties of the risk of damage to an effective co-parenting relationship inherent in any court proceeding. They may ask their clients to consider the direct impact on their children of the costs of a court proceeding: *could their legal fees be better spent on the children's post-secondary or private school education?*

Clients who are unable to settle the parenting issues may wish to pursue mediation, obtain an assessment with respect to the needs and preferences of the children and/or arbitrate the unresolved issues, while remaining in the collaborative process.

Agreement

A Parenting Plan is a comprehensive document that covers all aspects of the post-separation, parent-child relationship. The major headings are as follows:

1. **Background information** – This section includes the names of the parties, and the children's full legal names, birthplaces, and birthdates. It sets out the date of the parents' separation and their intent to work together cooperatively to parent their children post separation.

2. **Agreed Parenting Principles** – The principles developed by the parties in the process are inserted either as a preamble or under a separate heading.

3. **Parental Rights and Responsibilities** – This section describes the nature of the parenting arrangement, such as shared parenting, sole custody, or joint custody. The various parental rights and obligations will also be described including the obligation on the part of both parents to communicate effectively with each other and to share all relevant information relating to the children.

4. **Decision making** – Authority for making decisions in the areas of health, education, religion, and extracurricular activities should be described. Decisions may be made jointly or by the primary-residence parent or decision making may be allocated between the parents in different areas (one parent to decide on schooling and religious upbringing, the other on health issues and activities). The plan should also deal with emergency decision making.

5. **Children's Residential Schedule** – This issue typically requires the most detail. The Parenting Agreement should set out the time to be spent by each child with each parent both during the school

week, on normal weekends, and on long weekends. It should also specify how the children are to spend holidays with each parent, including Christmas, spring break, summer vacation, religious holidays, and special occasions such as the parents' and the children's birthdays, Mothers' and Fathers' days, and Halloween. The Parenting Agreement may also deal with transportation between the parents' homes and telephone contact with the other parent while the children are residing away from that parent.

6. **Dispute Resolution** – The Parenting Agreement should include a mechanism for the resolution of future disputes that may arise between the parents. Options here include CFL, mediation, arbitration, or mediation/arbitration. As the children grow older, provision may be made in the Parenting Agreement for them to have input into the dispute resolution process.

The lawyers may meet to prepare the Parenting Agreement together or, more commonly, one of them will undertake that responsibility. This draft document may be sent directly to all participants at the same time, by e-mail or fax, for review before the next meeting. The cover letter or e-mail memorandum should state that it is a first working draft that will no doubt require amendments and changes. This practice is consistent with the team approach, which invites input and involves all members in the writing of the agreement. At the next settlement meeting, the participants negotiate the final form of the Parenting Agreement. This agreement may stand on its own as a domestic contract or it may be appended to the Separation Agreement.

Parenting

Child Talk

Children are not prisoners
Children are not property
Children are people
Parenting Plans without Custody Clauses

CFL in Practice

Open with talk about the vhildren
Review the legal options
Review the parenting history
Establish the parenting principles
Identify and reframe the issues
Probe for underlying interests
Generate creative options
Select the option that is
consistent with the principles of the parties and
satisfies their common and individual interests.
Consider the alternatives
Prepare the agreement

ENDNOTES

1 Ryan, J.P. (1989). *Parents Forever: Making the Concept a Reality for Divorcing Parents and their Children.* A Report Submitted to the Department of Justice (Canada) on the Parental Responsibilities Legislation in Four Jurisdictions: Florida, Maine, Washington and Great Britain.

2 *Harsant v. Portnoi* (1990), 27 R.F.L. (3d) 216 (Ont. H.C.); *Davis v. Davis* (1986), 3 R.F.L. (3d) 30 (Man. Q.B.); *Abbott v. Taylor* (1986), 2 R.F.L. (3d) 163 (Man. C.A.). The federal government in Canada has prepared legislation for Parliament to amend the Divorce Act, R.S.C. 1985, c. 3 (2nd Supp.) to replace "custody and access orders" with "parenting orders".

14

Child Support

- *Beyond the Guidelines*
- *CFL in Practice*

BEYOND THE GUIDELINES

While most jurisdictions in Canada and the United States have enacted child support guidelines which provide a legislative framework for calculating child support based on the payor's taxable income and the number of children, many rich opportunities for collaborative negotiation remain. Traditionally, lawyers estimate guideline support in the very first meeting with the client. Indeed, clients often want to know how much they will receive or have to pay.

Many view the guidelines as presumptive in the determination of child support and consider child support to be an open and shut issue. A challenge for CFL lawyers is to help the parties avoid going straight to a calculation of guideline support before they understand all of the available options. The goal of CFL negotiation is to have both parties feel that the child support agreement they reach is the best possible result given their circumstances. To achieve this result, it is necessary for the lawyers to set the table for a creative discussion of child support. As with other issues, the suggested model is to gather information, share interests and goals, develop principles, and generate and analyze options before making agreements.

CFL IN PRACTICE

Information

Legislative Context

The CFL lawyers may open the topic of child support with a shared explanation of the history of child support law, the legislative intent behind the enactment of the child support guidelines in their jurisdiction, the application of those guidelines, and how the guidelines are used to calculate the table amount of support and the sharing of extraordinary expenses. For the purpose of our discussion, we consider the *Divorce Act*,[1] a statute in force throughout Canada, and the *Federal Child Support Guidelines*,[2] which are found in the regulations made pursuant to this legislation. Child support guidelines with varying provisions are common in other jurisdictions.

Pursuant to the *Divorce Act*, an order for the support of a child must be made in accordance with the guidelines. The table amount is determined by consulting the table and selecting the requisite child support payment based upon the income of the payor and the number of children eligible for support. In addition, the parties share special or extraordinary expenses in proportion to their incomes.

The legislation permits the court to deviate from the guidelines only if satisfied that reasonable arrangements have been made for the support of a child. Under the guidelines, the court may order an amount other than what is set out under the applicable table in certain situations: where a child is over the age of majority; the payor's income exceeds $150,000; and in a shared custody arrangement where a child spends at least 40 per cent of her time with one parent. In those cases, the court may take into account the conditions, means, needs, and other circumstances of the child and the financial ability of the parents. Where the parties wish to depart from the guidelines, they must provide reasons for such departure and demonstrate that the proposed arrangement directly benefits the child. For example, a parent may wish to transfer all of her interest in the matrimonial home to the other parent in lieu of or in return for reduced monthly child support payments.

Parties who intend to divorce after negotiating their Separation Agreement must be aware that the court is obligated to scrutinize the provisions of a Separation Agreement before granting a divorce to ensure that adequate arrangements have been made for the support of the children. Essentially, this means ensuring that the guidelines have been followed or that equivalent child support arrangements have been made.

The lawyers may choose to discuss with the parties some perceived problems with the guideline model. For example, the provision under the heading, "Shared Custody," or, as it has come to be known in practice, the *40 per cent rule*, can be problematic. Many family law practitioners criticize the legislation for linking the obligation to pay guideline support to the amount of parenting time, which sometimes fuels insincere claims for custody. Another difficulty with this provision is that it does not define how to make the time calculation. *Is all time to be taken into account, waking time only, the time when the child is not in school, or just the time when the child is actually with a parent?*

Another concern for some is that the guideline model does not take into account the non-primary-residence parent's costs for the children when they are with her, which may include housing, food, transportation, clothing, and entertainment. Given that the table amount in the guideline model is based upon the payor's income only, there is no consideration as to whether she can afford the prescribed payments or whether the payments meet the recipient's actual needs for the children.

The guidelines envision an annual sharing of income information and a re-adjustment of support in accordance with the guidelines. Some parents wish to avoid annual fluctuations resulting from child support adjustments. Where the calculation of income is complex or relations between the parties are strained, they may not welcome an annual process of income assessment and review of support. Instead, they may wish to negotiate a review after a longer interval, with a fixed percentage adjustment in the interim.

Methods of Payment

Before generating options for the payment of child support, the lawyers should finish *setting the table* by outlining various ways, which can be used in isolation or in combination, that child support can be paid. There are generally four methods for payment of child support, which offer some structure to the discussion.

1. Where one parent has primary care, the other parent pays a monthly amount of support toward basic expenses. This may be the table amount. In addition, the parents share certain other expenses, such as childcare, extracurricular activities, and non-covered medical and dental expenses. These expenses can be shared in some proportion as they are incurred, responsibility for payment of certain expenses can be allocated between the parties, or the non-primary-residence parent can pay her share of these expenses to the other parent on a monthly basis.

2. Where parenting time and incomes are about equal, the parents may share a schedule of agreed upon expenses for the children – daycare, clothing, activities, trips, summer camps, etc. – by paying the costs as they fall due, by allocating responsibility for paying certain costs, or by each contributing a monthly amount to a joint *children's account* to be drawn upon for these costs.

3. Where parenting time is about equal and one parent has a greater income than the other, the parent with the greater income may pay child support monthly to the other calculated by assessing the higher income earner's table support obligation less the lower income earner's table support obligation. This formula may be adjusted to take into account the increased costs of shared custody by way of a gross-up of the setoff amount and/or may be adjusted for the actual time that the child spends with each parent. In addition, the parents may share a schedule of agreed upon expenses for the children, proportionate to their incomes.

4. Child support can be paid as a lump sum or by a transfer of property, most commonly one parent waiving her interest in the matrimonial home or deferring receipt of her equity, to allow the children to remain in the home.

Incomes

After discussing the legislative background, the problems with the child guideline model, and methods for payment of support, the lawyers will assist the parties in the collection of all financial information that may impact on decisions about child support.

In most cases, each parent will prepare a Financial Statement. They can share detailed information about their income from employment – compensation arrangements including salary, entitlement to overtime, bonuses, commission, stock options, life insurance, health, car, and retirement benefits. *Upon what basis are these paid? What does each parent expect to receive in the upcoming year? Does either intend to upgrade qualifications, change employment, relocate, or take any other steps that will impact on the ability to contribute to support?*

If a parent is self-employed, additional issues with respect to determining income arise. Taxable income set out in a self-employed person's income tax return may not represent income for the purposes of calculating child support. It will be important to discuss whether or not a self-employed parent has personal expenses put through the business, leaves profit in the business in the form of retained earnings, reduces income tax by way of income-splitting, or receives the profit of the business by dividends, repayment of shareholder loans, or some other means.

Often, the business accountant can provide a calculation of income for support purposes for minimal cost. In some cases, the parties may jointly retain an independent accountant as discussed in chapter 12. The focus remains on gathering all relevant information about income without linking that information to a particular outcome. The inquiry is intended to provide the most comprehensive understanding of the financial circumstances, which will generate options and possibilities, rather than prematurely assigning some specific guideline support amount.

Expenses

As with income, the participants must discuss expenses, ask questions, and obtain documentation to support estimates or actual figures where needed. Frequently, one spouse assumed sole responsibility for bill payment in the household. The CFL process encourages the parties to work together, either on their own or with the assistance of their lawyers, to create two household budgets based, as far as income allows, on the family lifestyle before separation. The parent with greater budgeting experience can quickly and cost-effectively raise the knowledge and comfort level of the other. They can often agree to the budget for each of them and then turn to address the challenge of meeting the agreed expenses and/or looking for acceptable ways to reduce certain costs.

Issues

Under the guidelines there are many issues to be negotiated such as:

1. The determination of the income of a payor spouse who is self-employed, has fluctuating income, earns bonuses or commissions, or works outside Canada in a country with a different income tax regime;
2. The extraordinary expenses that the parents may choose to incur and how they will be paid;
3. The duration of child support payments for a child over the age of majority;
4. The continuing entitlement to child support if a child takes time away from school to work or travel;
5. The terms for payment of post-secondary education expenses;
6. The division or sharing of child-related tax benefits;

7.   The indexation, adjustment, or variation of the child support payments.

Interests

The topic of expenses for the children will lead to a discussion of the children's interests, activities and lifestyle, and the goals the parents share for them. This exercise is often one in which the parties reveal many areas of agreement.

The parents first consider the interests of their children. *Do the parents want their children to remain in the family home, be cared for by a nanny or daycare provider, continue in ballet and music classes, have new or used sports equipment, attend summer camp, obtain counselling, receive tutoring, or attend private school to maximize academic success? Do they wish their teenagers to have access to a car or to have their own vehicle or to take public transit? Do they want them to have the opportunity to attend school trips, to have use of a computer, to buy name brand clothing? Do they want their children to attend university or community college – at home or away from home? Do they wish to set aside funds for their post-secondary education? Do they expect the children to contribute to those costs?* Parents can often co-create a schedule of agreed upon goals and expenses for their children.

At the same time, parents will have their own goals and interests, which overlap those of their children. *The children should perceive each parent as contributing towards their support. Each parent should be left with sufficient funds to provide a home for the children. The children should be able to take a similar vacation with each parent. Each parent's cash flow requirements and limitations should be considered. The parents should share responsibility for and control over special or extraordinary expenses. A parent with a particular interest in a certain activity, such as a team sport, may wish to take sole responsibility for the costs related to that activity.*

It is essential that CFL lawyers assist the parties to canvas fully the interests and objectives that the parents hold for themselves, as well as their children, around the issue of child support payments.

Principles

In circumstances where one parent has primary care of the children, the parties will likely choose to adopt the guidelines as their objective standard. Alternatively, the parties may choose to develop their own principles for resolving child support such as:

- The children should experience comparable lifestyles in each household;
- The children's standard of living is to be maintained;
- The children are to perceive both parents as contributing to their financial support;
- Both parents must agree to the payment of special or extraordinary expenses with full exchange of information;
- In appropriate cases, such as where a child resides away from home to attend university, child support payments can be made to that child if she is over the age of majority;
- The parents promote post-secondary school education for their children;
- The children are expected to make some contribution to their post-secondary school education;
- The children are not to be overburdened with student loans;
- Private school education is to be a first priority; and
- The parents will share special or extraordinary expenses proportionate to their incomes.

Options

The parties can now generate options for child support that address the interests of the parties and their children. For example, if components of the income of either parent are comprised of bonuses, commissions, and stock options, which are variable and uncertain, that income could be estimated and adjusted retroactively or disclosed and dealt with by lump sum payments when received, based on some agreed formula. Another option is that the table amount be paid monthly with a percentage of gross commissions paid quarterly when received. Yet another possibility is to make a mutually beneficial trade, such as allowing one party to retain overtime earnings without any corresponding increase in child support, provided she makes annual contributions into a registered education savings plan for each child.

In many situations, the parties will wish to follow the guidelines but do so in a way that meets the interests of both parents and the children. For example, if the parties agree that the dependant spouse should remain in the house with the children for a certain period of time, the cost to the payor of leaving his equity in the home may be calculated and considered as a contribution toward child support. In another situation, the parties may agree that a contribution to a child's education fund be considered a payment on account of child support.

A strict application of the guidelines may be seen as one option among, or in combination with other options, to be assessed in terms of the extent to which the child support arrangements satisfy the goals and interests of the parents and their children.

Alternatives

The parties may reach impasse regarding child support. Their lawyers may remind them of their alternatives and, in particular, adjudication. If they do not resolve the issue themselves, the court will impose an outcome that conforms to the guidelines. In Canada, where the non-primary-residence parent spends at least 40 percent of the time over the course of a year with a child, where a child is over the age of majority, where the payor spouse earns more than $150,000, and with respect to special and extraordinary expenses, it may be helpful to inform the parties again that the courts have discretionary authority and there is a range of possible outcomes.

The collaborative lawyers may encourage the parties to consider procedural options for moving beyond impasse, such as jointly retaining a recognized expert to provide a written legal opinion with respect to the child support issue or pursuing arbitration, either within the CFL process on a single issue or as an alternative to litigation following termination of CFL.

Agreement

If the negotiated settlement does not accord with the guidelines, it is important that the Separation Agreement outlines the reasons for the child support arrangements and how they directly benefit the children. In certain jurisdictions, a court may refuse to grant a divorce if satisfactory financial arrangements for a child have not been made, which some judges interpret to mean strict compliance with the guidelines.

The Separation Agreement should set out a procedure for the exchange of financial information in the future, for the adjustment or variation of child support, and for resolving future disputes regarding child support.

> ## Child Support
> ### Beyond the Guidelines
> The Guidelines provide opportunities for
> negotiation.
> ### CFL in Practice
>
> Provide information to the parties
> about child support law.
> Obtain information from the parties
> about their incomes and expenses.
> Identify the issues.
> Share interests and goals.
> Develop child support principles.
> Generate creative options.
> Select the option that is
> consistent with the principles of the parties and
> satisfies their common and individual interests.
> Consider the alternatives.
> Prepare the agreement.

ENDNOTES

1 *Divorce Act*, R.S.C. 1985, c. 3 (2nd Supp.).
2 *Federal Child Support Guidelines*, SOR/97-175.

15

Spousal Support

- *The Challenges*
- *CFL in Practice*

THE CHALLENGES

Spousal support can be one of the most challenging issues to resolve in any family matter. The subject usually evokes strong feelings, with both sides perceiving themselves most aggrieved. Each has interests and objectives vastly different from those of the other. Experiencing a sense of mutuality here is often elusive. A dependant spouse frequently feels vulnerable, under the control of the payor spouse, lacking self-worth and dignity, and fearful about future financial security. A payor may feel encumbered by obligations and ongoing connections to the ex-spouse, frustrated by a lack of financial independence and freedom, denied an incentive to work hard, and worried about maintaining good relations with the children or a new partner.

Both spouses may feel burdened by the legacy of the roles and responsibilities assumed during the marriage and fearful about their future financial well being. There is a tendency for the parties to become entrenched in positions, with each side convinced that their interests are highly incompatible. The lawyers may prepare the parties to meet these challenges by *normalizing their feelings* and *revisiting communication protocol.*

Normalize Feelings

It is helpful at this stage to normalize the parties' perspectives and feelings about spousal support. Collaborative counsel may observe that since two households cost more than one, most separating couples experience financial struggles and worry about how they will manage after divorce. It is also common to have fundamental differences and strong feelings about this topic.

This issue affords a crucial opportunity to practise the virtues and reap the rewards of open-ended questioning and active listening. The lawyers may ask the parties to discuss, as fully as possible, each person's concerns, worries, and objectives about this issue. They may ask the parties whether they are willing to listen for the other person's interests and priorities, in order to propose settlement options attractive to the other that maximize the interests of both.

On the subject of spousal support in particular, each person may hold a unique and often contradictory perspective on the history of the marriage – which spouse made the greatest sacrifices and who was responsible for their lifestyle choices. It is important to acknowledge that both spouses made contributions to the marriage and that it is not necessary to reconcile their incompatible perspectives. The purpose of collaborative negotiation is to find solutions that meet the fundamental financial interests and objectives of both parties, without the need to determine who is right or wrong.

Revisit the Communication Protocol

Paying attention to effective communication at this stage will help avoid backsliding and unproductive argument. Nothing shuts down effective communication like accusatory statements that reach back to the early days of the relationship. Each lawyer may remind his or her client to speak in "I" rather than "You" statements, express concerns and objectives without blame, and avoid becoming mired in the past. While some discussion of the circumstances that brought this couple to the present is necessary, the negotiations are future-oriented.

CFL IN PRACTICE

Information

Legislative Context

An important role for lawyers is to provide the parties with information to place the issue under discussion in a context. Information is a powerful tool to open up the parties' thinking process, to moderate position-taking, and to balance power between the parties. A discussion of the historical and legislative development of spousal support may serve to ease the parties away from an anxious focus on the amount and duration of spousal support to an awareness of the complexity and possibilities inherent in the spousal support issue. This discussion may take place during client preparation and/ or in the settlement meetings.

Current spousal support legislation and case law have evolved in response to the awareness in the 1980s by judges and lawmakers that the standard of living of most women and children fell dramatically after divorce, while the standard of living of most men rose or stayed the same. The focus in awarding spousal support shifted away from an expectation of speedy economic independence and a *clean break* between most spouses, to an appreciation of the long-term economic cost of parenting and homecare responsibilities, often requiring an ongoing financial connection.

Spousal support legislation speaks in terms of general factors and objectives to be considered. Unlike child support and property division, there are no guidelines or formulas to determine entitlement and amount for spousal support. Broad judicial discretion results in different outcomes on similar facts. Lawyers may provide conflicting opinions and advice to their respective clients, while relying on the same legal authority.

At present in Ontario, the court may set aside an agreement by the parties to release rights to spousal support if the court determines that it did not meet the statutory objectives.[1] Case law can provide powerful incentives to create agreements around spousal support that address the real needs of the parties and recognize their respective contributions to the marriage. The CFL process involves a thorough consideration of the immediate and long-term needs of both parties. They seek outcomes that are durable. It is far more likely that parties who reach agreement by way of collaborative negotiation will perceive the results to be fair and balanced, *as they define those terms,* than those who have solutions imposed upon them by their lawyers or the court.

A discussion of the statutory criteria for spousal support awards often serves to modify extreme positions on the topic and gives objective credibility to the request for sufficient support. Explaining that spousal misconduct is not considered by the court when determining spousal support can sometimes assist in diffusing accusations and refocusing on problem solving.

A reference to the legislation will also demonstrate that the statutory criteria are sufficiently broad to permit a wide range of possible results. Clients will appreciate why lawyers cannot predict with certainty how the court might address spousal support in any particular case. This uncertainty can be seen as an opportunity for the parties to find arrangements through collaborative negotiation that meet their unique needs and circumstances.

Most spousal support orders lack any termination date, leaving it to the parties to return to court if circumstances change in the future. The court defines neither the extent of change necessary to trigger variation, nor the process for modification. Most separating couples want their financial arrangements to be clear, specific, and as predictable as possible, attributes a court can rarely provide.

Spousal Support Arrangements

The lawyers will review with the clients, either during preparation or at the settlement meeting, the various types of spousal support arrangements that can be made. In a court proceeding, the court can make one or more of the following orders:

- Interim periodic spousal support based on limited information, which may set a precedent for future decisions;
- Indefinite or time-limited periodic spousal support, which attempts to satisfy statutory criteria by considering factors such as the length of the marriage, the roles of the parties in the marriage, and their relative financial circumstances;
- Lump sum spousal support, which may be intended either to compensate a spouse for contributions made during the marriage or to effect a clean break;
- A variation of periodic spousal support, which follows a request by one or both parties to change an existing order or agreement due to a change in circumstances, although, the threshold to justify change and the scope of available change are uncertain and difficult to predict; and
- A review of periodic spousal support, which involves a fresh consideration of the matter at an agreed time or upon the occurrence of certain events.

In the CFL process, the parties can negotiate any of the above spousal support provisions. They can make immediate arrangements to pay bills and to maintain each household in the interim. They may agree that the final periodic spousal support agreement be retroactive to separation, in order to eliminate prejudice to a party as a result of the time necessary to conduct their negotiations. These arrangements will usually be made without the delay, cost, and hardship inherent in obtaining court orders.

The parties will negotiate spousal support to be effective after agreement is reached. These arrangements will meet as fully as possible the spousal support principles the parties adopt from the statute and/or create on their own. They will often define in detail the criteria for reviewing, changing, or terminating spousal support in the future, including what circumstances will permit a request for change and what circumstances will not, and the timing and procedure for review or variation.

Incomes and Expenses

As with child support, the parties provide information and exchange documents concerning their incomes and expenses. They may prepare current and anticipated budgets, either before a settlement meeting or as a joint effort during the meeting. Using the computer during meetings allows quick preparation and amendments to budgets. Counsel may encourage the parties to consider their needs for the following year, in two years, and perhaps in five years. This will encourage the parties to focus not only on their immediate situation, but also on the long term. Once the numbers have been discussed and as far as possible agreed, counsel may print and distribute copies of both budgets to everyone. It is also powerful to use a flip chart and tape each budget to the wall, as a graphic way of putting everyone on the team on the same side of the problem. Now the challenge of meeting any budget shortfall, in a manner consistent with the principles the parties have established, is squarely in front of both parties.

Some clients will adopt the principle that each should have equal after-tax incomes. If so, budgets may or may not be necessary, except as a check by each individual for affordability of certain expenditures. To assist the parties, income tax calculations should be made to ascertain the net disposable incomes of the parties at various levels of support.

Issues

There are at least five spousal support issues to be negotiated by the parties:

1. **Entitlement** – The parties must first agree as to whether it is appropriate in the circumstances that any spousal support be paid.

2. **Amount** – Once entitlement is determined, the amount of support is the most urgent question for both the payor and recipient spouse. Unlike child support, there are no charts or guidelines to determine the amount of spousal support. While there may be support practices in vogue at any particular time, the parties are free to agree to any amount of support that is acceptable to both of them.

3. **Duration** – The next element of support to be decided is how long it will be paid. Again, the parties can decide whether support will be paid indefinitely or for a specified period of time after which it

will end. They can define the assumptions and expectations that underpin their agreement.

4. **Method of Payment** – Support orders may be time-limited, indefinite, or by way of a lump sum. Support can be paid in regular, usually monthly, instalments which will be taxable to the recipient and deductible to the payor; by the payor making direct payments to a third party on behalf of the recipient for such things as mortgage payments, retraining costs, or pension contributions, which may or may not attract tax consequences; or in a lump sum, which does not attract tax consequences. CFL affords opportunities for creative tax planning that will maximize the after-tax positions of the parties.

5. **Variation or Review** – The parties can determine whether or not spousal support can be changed in the future and if so, when, under what circumstances, and by what procedure.

Interests

In our earlier discussion of the interest-based negotiation model in chapter 11, we offered our thoughts as to some possible interests of the parties on the issue of spousal support. A spouse has certain needs, desires, concerns, and fears, which may be unique to him, and others that are shared with his spouse. Each requires an ability to meet his or her immediate expenses to maintain an accustomed standard of living. As well, they share a concern about long-term financial security. A woman who has devoted her married life to the household needs of the family and the nurture of their children may seek recognition of her contributions. A man who spent a substantial amount of his time working to provide for his family may desire to reduce his hours at work to devote more time to his children after separation.

The interests of the parties related to spousal support issues can be as varied as the attributes and characters of any two people. The lawyers in a CFL process must be aware of this diversity of interests. They must broaden the inquiry beyond the substantive needs and means to include the psychological and procedural interests of the parties as well.

Principles

Rather than simply adopting the broad legislative criteria for deter-mining spousal support, the CFL process encourages the parties to develop unique principles by which they will assess their support options. Principles for spousal support will be fashioned from the parties' individual interests, values, and goals, as well as from the prevailing legal framework.

Some possible principles for spousal support are:

- The spouses should have comparable net disposable incomes and standards of living;
- The pre-separation standard of living should be maintained as far as possible for both spouses;
- A homemaker should be compensated for giving up her career;
- A homemaker should receive retraining in a career of her choosing, and support if she needs it until she can support herself;
- A spouse's contributions to the career or business development of the other should be recognized and compensated;
- The parties should each achieve future economic security;
- A spouse who invested his inheritance in the family home should have that recognized;
- The family cottage should be kept for the children, and the cost to do so should be borne by both parties;
- A spouse's obligation to care for the children or an elderly parent is a valued service, supported by the other;
- A parent should remain home fulltime until the children are in school;
- The primary income earner will not be required to take overtime on weekends, so that his time with the children is maximized; and
- The spousal support arrangement will be structured so as to maxi-mize the after-tax position of each party.

When options for spousal support arrangements are put forward, each party can be asked to explain how his or her proposal promotes their agreed principles. As with all other issues, the interests of these particular parties need to be elicited and understood by both.

Options

The parties are ready to create options for resolving spousal support when:

1. They are mindful of the guidelines for effective communication;
2. They understand the income available to each spouse and the budgets for each household;
3. They are aware of the interests and goals of each party; and
4. They have agreed to spousal support principles.

Family lawyers use computer software programs, which calculate the after-tax position of each spouse assuming various amounts for child and spousal support. These can be created in advance or during the settlement meetings.

Clients are assisted to generate spousal support options that satisfy the interests of both parties. For example, if the payor spouse seeks a termination of spousal support after a fixed period, counsel may ask what assets or issues of importance to the recipient spouse he might be willing to trade in exchange for that release. In the alternative, that spouse may be asked how a release of support after a fixed period can be structured to promote the agreed spousal support principles. *What would you be willing to do to ensure your spouse's economic security after support ends?*

If time-limited spousal support is not appropriate, the parties may consider a time period after which spousal support provisions may be reviewed. They may set a date for or the circumstances that will trigger a review or request for a variation as, for example, any of the following:

• Completion of a retraining program;
• A substantial change in the income of either party;
• The payor's retirement;
• A child ceasing to be dependant;
• A health issue affecting either person's ability to earn income; and
• The remarriage or cohabitation of one or both parties.

The parties may agree as to the obligations to be undertaken by the dependant spouse in the interim, such as pursuing retraining and/or employment, developing a new business, or obtaining counselling.

Their agreement may also set out the details of the review process, including the issues to be considered, the financial information to be exchanged, and the forum for review, which could be a return to the CFL process, mediation, or arbitration. The parties may also wish to specify what events will *not* permit variation, such as minor changes in income or parenting time, receipt of income from overtime or inheritance, or the recipient spouse earning income to a threshold amount.

As an alternative to a review or variation procedure, the parties may opt for a formula that adjusts spousal support automatically in accordance with changes in the incomes of the parties. In a CFL case recently negotiated, the parties inserted the following formula in their agreement:

> The amount of spousal support will be adjusted annually on the 15th day of May each year as follows:
>
> A = The recipient spouse's income from the previous year's income tax return
>
> B = The payor spouse's income from the previous year's income tax return
>
> C = Table amount of child support pursuant to this Agreement
>
> Monthly spousal support = C x (B-A) / B.

In this case, the parties began with a spousal support payment tied to the child support payment. If there are no changes in the incomes of the parties, the spousal support remains the same. If the income of the recipient spouse increases relative to that of the payor spouse, there is an automatic decrease in the spousal support paid without either a review or variation process.

While the law professes a strict separation of the parenting, property, and support issues, the clients may well see the issues as pieces of a puzzle, available to create an agreement that meets each person's own needs as well as those that are shared. A father who wants increased time with the children may agree not to reduce child support even if he has the children more than 40 per cent of the time. A secondary income earner may be willing to consider a release of spousal support if the other pays for her retraining, provides top-up support while she establishes employment, and/or contributes to her retirement fund. One party may be willing to give the other credit for an inheritance invested in the cottage, if she agrees that he can visit the cottage with the children for a week each summer and/or she bequests the cottage to the children.

Alternatives

As with other issues, a reminder of the alternative of a court imposed solution may assist the parties to overcome any negotiation barriers. Unlike child support, there are no guidelines to which the lawyers can refer their clients. With spousal support, the court has broad discretion, and, as a result, outcomes are less predictable.

Where a dependant spouse waives entitlement to support, releases the other from all future claims for support, or agrees to an amount which may be significantly less than what a court might award, some lawyers may consider it their obligation to review the alternatives available to their clients. The challenge for them is to advise their clients of the applicable law in a way that maintains their decision-making autonomy and promotes resolution.

Other lawyers may not feel this need. They see no conflict between skilful collaborative practice, which recognizes the right of clients to make their own decisions, based on their values, priorities, objectives, and their lawyers' duty to advocate for them in an interest-based context.[2]

Agreement

The CFL process affords creative opportunities for the parties to satisfy individual and shared interests around spousal support, both immediate and long term, with as much predictability and detail as the parties themselves desire.

The Separation Agreement may recite the spousal support principles the parties adopted or created, the assumptions and expectations upon which the Agreement is based, and any other background information that describes why and how the settlement was reached. Where the parties do not reconcile fundamental differences in perspectives, the agreement may set out what each party believed to be the circumstances and reasons for the agreement. This information may be useful at the time of any variation or review.

Spousal Support

Confront the Challenges
Normalize the feelings.
Revisit the communication protocol.

CFL in Practice
Provide information to the parties
about spousal support law.
Obtain information from the parties
about their incomes and expenses
Identify the issues.
Share interests and goals.
Develop spousal support principles.
Generate creative options.
Select the option that is
consistent with the principles of the parties and
satisfies their common and individual interests.
Consider the alternatives.
Prepare the agreement.

ENDNOTES

1 *Miglin v. Miglin* (2001), 198 D.L.R. (4th) 385 (Ont. C.A.); reversed in part 2003 CarswellOnt 1374, 2003 CarswellOnt 1375, [2003] S.C.J. No. 21, 2003 SCC 24, 34 R.F.L. (5th) 255, 224 D.L.R. (4th) 193, 302 N.R. 201 (S.C.C.). In summary, the Supreme Court of Canada held that the Ontario Court of Appeal erred in holding that the wife could receive further ongoing spousal support in the face of the parties' separation agreement containing a spousal support release.

The Court held that an initial application for spousal support inconsistent with a pre-existing agreement requires a two-stage investigation into all circumstances surrounding that agreement: first, at the time of its formation and secondly, at the time of application.

In the first stage, the court must look to the circumstances in which the agreement was negotiated and signed to determine whether there was any reason to discount it. The court must consider the terms of the agreement to determine whether they substantially comply with the spousal support objectives provided in the *Divorce Act*.

At the second stage, the court must assess the extent to which enforcement of the agreement still reflected the original intentions of the parties and the extent to which it was still in substantial compliance with the objectives of the *Divorce Act*.

2 Rose, C. (2002). Wrestling with the model, *Collaborative Review*, v4, n1, pp. 1-4.

16

Property

- *The Property Regime*
- *Unfreezing*
- *CFL in Practice*

THE PROPERTY REGIME

The term *property regime* refers to the prevailing legal framework that governs the distribution of property between spouses on separation and divorce. Unlike the issues pertaining to children and financial support, where a certain uniformity is pervasive throughout Canada and the United States, what is in place in one province or state may be different from that of any other. This observation reflects the constitutional reality of both nations. Jurisdiction over property is a matter of provincial or state rights and court orders are made pursuant to their legislation.

The same general laws that applied to all other persons formerly governed property division between spouses in many jurisdictions. With the exception of certain possessory rights to the matrimonial home, title was paramount. Over the past two decades, family law reform legislation displaced these earlier property regimes. In most jurisdictions, spouses are now entitled to share equally in the distribution of all property acquired over the course of their marriage.

Family property legislation provides either that all assets are to be divided between spouses irrespective of ownership or that the net value of all of their property is to be equalized. Notwithstanding the apparent simplicity of the legislative intent, disputes still arise. To take into account special circumstances surrounding the acquisition of particular property, credits or exclusions may apply. The recognition of these claims can radically alter the outcome, leaving one party with substantially less than her spouse. Other issues emerge as to the appropriate value of certain assets and whether discounts for taxes and other imputed disposition costs ought to be applied. Accordingly, an element of complexity surrounds the determination of these property issues. The outcome is not always apparent and it may not accord with the notion of justice and equity held by one or both spouses.

UNFREEZING

The property regimes currently in place have not always been the way in which property issues were determined on separation and divorce. In fact, some have been in place for shorter periods of time than the duration of the marriage or cohabitation of the parties who seek relief. Once a property regime is in place, lawyers soon become accustomed to its application in their jurisdiction. An outcome, which appears quite inappropriate to the parties, may be seen by their lawyers as legitimate solely because it conforms to the statutory scheme. For example, in a given case, a spouse may have to forego all of her tangible assets to offset her interest in a pension plan the benefit of which she will not realize until retirement.

CFL endorses an interest-based approach to the resolution of all issues in dispute including those pertaining to property. The outcome need not parallel what a court might award. The adjudicative alternative may not satisfy the interests of either party. To negotiate an interest-based outcome may require that the lawyers let go of a strict adherence to the mandates of the prevailing property regime.

In his research on group dynamics, Kurt Lewin identifies the three steps that groups must take to achieve sustainable change: *unfreezing*; *moving to a new level*; and *freezing at the new level*.[1] CFL lawyers adapt that process to their use. Before they can move ahead, they must first *unfreeze*. They are not bound to follow the process dictated under their property regimes; there may be other ways to resolve property disputes between spouses. An outcome is no less acceptable simply because it does not conform to what the legislation prescribes. What matters in the final analysis is whether the outcome achieves the goals of the parties. In the words of Edward de Bono, CFL encourages them to think *outside the box*.[2] They are capable of generating creative, original ideas that satisfy their shared and individual interests.

CFL IN PRACTICE

Issues

The parties usually bring to the process concerns about particular assets and debts. They seldom speak in terms of an overall scheme of distribution or equalization. The lawyers should record these concerns without implying any particular outcome. For example, rather than listing *an equalization of net family property*, consider framing the issue as *division of property*. Rather than *sale of the matrimonial home,* use *what to do with the matrimonial home*? Labelling the issues this way does not foreclose any options or predetermine any result.

Information

Lawyers routinely ask their clients to complete Financial Statements containing schedules of assets and liabilities. Lawyers operating within the adversarial paradigm generally take this disclosure process further than simply the preparation of preliminary Financial Statements. They request the production of a myriad of materials to support all of the entries, line by line. They may also demand formal appraisals or valuations of some of the listed assets. Quite apart from the cost and inconvenience, compliance inevitably results in a lengthy delay to the commencement of negotiations.

While the parties to a CFL process may begin to work on Financial Statements prior to their first settlement meeting, it is not necessary that they be completed. The lawyers do not make production demands as a condition precedent to their attendance at the first settlement meeting. They defer consideration of what is required until then. At that time, the participants determine what information they require to resolve their property issues. For example, if the parties have agreed to the sale of their home, an appraisal is unnecessary. They will only need statements from the mortgagee and any other creditors whose loans will be paid on closing. If support is not an issue, budgets are probably unnecessary. During these early phases of the CFL process, the participants decide what is necessary, following which they assign the task of who should obtain what.

If it is necessary to determine the value of certain assets or debts, the participants should follow the process discussed in chapter 12. They jointly select an appropriately qualified expert, agree whether her opinion is to be final and binding, decide how to pay for the investigation and the report, if any, and determine what is to be done with this expense in their property settlement.

To ensure that the parties are fully informed before making any decisions, the lawyers help them calculate a division of property according to the applicable law. The parties are then able to consider whether the statutory option satisfies their interests and objectives.

Interests

As with the other substantive issues, it is necessary for the lawyers to facilitate a comprehensive exploration of the underlying interests of the parties in respect of their property. Rather than discuss interests again in a general way, we propose to examine four of the more prominent generic assets that are typically the subject matter of discussion in any family dispute resolution process.

The Family Residence

With most families, the family residence is their principal asset. The spouses hold some interests in common. A primary interest of most parents is to minimize the disruption in the lives of their children that accompanies a move from their home. This concern is obviously linked to the parenting and support issues. Each parent needs a home appropriate for the children. Most spouses, whether they have children or not, want to have a residence consistent with the family income and accustomed standard of living.

In addition to these shared interests, there may be others unique to one or the other of the spouses alone. Over the course of their ownership and occupancy, one spouse may have devoted considerably more time than the other toward improvements and renovations. The house is no longer just a residential property but an extension of her identity. In another case, a spouse may have inherited a cottage that has been in her family for generations. By virtue of its character as an alternative family residence, each may be entitled to exercise possessory rights. However, the titled spouse cherishes it beyond its market value or recreational use; it is a family legacy.

Personal Use Property

This category of property encompasses everything that the spouses use in the course of their daily lives as matters of necessity, convenience, entertainment, and recreation. The primary items include their furniture, appliances, artwork, clothing, jewelry and motor vehicles.

What are the interests of the parties in respect of this category of property? Both probably want to maintain the standard of living enjoyed during their marriage or cohabitation. Each requires a car, furniture, and appliances. If there are children who will be spending significant amounts of time in each of their respective homes, they want to avoid any apparent diminution in the quality of their children's lives when they move from one residence to the other. Neither spouse wishes to feel that he or she is worse off than the other as a result of the allocation of their personal use property. They seek balance and proportionality.

From an individual perspective, each may miss something that is no longer his or hers to enjoy. Some possessions have special emotional significance to one or both of the spouses. For example, wedding gifts, items created by the children, family photographs and videos, and gifts from members of their extended families are important mementos of their lives together.

The Business

The spouses have interests in common when one owns a business that is the principal source of income for the family. They want to preserve the revenue generated by the business to support each of them and their children. They do not want to inhibit the incentive of the proprietor to work diligently for its continued success and growth. Other members of the family, notably the children of the parties, may also be looking to work for the business in the near future and ultimately succeed their parent or parents as owners.

As well, there are individual interests that must be recognized. The spouse who developed the business is proud of her accomplishment and she will want to preserve it as an ongoing enterprise. She may fear its loss as a result of the division or equalization process. From the perspective of the other spouse, he may have made a contribution toward the establishment, operation, and improvement of the business and he likely made other sacrifices for it to prosper. This spouse seeks recognition of his efforts toward this family enterprise.

Retirement Assets

For most spouses, the most significant assets, aside from the family residence, are their retirement savings and pensions. A party may be limited to what she will receive from a public pension plan and social security. Alternatively, she may also have accumulated substantial retirement savings in a private retirement savings plan. One or both may be a member of a private pension plan.

The parties share a common wish for a comfortable lifestyle in retirement. A spouse who is a pension plan member often wants a clean break with no obligation to the other. On the other hand, the non-member spouse may feel that she has contributed to the growth of these funds and is entitled to a share of the pension benefits. At the same time, most spouses want and need a balanced division of their other accumulated capital assets. They may not be content with the right to receive an income in retirement as their only property following a separation.

Principles

The parties may choose as their objective criteria or standard of legitimacy the framework provided under their property regime. However, this approach will limit their options and it may not satisfy all of their interests.

Alternatively, the parties may opt to create a statement of principles that will guide them in their deliberations. For example, they may agree that each should have a residence of comparable quality sufficient to accommodate themselves and their children. They might add that neither must divest him or herself of all liquid assets to equalize their property. They could commit themselves to the development of a retirement plan for each. These principles are not found in any legislation. They acquire their validity from the will of the parties who want to satisfy their interests to the maximum extent possible.

The participants may decide to involve one or more neutral third parties; individuals with expertise in some aspect of valuation, management, or investment. These persons introduce external standards, which are supplemental to whatever the law or the parties themselves may provide.

Options

The Family Residence

The options that are immediately apparent are the acquisition of the interest of one spouse by the other, an immediate sale and distribution of the proceeds between the spouses, or a deferred sale with one spouse retaining exclusive possession in the interim. Are there other choices that may satisfy the interests of both parties? As an illustration of what might be accomplished, we consider a family whose Parenting Plan provides that the children will be residing with each parent for equal amounts of time. The parents require two comparable homes. What are their options?

One option is for the parties to increase their mortgage on the existing family residence and use the funds as a down payment for a second house. One parent remains in the matrimonial home and the other moves into the new residence. They could hold title to both in their joint names and defer making any decision concerning the ultimate disposition of these properties until there are no longer dependant children living with them. Another option might be for them to sell the family residence and use the proceeds to purchase two similar properties that are each less expensive than the house they sold. A further option is the acquisition of a rental property in which each of the parties lives in alternate weeks while the other stays in the matrimonial home with the children.

Through the process of option generation, the participants develop several ideas. It is entirely possible that more will appear. The process is self-generating. Subsequent options may be adaptations of others that preceded them.

With the options before them, the parties look back at their interests. Which of their options maximizes their interest satisfaction? In our example, the parties may choose to retain the matrimonial home and acquire a second residence with an additional loan secured by both of them. This option realizes many of their goals: their children continue to live in their home; the parties use their joint equity to obtain another accommodation of comparable quality for the spouse who moves from the matrimonial home; they have not compromised their ultimate property settlement; and the proposal complements their Parenting Plan.

Personal Use Property

We outline a method of distribution of this category of property as an example of what could be developed by the parties working together. They begin with each party preparing a list of those chattels that he or she would like to keep. This process identifies the items that may be in dispute. The parties can then take turns choosing. They decide who makes the first selection and, in the event of disagreement, they can toss a coin. They continue in this fashion until all of their personal use property has been divided between them.

An alternative process has one party creating two lists with the other party selecting between them. It is often referred to as *final offer selection*. The process and outcome are similar in effect to *baseball arbitration*. It discourages an extreme position by the party who creates the list as someone other than her ultimately makes the final decision.

It may not be possible to divide the personal use property equally between the parties either in terms of quantity or value as a result of the circumstances of the separation. One of them may be moving a great distance and it is just not practical for her to transport furniture and appliances. The parties may agree to retain an auctioneer to value what one spouse retains. A monetary amount reflective of the difference in value of the personal use property each receives is negotiated with the assistance of this third party. That figure is then factored into the property settlement. The spouse might then receive that sum from the proceeds of sale of the matrimonial home or the disposition of some other property.

With personal use property that has sentimental value, a simple division between the parties is difficult. Photographs and videos may be duplicated; other items such as gifts from family members or creations by their children may not be. They must still be divided. However, the process is not as simple as provided above.

The traditional approach to personal use property division does not extend beyond what the parties have at separation. It does not consider the cost to replace items lost by a spouse in the division. However, the quality of the parties' post-separation lives depends in part upon the replacement of this property. In the CFL process, the parties could agree to share the cost to purchase essential items.

The Business

What options are available to the spouses to satisfy their interests with respect to a business asset? Surely, they are not limited to quantifying the value of the business as of the date of separation and requiring the owner spouse to make an equalization payment that she may not have the ability to pay. If the business developed over the course of a long marriage and each spouse contributed in one way or the other, they could consider bringing the other spouse in as an owner. Where the continued good fortune of the business is necessary to satisfy the interests of their children, they too could be introduced at a proper time and to a degree commensurate with their ages and commitments. An outcome of this nature is consistent with what is often done in families that are not divided by separation.

If the business is incorporated, another option is to issue a special class of non-voting shares in favour of the other spouse. The spouse's interest in the business could be realized through the redemption of the shares over a specified period during which dividend income is paid. Payments could be accelerated if the principal assets or the business itself is sold in the interim. The terms in respect of the payment of dividends and the redemption of the shares over time would likely be set out in a Shareholder Agreement.

Retirement Assets

Legislation may provide for the division of pension credits at source. In Canada, the *Canada Pension Plan*[3] and other federal pension plans contain this provision. Similarly, the *Income Tax Act*[4] allows a taxpayer to transfer funds directly from her private retirement savings plan to her spouse's plan without immediate income tax consequences in settlement of property rights on separation The division of these retirement assets does not usually present either conceptual or logistical difficulties.

Spouses do not have the same degree of freedom with respect to sharing the benefits of a private pension plan as they do with their other assets. The reason for this restriction is that these funds and the payments to be made from them are subject to legislation and the terms and conditions set out in the plans themselves. Essentially, there are really only two options available. First, the plan member spouse may pay a lump sum amount or transfer property to the other representing a share of her interest on the basis of its present after-tax value as determined by an actuary. Second, the pension benefits may be divided between the spouses as and when they are paid, either at source by the pension plan or upon receipt by the plan member spouse.

Another way to approach this issue is for the parties to retain a financial advisor to assist them in the preparation of a Retirement Plan. The objective is to develop appropriate retirement assets for both spouses sufficient to meet their anticipated needs at that time in their lives. As with their other property dispositions, they work together toward this end. The parties obtain information and suggestions from the advisor as to the choices available to them. With this input, they may choose to supplement what they have at the time of separation. For example, where one spouse is a member of a private pension plan, she could contribute to the private retirement savings plan of the other and/or the proceeds from the sale of a property could be deposited into that account. The goal is to create a fund that will provide an income to the spouse who is not a pension plan member comparable to what the other will receive from her pension.

Alternatives

If the parties reach impasse regarding the property issues, a review of the property division provisions according to statutory law may help them overcome negotiation barriers. As well, the areas of uncertainty and risk may be reviewed as a further reality check.

Where clients choose to resolve their property issues in a way that is substantially different from that set out in the statute, each lawyer must determine his or her approach. As discussed in chapter 15, some lawyers may see no need whatsoever to discuss the issue further, while some may feel an obligation to review the statutory alternatives prior to the client confirming the agreement. Many lawyers will wish to document any such deviations when reporting to their client.

Agreement

Before committing the negotiated agreement to writing, the lawyers should ensure that the following issues have been properly addressed. *Is this agreement viable – will it work? Is this agreement durable – will it hold up over time? Is this agreement enforceable – will a court be able to compel performance? Are the promises secured?*

The final step is the preparation of a draft Separation Agreement that embodies the terms and conditions of the negotiated outcome. The principles may be recited either in the preamble or in the body of the text. The parties may choose to list the interests that are recognized by the disposition of their property issues. Some matters require more precision than do others. For example, if the family residence is to be sold, the date upon which it is to be listed, the listing agent, the right of occupancy and possession, and the responsibility for maintenance ought to be specified. The variation and dispute resolution provisions of the Separation Agreement may apply where there is any form of continuing ownership and possession of their property. The proposed allocation of personal use property, and any ancillary or supplementary agreements such as a Shareholder Agreement or a Retirement Plan can all be attached as schedules or at least identified in the Separation Agreement.

Property

___The Property Regime___
Lawyers need to let go of their
strict adherence to the property regime.
Clients need to think outside the box.

___CFL in Practice___
Identify the issues.
Gather information about assets and liabilities.
Share interests and goals.
Develop property principles.
Generate creative options.
Select the option that is
consistent with the principles of the parties and
satisfies their common and individual interests.
Consider the alternatives
Prepare the agreement.

ENDNOTES

1 Lewin, K. (1947). Group decision and social change. In T.M. Newcomb & E.L. Hartley (Eds.) (1947). *Readings in Social Psychology*. New York: Henry Holt and Company, Inc.; Lewin, K. (1947). Frontiers in group dynamics. In K. Lewin (1997). *Resolving Social Conflicts* and *Field Theory in Social Science*. Washington, DC: American Psychological Association.
2 De Bono, E. (1970). *Lateral Thinking: A Textbook of Creativity*. New York: Penguin Books.
3 *Canada Pension Plan*, R.S.C. 1985, c. 8.
4 *Income Tax Act*, R.S.C. 1985, c. 1 (5th Supp.).

Part Six:

Final Thoughts

- *The Way to Collaboration*

17

The Way to Collaboration

- *A Conversation*
- *Becoming a CFL Lawyer*
- *Forming a CFL Association*
- *Creating a CFL Awareness*
- *Collaborating Beyond CFL*
- *Final Thoughts*

A CONVERSATION

At this juncture, we want to initiate a conversation among our colleagues about collaborative practice. Toward that end, we now speak in the second person. The collaborative way of resolving disputes is still evolving; our transformation to collaborative professionals is still underway. We encourage an ongoing exchange of ideas to achieve our common goal of excellence in our collaborative work.

In this chapter, we offer suggestions on becoming a CFL lawyer, on forming a CFL association, on creating a CFL awareness, and on collaborating beyond CFL. While these comments represent our final thoughts for this book, we intend that they comprise the first words in a continuing conversation.

BECOMING A CFL LAWYER

Obtain Your CFL Training

Once you have decided to become a CFL lawyer, you will require training in the collaborative process and the communication, negotiation, and intervention skills required for effective practice. Each CFL association establishes the minimum requirements for its members. Generally, CFL workshops consist of two days of process training and three to five days of skills training. Some practice groups encourage their members to obtain mediation training, which are usually forty hours in duration in accordance with the guidelines of the principal mediation associations in Canada and the United States.

In addition to basic training, it is extremely valuable for practitioners to learn about the psychosocial dynamics of separation and divorce for both parents and their children. It is also helpful for CFL lawyers to become familiar with the needs of children at their various ages and stages of development and what they experience when their parents separate and divorce. CFL lawyers should be able to recognize and screen for spousal abuse and intimidation. Mediators and child experts can offer insights and strategies for dealing with high conflict or particularly emotionally charged couples. Many CFL associations offer workshops on team building to improve working relationships with clients and professional colleagues. Many CFL lawyers also seek training in family counselling and divorce coaching. You may well consider it advantageous if not essential to pursue these other training opportunities.

As in the practice of law generally, continuing education in the CFL process and CFL skills development is a lifelong professional obligation.

Develop Your CFL Style

To embrace CFL requires that we let go of the directive, controlling approach to which we have become accustomed in traditional legal representation. Many lawyers, by temperament and training, are ill equipped and uncomfortable in the face of the strong emotions of their clients. We are accustomed to taking charge, providing advice, and steering the process along a familiar path. CFL requires us to adopt a profoundly different approach.

For many of us, becoming a CFL lawyer will involve moving into unfamiliar territory. Like mediation, CFL can be intense, highly focused work. It often requires that we connect with our clients and their spouses on an emotional and psychological level, as well as at the financial and legal levels with which we are more familiar. It requires that we slow down, let go of our assumptions, and stop trying to solve everything *for* our clients. As we truly listen to the parties, and become fully present in the process, we learn to handle with grace whatever comes along. We develop trust in the capacity of the parties to move beyond their fears, tap into their own wisdom, and make good decisions for themselves.

We each bring our own personality and values to our work and will develop our own CFL style. Some lawyers will conduct this process in a practical, business-like manner. They may find that simply taking more time to listen and reflect will enhance their ability to be present in the process. Others with a more therapeutic style may use meditation, yoga, or similar spiritual exercises to help them maintain a calm and centered presence. CFL lawyers are most effective when relaxed and comfortable in following the lead of their clients, or perhaps more accurately, *leading them from behind*. How you each achieve the state of mind to do this is a function of your personality and practice style. You will find and adopt a CFL style that works best for you and your clients.

Hone Your CFL Skills

Before taking your first CFL case it is beneficial to sit in on one or two CFL settlement meetings as an observer. Once you take on your own cases, you may find it helpful to approach an experienced CFL practitioner to act as a mentor or supervisor. While this may seem a somewhat unusual suggestion to make to lawyers who have been in practice for many years, it is an accepted approach in mediation skill development. Indeed, most family mediation associations require that candidates for certification receive up to 100 hours of supervision.

If you experience difficulty working effectively with the other CFL lawyer in a case or the interaction between the parties is particularly challenging, you may consider retaining an experienced CFL practitioner or mediator to observe a settlement meeting and debrief with you afterwards. You and the other lawyer will need to explain the purpose of this person's involvement to your clients and seek their prior consent. Alternatively, the mentor may meet with you and your colleague away from your clients to discuss their concerns and provide feedback and practice suggestions. The mentor's fees, if any, should be your responsibility and not your client's.

Your CFL associations may require that members provide a fixed number of voluntary mentoring hours each year as a condition of membership. Once you have passed the necessary experience threshold to serve as a mentor, doing so will further hone your CFL skills. The value of mentoring and supervision, for both the mentor and the recipient, cannot be overstated.

Some CFL associations organize monthly brown-bag lunches where CFL lawyers can share their cases while maintaining client confidentiality. These gatherings are consistent with a collaborative approach; lawyers working together to improve their skills and raise their self-awareness.

To further develop your CFL skills, we suggest that you familiarize yourself with the relevant and related literature. A suggested readings list is found in Appendix "I".

FORMING A CFL ASSOCIATION

CFL lawyers cannot practise alone. To introduce this alternative process into your area, you must form an association of like-minded lawyers. You may consider inviting a CFL lawyer from elsewhere to speak at a dinner or a lunch with colleagues who may be interested in learning more about this process. Most established CFL associations have websites, which provide extensive information about CFL. You may begin by sending out an invitation to lawyers you think may be appropriate for and interested in this process, along with an article about CFL or a reference to a CFL website.

Many CFL associations incorporate as non-profit organizations with officers, directors, and members; others remain as informal associations. Whatever the form, a CFL association must create and maintain standing committees to undertake various responsibilities on behalf of its members, which generally include the following:

1. Establishing and monitoring training and education requirements and opportunities;
2. Setting the criteria for membership;
3. Developing protocols and other internal communication among members; and
4. Public awareness and external communication with other professional, other CFL groups, and the judiciary.

CFL associations need to agree upon the terms of their Participation Agreement, and their protocols. A sample statement of protocols (for the conduct of a CFL case) is found in Appendix "J". Some groups have gone much further in what they offer their members. They may provide standard letters and information packages to send to prospective clients and their spouses, a code of conduct, agreements with respect to disclosure, criteria for withdrawal and termination, disciplinary procedures, data collection and client evaluation, and a draft CFL Separation Agreement or at least a preamble referring to the CFL process.

Whatever the degree of detail around protocols, it is important that all members of a CFL association share an understanding as to how a case will proceed in their community. When preparing a client to participate in a CFL process, it is helpful if his lawyer is able to explain that his spouse is receiving the same information and preparing in a similar way. It is essential that all members share an understanding of the principles that ground the process and know what to expect of each other at each stage and when challenging circumstances arise. New groups can access the protocols created by others from their websites or by direct request to assist them in formulating their own. Consistent with CFL philosophy, existing practice associations have demonstrated a willingness to share their experiences and precedents with new groups. A list of some of the websites in Canada and the United States are found in Appendix "K".

Once your CFL association is in place, you must keep it vibrant and dynamic. Some groups hold monthly meetings over dinner to promote rapport among their members; others meet at lunch or after work. Wherever and whenever meetings are held, they present opportunities for learning, mentoring, and relationship building among members. Your CFL association may decide to invite speakers, trainers, and various support professionals such as child experts, business valuators, and financial planners to enhance the knowledge and skills of your members.

When the members of your CFL association meet, they may conduct role plays followed by debriefs, discuss cases of interest, offer peer mentoring, and raise concerns that have arisen for feedback and guidance. Your group should ensure that the rules require reasonable attendance and commitment to the process. Members should be active and committed. Your CFL association might also consider developing client evaluation forms, which are useful to improve the quality of service, to instill enthusiasm among lawyers and to market CFL.

Some CFL associations create protocols for bringing difficulties back to the group for peer consultation and review. A corollary of this practice is the development of a procedure for responding to complaints, including investigation and a hearing where appropriate. A member who is found to have consistently acted in a manner contrary to the protocols established by his CFL association may be removed from its roster. A sample code of disciplinary procedures is found in Appendix "L".

CREATING A CFL AWARENESS

Although CFL has received positive coverage in the media, it is still a new process, relatively unknown to the public. CFL associations and individual CFL lawyers must each take responsibility for creating a public awareness of this process option. The development of a website is a cost-effective way in which to reach a large number of prospective users. Your CLF association website might provide information about the CFL process, articles written by your members, copies of your Participation Agreement, and the names of qualified CFL lawyers in your association. Many of these websites also have links to other CFL associations as well as individual CFL lawyer websites. If you already have your own individual or firm website, you should add CFL as another service you offer and link your website to that of your CFL association.

Each CFL association prepares a CFL brochure with the names, telephone numbers, and e-mail addresses of its members. Brochures are placed in law offices, the courthouse, and public libraries. You may also wish to forward copies to physicians, therapists, counsellors, clergy, and others who are routinely consulted by individuals following a separation, for display in their waiting rooms.

Either on your own initiative or through your CFL association, you may develop an information kit about the CFL process. It could contain your association brochure, your own business card, newspaper and other articles about CFL, preferably local, as well as a copy of the Participation Agreement and guidelines for effective communication and co-parenting.

Advertising in local newspapers professional newsletters, church bulletins, and the yellow pages of the telephone directory are excellent if your group can afford the cost. All ads should provide contact numbers and/or a website address.

You and your colleagues should make yourselves visible as CFL lawyers in your community by offering to speak at meetings of your bench and bar associations, annual general meetings of the lawyers in your area, your chamber of commerce and other business associations, as well as at your library, service clubs, community organizations, and support groups. You should learn to write press releases for the media, letters to the editor, and articles about CFL and you should make yourself available as a guest for cable TV and radio community interest programs.

Your CFL association ought not to overlook the judges of your family court. You will want to keep them informed about CFL and obtain their support. They may be invited to attend association meetings and conferences, and written materials may be provided to keep them informed and up to date. It is essential that judges understand the CFL process so that they will uphold CFL participation agreements and their confidentiality provisions if cases are taken to court. They can also be excellent referral sources. The courts in Western Canada now include information about CFL and mediation to parties when proceedings are commenced.

Mediators and counsellors should also be included in your extended CFL family. They will continue to serve an important role in the resolution of family disputes. Indeed mediators and collaborative lawyers share the belief that separating couples can be empowered to create their own settlements. Many separating couples will continue to choose mediation, while those who opt for CFL may mediate specific issues, such as parenting arrangements or communication strategies. CFL lawyers can enlist mediators as neutral intervenors to overcome impasse. Mediators and therapists are also excellent sources of cross-referral.

You may consider providing a brief complementary information session, either in person or by telephone, to prospective clients. In addition to building your own caseload, these consultations offer an opportunity to spread the word. You should explain that the purpose of the meeting is to provide information about the available process options: traditional lawyer-to-lawyer negotiation with litigation as a possible recourse, mediation, and CFL.

Finally, the most compelling and persuasive instrument for creating public awareness as well as marketing your practice is professional competency and client satisfaction.

COLLABORATING BEYOND CFL

Collaborative practice is by no means restricted to the process described in this book. Within the family law domain is another model, Collaborative Divorce, which is in place in California, Wisconsin, British Columbia, and elsewhere.

The Collaborative Divorce practice model involves a multidisciplinary team of professionals comprised of the lawyers for the parties, divorce coaches, a parenting coordinator, and a neutral financial planner. If your CFL association considers Collaborative Divorce as its ultimate destination, you may consider offering process training to other professionals in your community, who you consider might be interested. Your practice group may invite them in as members.

While the primary focus of this book is family dispute resolution, the collaborative way is equally effective in other practice areas where an ongoing positive relationship between the parties is valued by them. Estate matters involve members of the same family. Organizational conflict occurs within a workplace setting where the parties interact on a daily basis. Commercial disputes may compromise or damage mutually beneficial business relationships. Conflict and disputes of these kinds are being resolved collaboratively in some cities in Western Canada and the United States.

FINAL THOUGHTS

We hope that this book will provide you with a sound foundation for collaborative thinking and practice. As this approach to our work attracts more practitioners and clients and its application extends into other areas of law, questions, challenges, and issues will continue to emerge. There are many ways to fulfill the mandate of collaborative practice. We look forward to continuing this conversation as we work together toward excellence in our transformation from the adversarial way to the collaborative way.

The Way to Collaboration

Becoming a CFL Lawyer

Obtain your CFL training.
Develop your CFL style.
Hone your CFL skills.

Forming a CFL Association

Find other interested practitioners.
Create an organization.
Invite others to join your association.
Establish your training requirements.
Set your criteria for membership.
Develop your practice protocols.
Meet regularly.
Share your CFL experiences.
Include other professionals.
Commit to continuing education.

Creating a CFL Awareness

Develop your CFL association website.
Create and distribute your CFL association brochures.
Assemble a CFL information kit for clients and others.
Advertise in local print media and yellow pages.
Write articles and opinion letters for publication.
Appear on local cable TV and radio community interest programs.
Speak at meetings of area business and social service groups.
Enlist the support of your judiciary.

Collaboration Beyond CFL

The multidiscipline practice model.
Estate, organizational, and commercial practice areas.

Appendices

APPENDIX "A"

Questions Clients Ask

Q: *Why can't you go to court if I need to? Why should I retain you as a CFL lawyer when I can retain a lawyer to do the whole job?*

A: When litigation is an option, lawyers tend to go to court when they encounter problems. If we take a case that may go to court, we have to spend some time preparing to go to court, just in case. A lawyer involved in a litigation case acts differently, follows different procedures, and involves his or her client less than in a collaborative case. When the parties have given up the right to go to court, all of the lawyer's problem-solving abilities are focused solely on settlement. When court is not an option, the parties and their lawyers stay at the table and keep talking. Generally, they are able to come up with creative settlements that are far better and more customized than a court could create. Even if the collaborative process doesn't succeed and you have to go to court, you have had the best of all worlds — a lawyer who specializes in settlement and, if trial is necessary, a lawyer who specializes in court. It is rare for a lawyer to be as effective as a negotiator and as a trial lawyer.

Q: *I'm interested in CFL, but my spouse and I aren't talking and I'm worried he won't listen to me. Is CFL for us?*

A: When people go through a divorce their minds are very busy dealing with a lot of unknowns. People usually feel very worried and fearful about their future. It's hard to get the psychological space to think and make good decisions. And it can be really difficult to talk with each other. In the collaborative process, you'll have time to breathe deeply, think, and make the best possible decisions. I'll be there to support you, to keep the negotiating space safe and clear. There'll be no yelling, intimidation, or disrespectful behaviour. Your husband's lawyer will be discussing appropriate behaviour with him as well. Often, once a proper negotiation climate is established and each spouse realizes that the goal is to get both of your needs met, each person can begin to really listen to the other and to move forward successfully.

Q: *How do the costs of CFL compare with mediation or court?*

A: CFL is far cheaper than a court proceeding that goes all the way to a trial. Although many are settled before trial, the legal fees for each party will not likely be less than $20,000 and it is not uncommon for them to be as high as $50,000. I know of cases where they have even been much greater. Some people think that mediation is cheaper than collaborative law because the parties share the cost of the mediator as opposed to each paying for their own collaborative lawyer only. This is often true. However, some people require that their lawyers be quite involved while they go through mediation, providing legal advice, and perhaps attending the mediation sessions. If that happens, mediation may even be more expensive than CFL. Although I cannot predict your costs in a CFL process, as the number of meetings vary from case to case, we generally find that the fees range from about $3,000.00 to $12,000.00 for each side, with most people spending about $6,000.00 each for a comprehensive settlement of all of the issues. We suggest that you choose mediation or collaborative law based on which process you think is most appropriate for you, rather than because one may be cheaper than the other.

Q: *My lawyer says he settles most of his cases. How is collaborative law different from settling a traditional legal case?*

A: CFL settlements tend to be negotiated in quite a different way than cases that proceed through the courts. While most family cases do settle before trial, settlement usually occurs only after each party has spent a great deal of money and suffered emotionally from the experience. Settlements are often reached while everyone is under stress, to avoid the next court appearance. In an adversarial proceeding, lawyers negotiate settlements based on what they predict will happen in court. From the outset of a CLF case, all of our efforts are made toward achieving an early settlement. Our goal is to negotiate a settlement that satisfies each party's needs and interests rather than what a judge might order. You and your spouse, not your lawyers, create the settlement. Fourth, CFL negotiations are generally more respectful and open than what you might see in an adversarial proceeding. Unlike court, which is scheduled according to the lawyers' and the court's timetable, CFL meetings are scheduled to suit you and your spouse. You will both have time to think and make good decisions. Finally,

CFL settlements are customized to suit your particular family, are arrived at more quickly and usually with less cost than settlements reached in a traditional negotiation.

Q: *How do I know if CFL is for me?*

A: CFL may or may not be the most appropriate process for you. It may be helpful for you to consider certain factors before you make your choice. First, CFL will be of interest to you if you and your spouse want to keep control over the decisions made about you and your family, rather than giving authority for decision making over to a lawyer or a judge. Second, you should only choose CFL if you and your spouse each accept that the other has legitimate needs and interests that must be addressed as well as your own. Third, CFL is probably for you if maintaining civility, dignity, and mutual respect throughout the process is important for you. Fourth, if you want to maintain a positive relationship with your spouse after the divorce, CFL is preferable to court. Fifth, CFL offers a greater assurance that your children will be sheltered from the emotional damage often caused by a separation of their parents. Sixth, if the goal of you and your spouse is to co-parent your children, there is a greater likelihood of obtaining that outcome and developing an effective parenting plan through CFL. Seventh, before you commit to CFL, you and your spouse must be willing to exchange all important information.

Q: *How do I know my spouse will be honest and won't hide information?*

A: There are no guarantees of honesty in any legal process. CFL relies on undertakings by both parties to make voluntary disclosure of all important information. CFL lawyers do not focus on rooting out hidden assets or income. Although you may see any financial documentation you feel is important, if you do not trust in the basic honesty of your partner, CFL is likely not appropriate for you. Remember that the cost to find hidden assets is often very high. Regardless of the process you choose, you will need to conduct a cost-benefit analysis and decide whether such a search is worth the expense. A CFL lawyer will withdraw or terminate the process if he or she feels his or her client is refusing to make full disclosure. There is no such requirement in a traditional negotiation.

Q: *What if we settle everything but one issue in CFL – do we have to lose our lawyers to go to court?*

A: If all but one or two issues have been resolved in the CFL process, it is possible to refer those issues to an arbitrator who will make a final and binding decision. If you and your spouse agree upon the facts, the issues that need to be resolved, and to arbitration as a dispute resolution process, your lawyers may then be able to continue to represent you and your spouse. The Participation Agreement approved by our CFL association permits arbitration in those circumstances.

Q: Which is more appropriate for us – mediation or CFL?

A: Mediation is appropriate for spouses who can negotiate on their own behalf with the help of a neutral third party who does not provide legal advice. They are willing to consult with their lawyers when needed and to take their mediated agreement to their lawyers for legal advice before it is confirmed. CFL is appropriate for those who want to negotiate for themselves, but want their lawyers with them every step of the way to provide legal advice and negotiation support. CFL may also be suitable where the issues are technical or complex, there is a perceived power imbalance between the parties, where there has been past abuse, or where there are strong emotions and low trust.

APPENDIX "B"

Information Letter to Prospective CFL Client

Dear Client:

Re: Collaborative Family Law

I have suggested that you consider resolving your separation issues by using Collaborative Family Law or CFL. I am pleased to provide you with some information about how CFL works and how it differs from other dispute resolution processes.

In traditional legal representation, the lawyers attempt to negotiate a settlement of the issues and, if negotiations fail, litigation is commenced. In this process, the lawyers are in charge of the discussions. While they may focus on settling the case, they must also spend time preparing for the possibility of a trial.

Mediation is an alternative to negotiation between lawyers and litigation. A mediator is a neutral third party who assists the parties to reach a mutually acceptable settlement. Mediators are usually either lawyers or mental health professionals with experience in family dispute resolution. The mediator does not give legal advice or have any decision-making authority. The mediator may or may not prepare the draft Separation Agreement. Usually, the parties attend mediation without their lawyers. A mediated agreement is reviewed by the parties' lawyers before the terms are finalized and it is signed.

Like mediation, CFL is distinguished from litigation and lawyer-to-lawyer negotiation in the shadow of litigation by employing an interest-based, non-adversarial approach. The parties conduct their settlement negotiations directly with each other although their lawyers are by their side, every step of the way. Negotiations take place in a series of face-to-face meetings with both lawyers and parties present. CFL lawyers act as negotiation coaches, information resources, and legal advisors. The parties disclose all of their important information, undertake to negotiate in good faith , and work together to develop a full array of options for settling their case.

Fundamental to the understanding of CFL is the contract entered into by the lawyers and the parties, the Participation Agreement. This agreement provides that if settlement is not reached and a party wishes to go to court, both lawyers must withdraw and neither may represent his or her client in litigation. This agreement ensures that the lawyers are fully committed to settlement and their only role in the process is to help the parties arrive at a settlement that satisfies the interests of both.

CFL lawyers are trained in interest-based negotiation skills, mediation techniques, and the CFL process. If other experts are required, such as counselors or financial experts, they are jointly retained as part of the collaborative team.

Many benefits flow from the collaborative approach. Separating spouses have the opportunity to create customized solutions, generally more quickly and at less expense than if they were to proceed through the traditional court process. Their participation in this process improves their ability to communicate effectively, to co-parent their children, to develop an appreciation of each other's perspectives and concerns, and to achieve a dignified closure to their relationship. Lessons learned about effective conflict management will carry over into their post-separation lives to resolve future issues which may arise.

I enclose two copies of our CFL brochure and an information package, one for yourself and another that you may pass on to your spouse. You can visit our CFL association website at www.collaborativefamilylawassociation .com. I would be pleased to answer any further questions you may have.

I look forward to hearing from you.

Sincerely,

CFL Lawyer

APPENDIX "C"

Letter to Client's Spouse to Participate in CFL

Your File:
Our File: «OurFileNumber»
«RespLawyerInitials»/«SecretaryInitials»

March 4, 2003

«SpouseFirstName» «SpouseLastName»
«SpouseAddress1»
«SpouseAddress2»

Dear #Mr./Mrs. «SpouseLastName»:

Re: «ClientFirstName» «ClientLastName» and «SpouseFirstName» «SpouseLastName»

«MrMrsMs». «ClientLastName» has retained me to represent «Clienthim-her» concerning your matrimonial difficulties. «MrMrsMs» «Client-LastName» would like to solve your matrimonial differences as amicably, quickly and inexpensively as possible.

Therefore, «MrMrsMs». «ClientLastName» would like to try to keep your differences out of the court system. «MrMrsMs». «ClientLastName» would like to try to work with you to solve the problems you both face about:

- how you will each parent your children;
- how you will each financially support your children;
- how you will each have sufficient income to support yourselves;
- how you will divide your property; and
- how you will dissolve your marriage.

We strongly encourage you to immediately consult a lawyer for legal advice about each of these issues. In fact, you and «MrMrsMs». «ClientLastName» cannot enter into a binding contract to divide your matrimonial property without each of you having independent legal advice from your own lawyer.

There are 3 process choices available to you and «MrMrsMs». «ClientLastName» to solve your matrimonial differences:

1. **The Collaborative Family Law Process**

    This is a process available in Medicine Hat and other areas of Alberta. In Collaborative Law, you, «MrMrsMs». «ClientLastName» and both of your lawyers formally agree to stay out of the court system to solve your matrimonial differences. «MrMrsMs». «ClientLastName» and I would meet in the immediate future with you and your lawyer to begin to solve your matrimonial differences.

    I enclose for your information a Brochure about Collaborative Law in Medicine Hat. It sets out:

    • a list of Medicine Hat lawyers qualified as Collaborative Law Lawyers, who could assist you in the Collaborative Law Process; and

    • useful information about the Collaborative Law Process.

    In the Collaborative Law Process, you and «MrMrsMs». «ClientLastName» would control the result, the timing and the costs. The Collaborative Law Process is private and confidential and takes an average of 2 to 6 months to reach a conclusion. The Collaborative Law Process is generally much less expensive than going to Court.

    If you are interested in Collaborative Law, please contact any lawyer on the list of Collaborative Lawyers to make an appointment . At the time you make the appointment, make sure you tell the lawyer you are investigating the Collaborative Law Process. If you present this letter at the time of your appointment the Collaborative Lawyer will give you a **free**

half hour to give you advice about the choices available to solve your matrimonial differences.

2. The Mediation Process

In Mediation, you and «MrMrsMs». «ClientLastName» would meet, in the immediate future, with a trained Family Mediator. You and «MrMrsMs». «ClientLastName» would formally agree to stay out of the court system to solve your matrimonial differences.

You will also each need a lawyer to give you legal advice while you are in Mediation and at the end of Mediation, to give you independent legal advice when you sign your agreement. If you choose Mediation you will need to immediately retain a lawyer to assist you. In Mediation, you and «MrMrsMs». «ClientLastName» would control the result, the timing and the cost. Mediation is private and confidential and takes an average of 4 to 10 months to reach a conclusion. This Process is also generally much less expensive than the Legal Process.

3. Court

If you and «MrMrsMs». «ClientLastName» choose this option, our next step, as «MrMrsMs». «ClientLastName»'s lawyers, would be to immediately serve you with a Statement of Claim for Divorce and Division of Matrimonial Property and a Court application for you to pay monthly #child and #spousal support to «MrMrsMs». «ClientLastName». In addition, you and «MrMrsMs». «ClientLastName» may have to proceed to trial for a Judge to finalize the child #and spousal support issues and divide your assets and debts for you. In this option, you and «MrMrsMs». «ClientLastName» do not control the result, the Process, the timing or the costs. The lawyers and the Judges control all of these things. The Legal Process is a public process and everything heard and filed is public record. It takes an of average 1 to 4 years for the Legal Process to reach a conclusion and the Legal Process is substantially more expensive than either the Collaborative Law Process or Mediation.

I am sure you are as interested as «MrMrsMs». «ClientLastName» in resolving your matrimonial differences as amicably, quickly and inexpensively as possible. Please
discuss these 3 options with «MrMrsMs». «ClientLastName» and with a lawyer as soon as possible.

Please contact me, or ask your lawyer to contact me, immediately by phone, letter or e-mail if you are interested in considering Collaborative Law to resolve your matrimonial differences with «MrMrsMs». «ClientLastName».

Please respond before 12:00 noon on #, 200#.

Yours truly,

Pritchard & Company LLP

«ResponsibleLawyer»

«RespLawyerInitials»/«SecretaryInitials»
Enclosures
c «ClientFirstName» «ClientLastName»

APPENDIX "D"

Collaborative Family Law
Retainer Agreement

Scope and Duties

You have retained me to assist you in negotiating a settlement of your family law matters in accordance with the terms of the Participation Agreement attached as Schedule "A".

Your retainer of me as a collaborative lawyer differs in some important ways from representation by a litigation lawyer. You are retaining me specifically to assist you in reaching a settlement with your spouse or partner and for no other purpose. Although you retain the right to terminate the collaborative process at any time and go to court, doing so will end my representation of you. If your spouse or partner should elect to go to court, this also terminates the collaborative process and you would need to retain new litigation counsel to represent you in court. Neither I nor any lawyer in my firm will represent you in litigation and my retainer is terminated by either party's decision to litigate, whether or not it was your decision.

We will work together to take whatever steps are most appropriate to advance settlement of your case. This will include settlement meetings with your spouse and his or her lawyer and meetings on our own. I will give you legal information concerning the issues you are resolving. I will send you copies of all letters and other documents. You will let me know if you have any questions or do not understand any matter in connection with your case. We will work together to clarify your needs and satisfy your interests.

Payment Arrangement

You have agreed to pay me $ _____ per hour plus 7% GST for any time I spend working on your case, including meetings, telephone and office time, correspondence, travel, research and consultation with other lawyers and experts and the preparation of documents and agreements and any other work done in connection with your file. Work done by my legal assistant will be billed at the rate of $ _____ per hour plus 7% GST.

Retainer

This letter will confirm our financial arrangement. You have agreed to pay my fees, disbursements and GST in one of the following ways:

<u>By retainer</u>

_____   Provide a retainer in the amount of $ _____ (including GST) and to replenish that retainer as necessary; or

<u>Pay as you go</u>

_____   Provide a retainer of $ _____ (including GST) to cover work I do in between meetings, and to pay my fees, disbursements and GST at the end of each meeting for the cost of the meeting and any outstanding amounts from previous accounts.

Please make all cheques payable to _____ . At the conclusion of your case, any money remaining in trust will be returned to you.

Disbursements

You have authorized payment for all necessary disbursements, which may include such items as courier charges, photocopying, faxes and long distance telephone calls, and any applicable GST. Photocopies and faxes are charged at $0.25 per page.

Disbursements may also include the cost to retain experts on your behalf. You have authorized me to retain experts such as mediators, counsellors, parenting coaches, child specialists, financial planners, actuaries, business valuators and income tax experts. I will not retain any experts on your behalf without your prior approval.

Billing

Bills are due and payable when rendered. Any accounts which are thirty days overdue will be charged interest at the current rate pursuant to the Solicitors Act calculated from the date the account is rendered. If you have any questions about your account, please contact my assistant. Please keep my office advised of any changes in your address and/or telephone number(s).

Termination of the Collaborative Process

Should settlement efforts break down to the extent that, in the opinion of either of us, the matter needs to move to court, either of us may terminate our relationship on notice to the other. I will assist you to obtain a litigation lawyer and help you to make a smooth transition into the litigation process in accordance with the Participation Agreement.

Right to Withdraw

I have the right to withdraw from your case if you do not pay my account, or our professional relationship is no longer productive. If you have misrepresented or failed to disclose important information regarding the collaborative process or the issues to be resolved and continue to withhold or misrepresent such information, or if you unreasonably delay or otherwise act in bad faith, I will alert you to any suspicion of bad faith and I will either withdraw as your counsel or terminate the collaborative law process, at my discretion. In signing this Agreement, you are authorizing me to withdraw or terminate the collaborative process if, in my judgment, you are failing to participate in good faith.

You and I both have the right to withdraw from this Agreement if either of us feels we cannot abide by the principles of collaborative law or that the collaborative law process is not working to our satisfaction.

Your Termination of my Retainer

You are free to terminate my retainer at any time. If you wish to continue with the collaborative law process, you will need to retain a new collaborative lawyer in accordance with the terms of the Participation Agreement.

Closing Your File

When your matter is completed, your file will be closed. If you need any original documents from the file, these will be returned to you at your request. I may take copies of these documents for my records. I will put your file in storage for seven years, after which time it may be destroyed. If you need access to your file during this time, there will be a fee charged to you to retrieve the file from storage.

_____

Lawyer

I have read the retainer agreement and have received a copy. I understand this agreement and I agree to it.

_____   _____

Date: Client

Alternate Covering Letter

Clyde Barrow
123 - 4 Street SE
Medicine Hat, Alberta T1B 3X2

Dear Mr. Barrow:

Re: Your Separation

Thank you for consulting me.

I enclose two copies of my *Contract for Legal Services and Fees.* **Please read the *Contract for Legal Services and Fees* carefully.** It details the work my firm will do and the fees I will charge based on the discussions we had at our meeting. If you are satisfied with the contract, **please sign and date one copy and return it to me** so that I can begin work for you.

Returning letters and phone calls

I try to return all telephone calls the same day I receive them. If I am unable to call you, my Legal Assistant will return your call. Often you can get the information you need by asking to speak directly with her.
If you wish to communicate with me by e-mail, my e-mail address and my Legal Assistant's e-mail address are set out above.
I will send you copies of all letters and documents I receive and send out. If it isn't practical to mail long letters or documents to you, you'll be able to read them in my office.
Please contact me anytime you have questions.
I appreciate that you chose me to represent you. My staff and I work hard to help our clients receive the best service we can provide.

I look forward to working with you.

Yours truly,

Pritchard & Company LLP

Janis M. Pritchard

JP/ka
Enclosures

Contract for Legal Services and Fees

Part 1: Services

Course of action
How long will this take?
Your role as client
Legal services not covered by this contract

Part 2: Fees, Expenses, and Billing Arrangements

Cash advance on fees
My legal fees are based mostly on time spent on your file
Hourly rate
Lawyers
Legal assistants
Other charges:
    Minor expenses
    Major expenses
You must pay interim bills as your file progresses
G.S.T.
I charge interest on outstanding bills
Taxing a bill
Trust accounts

Part 3: Dealing with Each Other

Communication
Confidentiality
No guarantees of success
Last half hour free

Part 4: Signing this Contract

Part 1: Services

I agree to be your lawyer in the Collaborative Law Process once I receive a signed and dated copy of this Contract. I will then be your lawyer throughout the whole Collaborative Law Process. You and your Wife will each have your own lawyer. I confirm both of you have a commitment to avoid going to Court.

The Collaborative Law Process mostly involves informal meetings and discussions with you, me, your Wife and your Wife's lawyer all present. The focus of our discussions will be to find an acceptable settlement of all issues between you and your Wife.

Assuming your Wife agrees to proceed with the Collaborative Law Process, I will:

- represent your interests in this process;
- keep you informed about matters that arise;
- discuss with you any important decisions you must make;
- give you my best legal advice. However, you must make the final decisions and you will authorize any settlement; and
- file divorce documents or other documents once you and your Wife reach an agreement.

I will not be your lawyer in Court proceedings if either you or your Wife decides to go to Court. However, I will cooperate with you in transferring your file to a new lawyer for you if you or your Wife decide to use the Court Process instead of the Collaborative Law Process.

You acknowledge and agree that for so long as you participate in the Collaborative Law Process, you are giving up your right to:

- access the Court system;
- have your own expert(s); and
- formally object to produce any documents or provide any information to your Wife and her lawyer that I determine is appropriate.

You agree to make full disclosure of all of your assets, debts, income and expenses and any changes that occur in these while you are in the Collaborative Law Process. You authorize me to fully disclose all information, which in my discretion must be provided to your Wife and her lawyer.

You and I both retain the right to withdraw from this Retainer Contract if either of us feels we cannot abide by the principles of the Collaborative Law Process. I agree to give you 15 days notice by letter of my intention to withdraw as your lawyer in the Collaborative Law Process. I require notice in writing from you if you wish to withdraw from the Collaborative Family Law Process.

If your Wife declines to proceed in the Collaborative Family Law Process, this Retainer Contract will be of no effect and you and I will need to enter into a new Retainer Contract for conventional divorce representation before I can proceed to represent you.

How long will this take?

The Collaborative Family Law Process will take as long as you and your Wife decide you need in order to:
• share all the information each of you need to make informed decisions;
• discuss all options or choices you might make; and
• effectively negotiate to an acceptable settlement.

Typically this process can take as little as 1 month or as long as 6 months to 1 year, depending on you and your Wife's concerns, questions you need to answer and schedules.

Your role as client

You understand the importance of giving me all the facts and being totally honest with me. I can only do my best job for you if I have your trust and you fully inform me.

I ask you to give me all the information you have, or have access to, which could help assist you in making a decision about an acceptable settlement to your problems. You will need to gather all of the information I asked for in the Information to Gather Checklist I gave you.

It is your responsibility to keep me informed about any changes in your address, telephone numbers (home, work and cellular), e-mail address or other means of contact.

Your signature on this contract means that I may communicate with you by e-mail, if you have given me your e-mail address.

Legal services not covered by this contract

I have not agreed to give you legal advice or perform legal services for you relating to any other matter.

Part 2: My Fees, Expenses, and Billing Arrangements

Cash advance

I require my clients to pay some "up front" money to cover the fees and other charges for the next block of work I will do. I must have a cash retainer of $1,500.00 for fees and other charges before I begin to work for you. I will hold your $1,500.00 cash advance in my trust account and use it to begin work on your file. I will use it to pay my legal fees and other charges on your file when I send you an account.

My legal fees are based mostly on time spent on your file

The starting point for determining the legal fees I will charge you in this matter will be the time I spend on your file. Your final account may be adjusted up or down to a fair and reasonable amount, based on various factors, including:
• the legal difficulty of the matters we must deal with;
• the urgency of the matter;
• your co-operation or lack of co-operation in moving your file along;
• the monetary value of the matters in dispute;
• the importance of the matter to you;
• the need for special skills or services; and
• whether or not your file affected my firm's ability to take other files.

Hourly rates

I will bill you at my **hourly billing rate of $225.00 per hour for all in-office work**, whether there is no dispute, some dispute or dispute on all issues. This **$225.00** hourly rate applies to all in-office time spent on providing legal services to you. It covers many activities including:
• meetings;
• preparation time;
• drafting and reviewing documents;
• preparing and sending letters;

- receiving and reviewing letters;
- reviewing your file
- research;
- travel time out of town;
- preparing and sending my accounts and report letters to you; and
- generally all time spent in providing legal services to you in this matter.

Hourly rates may change from time to time without notice to you. The hourly rates of other lawyers in my office relate to their length of experience and specialized skills.

Legal Assistants

There are also many services such as preparing documents that my legal assistant is well qualified to perform. I will charge you for work my legal assistant does at $70.00 per hour. I will not charge you when the work is of a general secretarial nature. My legal assistant works under my supervision, but she **can not** give you legal advice. My legal assistant can often serve you at a lower cost than I can.

Other charges

Under the *Alberta Law Society Code of Professional Conduct*, I am allowed to recover certain "other charges" for non-legal services.

a) Minor expenses

I will charge you for the minor on-going expenses that I have to pay. Some of these expenses are:
- long distance telephone calls;
- photocopying costs;
- costs to deliver documents to the other lawyer;
- faxes;
- necessary land or company registry searches (e.g. — to find out the proper name of a company); and
- travel expenses, if necessary.

I will regularly bill you for these minor expenses as soon as they total $100.00. I will detail all expenses in my bills. Please pay my bills within 30 days.

b) Major expenses

You and your Wife may agree in the Collaborative Law Process to hire other people such as expert witnesses, accountants, and property appraisers to help you obtain facts and information. If such experts are necessary you and your Wife will be responsible for these costs.

I will usually ask you to pay for your share of these major expenses in advance.

You must pay interim bills as your file progresses

(CHOOSE EITHER OPTION "A" or "B" WHEN PREPARING THE LETTER)

_____ *OPTION "A"* _____

Legal matters often take considerable time to resolve. To keep you informed as to how much this matter is costing you and so you can plan financially while your matter proceeds, I will send you an interim bill if you owe me more than $300.00 in unbilled legal fees and $100.00 in other charges. I will detail all of my fees and other charges in my bills. I will pay your account from your cash advance in my trust account. I will ask you to replenish your cash advance on fees and other charges to $1,000.00 once your initial cash advance is used up.

If you do not bring your retainer back up to $1,000.00 within 30 days, I will not do more work for you until you make satisfactory arrangements with me.

Please call us any time to find out what your unbilled legal fees and other charges are.

_____ *OPTION "B"* _____

You will be paying all legal fees from the settlement proceeds you will be receiving from your Wife. I enclose an **Irrevocable Direction to Pay** for you to sign confirming this arrangement. This arrangement means I will be carrying you for fees over and above your retainer of $1,500.00. Therefore, I will be charging a premium of 10% on my fees when I send you my final Statement of Account.

I will send you a statement of unbilled fees if your fees are more than $300.00. This will be an information statement only and **not** a bill for you to pay.

I will send you an interim bill if you owe me more than $100.00 in other charges. I will detail all other charges in our bills. I will pay these other charges from your cash advance retainer in my trust account. I will ask you to replenish your $1000.00 cash advance on other charges once it is used up. **I will not carry you for other charges as I am carrying you for legal fees**.

Please call me any time to find out what your unbilled legal fees and other charges are.

_____ (Option "B" ends here) _____

G.S.T.

In addition to my legal fees and other charges, you agree to pay any Goods and Services Tax (G.S.T.) that I must charge you.

There are some other charges that I will pay for you, that are G.S.T. exempt. I confirm that your signature on this agreement authorizes my office to pay any of these other charges as your agent. Some examples of G.S.T. exempt charges are:
- marriage certificates; and
- services provided by the Land Titles office such as title and document searches and document registration.

I charge interest on outstanding bills

I will charge interest on outstanding bills. You agree to pay all my bills when I send them to you.

If you do not pay your bills within 30 days, I will charge interest on the outstanding balance at 18% per year from the date of the bill until you pay it in full.

Taxing a bill

I have attached Rules 613 and 614 of the *Alberta Rules of Court* for your information. They set out your rights about solicitor/client accounts.

Trust accounts

I maintain a separate bank account for money I hold in trust for my clients. This account is called a trust account. The Law Society has established very strict standards for lawyers' trust accounts. Trust accounts are audited annually by a professional accountant and the results of the audit are reported to the Law Society. The Law Society also conducts spot audits.

In most cases, the interest on trust accounts goes to the Law Foundation of Alberta and is used for law reform and public legal education. However, if a large sum of money is to be held in trust for you for an extended period of time, a specific interest-bearing account may be opened for the money, with the interest payable to you.

Part 3: Dealing with Each Other

I want to handle your legal problems in a prompt and effective manner. I hope you will let me know if there is any way I or my staff can improve in the service we provide you.

I cannot accept instructions that are in conflict with the Collaborative Family Law Process, as well as my duties to the courts, other lawyers and the public, as set out in the *Code of Professional Conduct* of the Law Society of Alberta.

Communication

Two-way communication will be very important in our relationship. If you ever feel you do not fully understand what is going on, please call or make an appointment for a meeting. If you have any information that might be of assistance to me assisting you, please call and let me know.

You will receive copies of most letters sent and received and most documents prepared on your matter. If you do not understand a document or letter you receive from me, please call.

Confidentiality

Certain communications between lawyer and client are absolutely confidential. This confidentiality is known as the "solicitor-client privilege." Because of it, you can give me all the facts relevant to your concerns without fear that prejudicial information will become public. I cannot be compelled by the tax department, the police, the government or the courts to divulge information that is subject to solicitor/client privilege.

The solicitor/client privilege is your privilege, not mine, so only you can waive it.

Not all solicitor/client communications are privileged. The privilege only arises when you reveal information in confidence to obtain legal advice or services. Information you give me that is not privileged is treated as confidential.

If you have any questions about privilege or confidentiality, please don't hesitate to ask me.

As your lawyer, I must share relevant and appropriate information about your case with your Wife and your Wife's lawyer in the Collaborative Law Process. As a condition of employment, all employees of Pritchard & Company must follow this confidentiality rule. Respecting your privacy and the confidentiality of your information is very important to me.

No guarantees of success

I will give you my best legal advice. However, you understand that I cannot guarantee any results whatever process you choose to solve your problems. All legal problems involve risks and uncertainties in the law and the facts.

Last half hour free

Please come in to see me for a **free ½ hour meeting** when your file is completed, to review my report letter and final bill. We will:
• review what has happened on your file;
• point out any future implications;
• review your bill;
• finalize payment arrangements; and
• answer any other questions you may have.

Part 4: Signing this Contract

This contract contains the whole agreement between us about our relationship with each other and our legal fees and other charges. This contract can only be changed if we both agree and sign any changes. This contract legally binds anyone such as your heirs or legal representatives who replace either you or us, but it does not legally bind other lawyers who might act for you if you decide to end our relationship.

If you are satisfied with this contract, please sign and date both copies and return one of them to me.

Please keep one copy for your records. If there is anything you do not agree with, or if there is anything you would like to discuss before you sign, please write or call me.

_____   _____
Lawyer   **(Date)**

I have read this contract carefully and I agree with it.

_____   _____
Client   **(Date)**

SOLICITOR AND CLIENT COSTS

Costs to be
reasonable

613. Barristers and solicitors are entitled to such compensation as may appear to be a reasonable amount to be paid by the client for the services performed having regard to:

(a) the nature, importance and urgency of the matters involved,
(b) the circumstances and interest of the person by whom the costs are payable,
(c) the fund out of which they are payable,
(d) the general conduct and costs of the proceedings,
(e) the skill, labour and responsibility involved, and
(f) all other circumstances, including, to the extent hereinafter authorized, the contingencies involved.

Subject to
taxation

614. The charges of barristers and solicitors for services performed by them are, notwithstanding any agreement to the contrary, subject to taxation as provided by these Rules.

[This contract was prepared by the Medicine Hat practice group and it is reproduced in this book with their permission and our grateful appreciation.]

APPENDIX "E"

Collaborative Family Law Participation Agreement

Jane Brown and John Smith
and
their lawyers

have chosen to enter into this Agreement to use the principles of the Collaborative Law process to settle the issues arising from the dissolution of their relationship.

I. Purpose

The goal of the Collaborative Law process is to settle the issues in a non-adversarial manner. The parties agree to use their best efforts to negotiate a mutually acceptable settlement by focusing on the merits and exploring interests. This approach is intended to minimize, if not eliminate, the negative economic, social and emotional consequences of litigation to the parties and their family and to create the best possible outcome. The parties have retained Collaborative Lawyers to assist them in reaching this goal.

II. Children's Issues

In resolving issues about sharing the enjoyment of and responsibility for their children, the parties agree to make every effort to reach amicable solutions that promote the children's best interests. The parties agree to act quickly to resolve differences related to the children to promote a caring, loving and involved relationship between the children and both parents.

The parties acknowledge that conflict between them is harmful to their children. They will refrain from criticizing the other parent, or his or her partner or family to the children or in their presence. They will support the other's relationship with the children. The parties will not use the children to communicate with each other but will communicate directly. They agree that separation issues will not be discussed in the presence of their children and that communication with the children regarding separation issues will occur only if appropriate and done by agreement, or with the advice of a child specialist.

III. Principles Governing Participation in the Collaborative Law Process

Written and verbal communication will be respectful and constructive. Communication during settlement meetings will be focused on the economic and parenting issues arising out of the dissolution of the relationship and the constructive resolution of those issues.

Neither party nor their lawyers will use the threat to withdraw from the process or to go to court as a means of achieving a desired outcome or forcing a settlement.

The parties and their lawyers agree to deal with each other in good faith.

Neither party will take advantage of inconsistencies or miscalculations in information provided by the other but will disclose them and seek to have them corrected. Any changes or corrections which are required to information previously provided, will be immediately disclosed to the other party.

Each party is encouraged to express his or her interests, needs, objectives and proposals and to seek to understand those of the other.

The parties are encouraged to develop an array of options for settlement and to negotiate a mutually acceptable settlement.

The lawyers' representation is limited to providing services within the Collaborative Family Law process. Both lawyers are disqualified from representing their respective clients in a contested court proceeding against the other spouse.

The agreement of the parties and their lawyers to participate in the Collaborative Family Law process does not preclude the parties from participating in any other alternate dispute resolution process such as mediation or arbitration.

IV. Exchange of Information

The parties agree to promptly provide to the other all important information which may affect any of the choices either party has to make regarding the collaborative process or the issues to be resolved. The parties agree to provide sworn Financial Statements making full and fair disclosure of their income, assets, and debts if requested.

No formal discovery procedures such as examination under oath will be used unless specifically agreed to in advance by the parties.

V. Use of Experts

The parties may retain neutral experts such as mediators, counsellors, parenting coaches, child specialists, financial planners, actuaries, business valuators and income tax experts. All experts retained in the Collaborative Law process will be jointly retained by the parties and will be directed to work for both parties to resolve the issues.

VI. Cautions and Limitations

In electing the Collaborative Family Law process, the parties understand that there is no guarantee that the process will be successful in resolving their case. The parties further understand that while the Collaborative Lawyers share a commitment to the process described in this document, each of them has a professional duty to represent his or her own client diligently, and is not the lawyer for the other party.

VII. No Court Intervention

Neither lawyer nor any member of his or her law firm may represent either party in any contested court proceeding by the other spouse.

VIII. Withdrawal of Party or Lawyer from Collaborative Family Law Process

If a party decides to withdraw from the Collaborative Family Law process, written notice will be given to the other party through his or her lawyer. On termination of the Collaborative Family Law process by a party or a lawyer, there will be a thirty (30) day waiting period (unless there is an emergency) before any court hearing to permit the parties to retain new lawyers and make an orderly transition. All temporary agreements will remain in full force during this period. The intent of this provision is to avoid surprise and prejudice to the rights of the other party. Either party may bring this provision to the attention of the court to request a postponement of a hearing.

If a party wishes to withdraw from the Collaborative Family Law process with their current lawyer, and retain a new lawyer to continue with the Collaborative Family Law process, the party will give written notice to the other party of the intention to obtain a new Collaborative Lawyer. The new lawyer will execute a new Participation Agreement within 30 days of the party giving notice. If a new Agreement is not executed within 30 days, the other party will be entitled to proceed as if the Collaborative Family Law process was terminated as of the date written notice was given.

If either lawyer withdraws from the process for any reason except those set out in the Mandatory Termination clause of this Agreement, the withdrawing lawyer will give written notice to his or her client and to the other party through his or her lawyer. If the party whose lawyer has withdrawn elects to continue with the process, he or she will give written notice of this intention to the other party through his or her lawyer. The new lawyer will execute a new Collaborative Family Law Participation Agreement within 30 days. If a new Agreement is not executed within 30 days, the other party will be entitled to proceed as if the Collaborative Family Law process was terminated as of the date the first written notice was given.

IX. Mandatory Termination of the Collaborative Family Law process

A lawyer must withdraw from the Collaborative Family Law process if his or her client has withheld or misrepresented important information and continues to do so, refuses to honour interim agreements, delays unreasonably, or otherwise acts contrary to the principles of the collaborative law process. The lawyer withdrawing will advise the other lawyer only that the Collaborative Law process has terminated.

X. Confidentiality

All communication and information exchanged within the Collaborative Family Law process is confidential and without prejudice. If subsequent litigation occurs, the parties agree that:

(a) neither party will introduce as evidence in court information disclosed during the Collaborative Family Law process, except documents otherwise compellable by law including any sworn financial statements made by the parties;

(b) neither party will introduce as evidence in court information disclosed during the Collaborative Family Law process with respect to either party's behaviour or proposals for settlement;

(c) neither party will introduce as evidence in court any reports, opinions or notes of any expert prepared in the Collaborative Family Law process unless both parties accept, in writing, the opinion of the expert; and

(d) neither party will require the production at any court proceedings of any notes, records or documents in the lawyer's possession or any reports, opinions or notes of any expert prepared in the Collaborative Family Law process.

(e) neither party will request or compel either lawyer or any expert to attend court to testify in any court proceedings or attend for examination under oath, with regard to matters disclosed during the Collaborative Law process;

XI. Rights and Obligations Pending Settlement

While the Collaborative Family Law process is ongoing, unless otherwise agreed in writing, the parties agree that:

(a) neither party will dispose of any assets, change beneficiaries or title to property, except as may be required for usual household expenses or in connection with the operation of an existing business;

(b) all existing insurance coverage will be maintained and continue without change in coverage or beneficiary designations;

(c) all existing extended health and dental benefits will be maintained in force for the spouse and the children;

(d) the ordinary residence of the children will not be changed nor the children removed from the Province of Ontario;

(e) neither party will incur any debts or liabilities for which the other may be held responsible; and

(f) both parties will respect each other's privacy.

XII. Enforceability of Agreements

If the parties require a temporary agreement during the Collaborative Law process, the agreement will be in writing and signed by the parties. If either party withdraws from the Collaborative Family Law process, the temporary agreement is enforceable and may be presented to the court as a basis for an Order.

Any final agreement signed by the parties may be filed with the court for enforcement.

XIII. Acknowledgement

Both parties and their lawyers acknowledge that they have read this Agreement, understand its terms and conditions and agree to abide by them.

Dated at (*insert municipality*) on (*d/m/y*)

_____   _____

Jane Brown   **Jane Brown's Lawyer**

_____   _____

John Smith   **John Smith's Lawyer**

Collaborative Law Contract
(Family)

Among:

_____

Client – Husband/Father

-and-

_____

Lawyer for Husband/Father

-and-

_____

Client – Wife/Mother

-and-

_____

Lawyer for Wife/Mother

1   Goals

1.1   We believe that it is in the best interests of _____ and _____ and their children to resolve their differences by discussing what is important to _____ and _____ rather then going to court.

1.2   We agree to use the Collaborative Law Process (called the "Process" in this Contract) to resolve our differences. This Process is based on:
- honesty;
- compromise;
- co-operation;
- moderation;
- integrity; and
- professionalism.

This Process is focused on the **future** wellbeing of _____ and _____ and their child(ren).

This Process does **not** rely on Court imposed solutions.

1.3   Our goals are:
- to resolve all of _____'s and _____'s differences in the best interests of their child(ren);
- to eliminate the negative financial, social and emotional consequences of litigation; and
- to find solutions that are acceptable to _____ and _____ .

2   We Will Not Go To Court

2.1   We commit ourselves to settling this case without going to Court.

2.2   We agree to give complete, honest and open disclosure of all information, whether requested or not. Any request for information will be made informally. _____ and _____ will provide this information immediately.

2.3   We agree to engage in informal discussions and conferences to settle all issues.

3   Cautions

3.1   _____ and _____ understand there is no guarantee that they will successfully resolve their differences with this Process.

3.2   _____ and _____ understand this Process is designed to solve only the legal problems of _____ and _____ arising from the breakdown of their relationship. This Process is not personal or marriage counselling.

3.3   _____ and _____ understand they are still expected to state their individual concerns and what is important to each of them and that both lawyers will help each of them do this.

3.4   _____ and _____ understand that they should not lapse into a false sense of security that the Process will protect them.

3.5   _____ and _____ understand that each of their lawyers has a professional duty to represent his or her own client diligently and is not the lawyer for the other client, even though their Collaborative Lawyers share a commitment to this Process.

4   Lawyers' Fees and Costs

4.1   _____ and _____ agree that their lawyers are entitled to be paid for their services. _____ and _____ will each pay their own lawyer.

OR

4.1   _____ and _____ agree that their lawyers are entitled to be paid for their services. _____ will pay _____% and _____ will pay _____ % of the amount owed to each lawyer.

5   Participation With Integrity

5.1   We will respect each other.

5.2   We will work to protect the privacy and dignity of everyone involved in this Process.

5.3   We will maintain a high standard of integrity.

5.4   We will not take advantage of any mistakes anyone makes in this Process.

5.5   We will immediately identify and correct any mistakes.

6   Experts

6.1   If we need experts, _____ and _____ will hire them jointly unless they agree otherwise in writing.

6.2   We agree to direct all experts to help _____ and _____ to resolve their differences without going to court.

7   Child(rens)' Issues (If Applicable)

7.1   We agree:
         • to act quickly to resolve differences related to _____'s and _____'s children;
         • to promote a caring, loving and involved relationship between _____'s and _____'s children and each parent;
         • not to seek a custody evaluation during this Process;
         • not to involve _____'s and _____'s children in their differences; and
         • _____ and _____ will attend the Parenting After Separation Seminar.

8   We Will Negotiate In Good Faith

8.1   We acknowledge that each lawyer represents only one client in this Process.

8.2   We understand that this Process will involve vigorous good faith negotiation, even with full and honest disclosure of information.

8.3   Each of us will be expected to take a moderate approach in all differences. Where what is important to _____'s and _____'s is different, each of us will use our best efforts to create proposals which are acceptable to _____ and _____. If necessary, we will compromise to reach a settlement of all problems.

8.4   None of us will use threats of litigation as a way to force settlement, although each of us may discuss the likely outcome of going to court.

9   Abuse of the Collaborative Law Process

9.1   We understand that both lawyers must withdraw from this case if either lawyer learns that either _____ or _____ has taken unfair advantage of this Process. Some examples of such violations of this Process are:
   • _____ or _____ abusing their child(ren);
   • _____ or _____ planning or threatening to flee the jurisdiction of the Court with their children;
   • disposing of property without the consent of the other person;
   • withholding or misrepresenting information;
   • failing to disclose the existence or the true nature of assets or debts; or
   • failing to participate in the spirit of this Process.

9.2   If either lawyer withdraws from the Collaborative Law Process, he/she will give written notice of their withdrawal to the other lawyer and to their own client.

10   What Happens If Someone Goes To Court

10.1   _____ and _____ understand that their lawyer's representation is limited to this Collaborative Law Process. Neither of the lawyers can ever represent their own client in Court in a proceeding against the other client.

10.2   However, if _____ and _____
agree, the lawyers may file divorce documents or other documents
reflecting the terms of _____'s and _____'s
agreement reached in this Process.

10.3   If either _____ or _____ goes to
court, both lawyers will be disqualified from representing either
_____ or _____ .

10.4   If either _____ or _____ goes to
court, they must give the other client and both lawyers written
notice of their withdrawal from the Collaborative Law Process.
Neither _____ nor _____ can bring a court application
within 30 day of giving written notice of their withdrawal from the
Collaborative Law Process. However, if either _____
or _____ satisfies a court that there is an emergency requiring immediate action, which must be dealt with before
the 30 day period expires, then that court application will not be a
breach of this contract.

10.5   If this Process ends, both lawyers will be disqualified as witnesses,
even if _____ and _____ agree
otherwise in writing.

10.6   If this Process ends, all experts will be disqualified as witnesses
and their opinions and reports will be inadmissible as evidence,
unless _____ and _____ and the
expert agree otherwise in writing.

**11   What Happens If _____ or _____
Dies During the Collaborative Law Process**

11.1   _____ and _____ acknowledge
that they have received legal advice about the effect of a death of
either _____ or _____ during the
Collaborative Law Process.

11.2   If either _____ or _____ dies dur-
ing the Collaborative Law Process and before a final Divorce and
Property Contract is signed, then the surviving client and the Personal Representative of the deceased client may continue the Collaborative Law Process. They will need to enter into a new Collaborative Law Contract with their respective lawyers.

11.3   If either the surviving client or the Personal Representative of the deceased client does not wish to continue in the Collaborative Law Process, the surviving client will file a Statement of Claim for the Division of Matrimonial Property within _____ days of the death of the deceased client. (Delete clause and initial)

or

11.4   _____ and _____ acknowledge that they have each discussed with their Collaborative lawyers the issue of the death of one of them during the Collaborative Law Process and prior to the signing of a Divorce and Property Contract, and both agree that they will make no agreement now about what might happen if one of them dies during the Collaborative Law Process. (Delete clause and initial.)

or

11.5   _____ and _____ direct their lawyers to file a Joint Statement of Claim for (Divorce and) Division of Matrimonial Property. (Delete clause and initial.)

12   Promise to Follow Contract

12.1   _____, _____, _____ and _____ agree to follow this Contract and to promote both the spirit and the written word of this Contract.

Dated at Medicine Hat, Alberta on _____, 2002.

_____   _____
Client - Husband/Father   Lawyer for Husband/Father

_____   _____
Client - Wife/Mother   Lawyer for Wife/Mother

APPENDIX "F"

Client Preparation Handout

Contents

- CFL Association Brochure
- Article on Collaborative Family Law (Preferably published in a journal or association newsletter)
- What is Collaborative Family Law? (Attached below)
- Collaborative Family Law Retainer Agreement (Appendix "I")
- Collaborative Family Law Participation Agreement
- (Appendix "E")
- Collaborative Family Law Principles (Attached below)
- Role of Lawyers (Attached below)
- Role of Clients (Attached below)
- Guidelines for Effective Participation (Attached below)

WHAT IS COLLABORATIVE FAMILY LAW?

- The practice of family law using interest-based negotiation where lawyers are retained solely to help the parties achieve a mutually acceptable settlement.

- The lawyers and parties sign a contract agreeing not to go to court.

- The parties and lawyers work as a team.

- The clients are responsible for:

  - Deciding issues to resolve;
  - Exchanging important information;
  - Sharing interests, needs, objectives, and proposals with the other spouse;

- Understanding interests, needs, objectives, and proposals of the other spouse;
- Generating settlement proposals;
- Creating mutually acceptable outcome.

- The lawyers are responsible for:

  - Creating a safe negotiating environment;
  - Advocating interests;
  - Advocating for collaborative process;
  - Acting as a negotiation coach;
  - Acting as an information resource.

- Negotiations take place in a series of four-way settlement meetings to exchange information, express interests, goals and concerns, develop options for settlement, and negotiate mutually acceptable agreements.

- During settlement negotiations, all parties treat each other with respect and they negotiate in good faith.

COLLABORATIVE FAMILY LAW PRINCIPLES

- *Team approach* – The lawyers and the clients work together as a team of equals, all pulling together on the same side of the problem.

- *Court is not an option* – Neither lawyer can commence a legal proceeding or threaten to do so during the CFL process. This provides an incentive for the lawyers and their clients to keep working together to find acceptable solutions and unleashes creative, *out of the box* problem solving. The team may include neutral experts when needed.

- *Recognition of the interdependence of the parties* – There is a shared belief that the best possible outcome can only be achieved if the needs and interests of both parties are met. Clients are not expected to agree with each other, but to accept that the other, along with his or her perspective and belief system, is a necessary partner in creating a solution.

- *Focus on interests* – Collaborative negotiations are interest-based, rather than adversarial. The parties exchange information and consider all available options before choosing the best solution to meet their identified interests.

- *Law is not the only standard* – Although CFL lawyers inform their clients about their legal rights and obligations, they encourage the parties not to limit themselves to outcomes dictated by the law.

- *Process and outcome are of equal importance* – In collaborative negotiation, the parties seek to understand and to be understood. The lawyers, in consultation with the parties, bear responsibility for creating a respectful, effective negotiation process. The parties own the outcome.

ROLE OF LAWYERS

- Advise clients of the law that applies to their circumstances.
- Guide clients through a process of effective conflict resolution using interest-based negotiation.
- Establish a safe environment for negotiation.
- Model for clients a commitment to honesty, mutual respect, and dignified behaviour.
- Model the ability to hear and understand (active listening) what is important to the other side so that the interests of both are promoted.
- Help clients communicate effectively.
- Use clear, neutral language in speaking and writing.
- Coordinate with other lawyer regarding ground rules, agenda development, and creation of a positive process.
- Get to know own client and establish rapport.
- Get to know the other party and establish rapport.
- Help identify facts, issues, interests of both sides.
- Cooperate to provide all important information and full disclosure.
- Help develop the widest range of possible choices.
- Represent own client's interests and choices while validating the other party's interests and choices.
- Assist parties to analyze consequences of possible choices and competing values.
- Respect choices made by the parties, even if they are choices different than the law may provide.
- Bring stability and reason to emotionally charged situations.
- Pre-empt crises.
- Be committed to finding effective ways to assist parties to reach agreement and overcome impasses (i.e. mediation, neutral experts, neutral lawyers to provide a third opinion).
- Remain committed to settlement and refrain from using adversarial techniques, tactics, or threats.

ROLE OF CLIENTS

- Commit to the process.
- Adhere to the principles of the collaborative approach.
- Respect the process needs of the other.
- Honour the agreed upon process rules.
- Help develop information and provide disclosure of all important information.
- Undertake tasks to keep costs down.
- Express needs clearly without blaming or judging.
- Respect the perspectives, interests, and values of the other party.
- Explore differences in perspectives, interests, and desired outcomes rather than react to them.
- Let go of positions and focus on interests.
- Generate as many options for settlement as possible.
- Look for solutions that meet the interests of both parties.
- Let go of past frustrations and focus on the future.
- Take responsibility for the outcome.

GUIDELINES FOR EFFECTIVE PARTICIPATION

- Identify your perspectives, interests, and beliefs.
- Listen to learn about the other party's perspectives, interests, and beliefs.
- Avoid taking positions.
- Respect the values and perspectives of the other person whether or not you agree.
- Don't try to change the other person's values and perspectives.
- Recognize your own process needs.
- Respect the process needs of the other person.
- Use "I" statements to speak for yourself.
- Don't use "you" statements to accuse or blame the other person.
- Don't argue.
- Don't be critical, judgmental, or sarcastic.
- Allow the other person to speak without interruption.
- Try to control anger and emotions.
- Take a break when you need it.
- Commit to the fullest development of choices and options before making decisions.
- Look for solutions that meet the interests of you and your spouse.
- Measure the value of everything you do by asking whether it is effective in advancing you to your desired objectives.
- Take responsibility for your feelings, interests, and choices.

APPENDIX "G"

Separation Agreement
(Victoria Smith and Sharon Cohen)

This sample Separation Agreement was prepared by Victoria Smith and Toronto collaborative lawyer Sharon Cohen at the conclusion of one of their collaborative cases (the actual agreement has been changed to protect their clients' confidentiality). This couple had been separated for over three years and had pursued mediation and counselling before they entered into the collaborative process. Their communication was nonetheless limited and ineffective, and their emotional dynamics strong, which threatened the viability of their co-parenting agreement and emotional well-being. Although the husband was initially reluctant to meet the wife face-to-face, he agreed to do so. They were able to negotiate their agreement in three collaborative meetings. Since completion of the process, they have each reported a significant improvement in their ability to communicate and co-parent their children, and a sense of bringing appropriate closure to their relationship.

We have included this sample agreement because it provides an example of the use of simple, clear language consistent with the principles of CFL. Victoria and Sharon worked together to draft the agreement, a practice that we recommend until we become more comfortable with a new way of documenting agreements. Note the use of "WE" as opposed to "The Husband" and "The Wife" or even the first names of the parties. "We" emphasizes that the agreement belongs to and was created by the parties themselves. The sample agreement illustrates the inclusion of parenting principles, clear arrangements for communication and co-parenting, and creative child support arrangements. It explains that the agreement was reached in the collaborative process, and an Issue Resolution clause which allows the parties to attend mediation or return to the collaborative process. We have adopted clauses from the Law Society of Upper Canada precedent Separation Agreement recently released in Ontario. We gratefully acknowledge their permission to reproduce those clauses. Please note that the schedules referred to in the agreement are not included in this appendix.

We are grateful to Pauline Tessler for her preamble clauses referring to the collaborative process, which helped us to shape our own.

THIS IS A SEPARATION AGREEMENT made this 31ˢᵗ day of
October, 2002.

B E T W E E N:

JANE BROWN

("Jane")

- and -

JOHN SMITH

("John")

1.   BACKGROUND

(1)   We were married to each other in Mytown, Ontario on June 17,
1985.

(2)   We have two children, Jennifer Smith, born August 19, 1989 and
Dylan Smith, born May 16, 1992.

(3)   We separated on February 1, 2002. We will continue living separate
and apart.

(4)   We have agreed to settle all issues between us.

(5)   We have agreed to enter into the following agreement which is a
domestic contract within the meaning of the Family Law Act,
R.S.O. 1990, c. F.3.

(6)   We agree to be bound by the terms of this Agreement.

(7)   We arrived at this agreement through the process of Collaborative
Law. At the commencement of the process, and throughout it, we
agreed that the Collaborative Law Process was to focus upon reaching a comprehensive resolution of all issues relating to our marriage
and separation. Our Participation Agreement is attached as Schedule "A".

(8)   In arriving at our Agreement, we have each applied our individual standards of reasonableness and acceptability. The conclusions we have reached are based in part on our respect and regard for each other. From time to time, we have considered what might happen if the matter were adjudicated in court, but we have elected to make our agreement without regard to whether a court might have adjudicated issues in the same manner. Throughout the Collaborative Law process our negotiations were in good faith and we each fully and completely disclosed all information necessary or requested in order to resolve our property and support rights.

2.   DEFINITIONS

Any legislation defined includes its regulations and any amending or successor legislation:

(a)   "income tax" and "income taxes" includes tax, interest and penalties owing under the provisions of the Income Tax Act and any tax owing under similar federal or provincial legislation, it includes tax on both income and on capital gains;

(b)   "matrimonial home" means the family home at 123 Any Street, Mytown, Ontario.

(c)   "net family property" and "equalization of net family properties" have the meanings given to those terms in the Family Law Act;

(d)   "property" means any interest, present or future, vested or contingent, in real or personal property;

(e)   "Canada Pension Plan Act" means the Canada Pension Plan Act, R.S.O. 1990, c. C.8;

(f)   "Change of Name Act" means the Change of Name Act, R.S.O. 1990, c. C.4;

(g)   "Children's Law Reform Act" means the Children's Law Reform Act, R.S.O. 1990, c. C.12;

(h)   "Divorce Act" means the Divorce Act, R.S.C. 1985, c. D.3.4;

(i)   "Family Law Act" means the Family Law Act, R.S.O. 1990, c. F.3;

(j)   "Health Care Consent Act" means the Health Care Consent Act, 1996, S.O. 1996, c. 2, Sch. A;

(k)   "Income Tax Act" means the Income Tax Act, R.S.C. 1985, c. 1 (5th supp.);

(l)   "Insurance Act" means the Insurance Act, R.S.O. 1990, c. I.8;

(m) "Pension Benefits Act" means the Pension Benefits Act, R.S.O. 1990, c. P.8;

(n) "Substitute Decisions Act" means the Substitute Decisions Act, 1992, S.O. 1992, c. 30;

(o) "Succession Law Reform Act" means the Succession Law Reform Act, R.S.O. 1990, c. S.26;

(p) "Trustee Act" means the Trustee Act, R.S.O. 1990, c. T.23.

3.   A MUTUAL RESPECT FOR PRIVACY

We agree that we will in every way respect each other's privacy.

4.   PARENTING

Parenting Principles

(1)   We agree that our children need the following:

(a) To know we both love them.

(b) To have the benefit of involvement of both parents.

(c) To have two "homes" in every sense of the word.

(d) To be left out of conflict between us.

(e) For us to live in close enough proximity to each other to co-parent effectively.

(f) To be emotionally, physically and financially secure.

(g) To be supported to achieve academic and personal success, based on their goals and interests.

(h) To have their ages and stages of development respected.

(i) To have the benefit of expert advice, when needed, to assist in determining their best interests.

(j) To have their wishes taken into consideration, when appropriate.

(2)   We will make major decisions affecting the children jointly. Major decisions include decisions with respect to education, non-emergency health care, religious upbringing and extracurricular activities.

(3)   We will support each other's parenting and positively encourage the children in their relationship with each of us and our extended family and friends.

(4)   We will provide each other with all important information regarding the children and confer as often as necessary.

(5)   We will work co-operatively in further plans consistent with the best interests of the children and in amicably resolving concerns and issues that arise.

Parenting Scheduling

Regular Times

(6)   The children will reside with each of us on a relatively equal basis.

(7)   The children will reside with each of us for seven days from Friday to Friday on alternating weeks.

Holidays

(8)   We will each have three weeks of vacation with the children each year, with no more than two weeks in a row without the agreement of the other parent. We will share holiday time with the children equitably, including Christmas, Easter and Thanksgiving. The children may be with each of us on our birthdays. We will share school professional development days and statutory holidays equally.

(9)   We agree that it is in the children's best interests that we both participate in special occasions involving the children including school trips, activities and birthday parties. We will inform each other of these opportunities as soon as possible. The children's requests will be taken into account in making decisions with respect to special events.

(10)   When the scheduled parent plans to be away without the children, the other parent has right of first refusal for their care. If the other parent is unable to care for the children, the scheduled parent is responsible to make alternate arrangements for their care.

(11)   The scheduled parent on any given day is responsible for taking the children or arranging to have them taken to doctors appointments and activities. We may ask the other parent to substitute if we are unable to take the child.

Communication

(12)   We agree to notify each other of all issues likely to affect the children. Our protocol for communication will be to communicate first by email. When necessary, we will schedule a telephone appointment or personal meeting.

(13)   When we are away on vacation with the children, the children will:

(a) telephone the other parent on arrival;
(b) telephone the other parent every three days or more if the children so request and if it is feasible.
(c) call the other parent upon their return home.

(14)   When either of us is away without the children, we may call the children every three days.

(15)   When we are both in town, the parent without care of the children may call the children after supper. The children may call or email the other parent at any reasonable time they wish, in private.

(16)   We will communicate with each other about critical events, milestones, illnesses, symptoms and medications. Essential documents, such as the children's health cards, will be transferred between us when the children are transferring from one home to the other.

New partners

(17)   We understand that our children require an opportunity to adjust to our separation. We agree not to introduce any new partner to the children for a period of one year from the date of our separation unless otherwise discussed and agreed upon in advance. We will notify the other parent of our intention to introduce the children to a new partner before we do so.

5.   NAME OF CHILDREN

We agree that we will not change the children's names.

6.   CHILD SUPPORT

(1)   Financial arrangements for the children are based on the following:

(2)   Jane's total income consists of:

Base salary	$70,000.00
Bonus/commissions	$10,000.00
Consulting	$3,000.00
Car allowance	$4,800.00
Stock options	$15,000.00
Total	$102,800.00

(3)   Jane's total income for the last three years has been:

1999:	$89,000.00
2000:	$95,000.00
2001:	$97,000.00

(4)   John's total income consists of:

Base salary	$65,000.00
Bonus/commissions	$20,000.00

Consulting	$10,000.00
Car allowance	$6,000.00
Total	$101,000.00

(5)   John's total income for the last three years has been:

1999:	$98,000.00
2000:	$108,000.00
2001:	$99,000.00

(6)   We will each pay for the children's day to day expenses while they are in our care.

(7)   We will maintain a joint account for the children's expenses and will deposit an agreed upon amount into the joint account on a monthly basis (currently $950.00 each, monthly). The expenses to be paid from this account include:

> major clothing items, such as shoes, jackets, ski and snow suits;
> activities;
> clothing and equipment for agreed upon activities;
> school related expenses;
> tutor;
> allowances;
> caregiver; and
> other expenses agreed to in advance.

(8)   We will share statements, receipts and documentation regarding this account and payments made out of this account.

(9)   Child support will be reviewed when each child finishes high school.

(10)   We acknowledge our obligation to contribute to the support of our children so long as they are financially dependent within the meaning of the Divorce Act.

(11)   Any future issues or concerns with respect to child support arrangements will be resolved pursuant to the Issue Resolution paragraph 11 of this Agreement.

7.   REVIEW OF CHILD SUPPORT

(1)   If either of us requests it, we will exchange income tax returns and any other documentation required by the Child Support Guidelines on May 1st each year.

(2)   If our incomes change, parenting arrangements change or any other circumstances affecting the financial arrangements of the children change, we may change the child support arrangements in this Agreement.

(3)   This issue will be resolved under the Issue Resolution paragraph 11 of this Agreement.

8.   POST-SECONDARY EDUCATION

(1)   We will each deposit $170.00 (or such other amount as we agree) each month into the RESPs for the children, held in our joint names, and will invest these monies as we agree.

(2)   We will contribute to the post-secondary education for the children proportionate to our income, after taking into account the proceeds of the RESP and the children's own contributions, in accordance with the Child Support Guidelines.

9.   EXTRAORDINARY MEDICAL AND DENTAL EXPENSES

(1)   We each have extended health benefits through our employment. We will each cover the children under our plans for as long as those plans are available to the children through our employment. We will co-ordinate coverage so that the children receive maximum benefits.

(2)   We will share, proportionate to our incomes, any extraordinary medical or dental costs not covered by any plans.

(3)   We will both maintain the children as beneficiaries of extended health insurance through our employment, and will sign documentation authorizing the other to make claims directly to our respective insurers. When either of us is reimbursed for a medical expense paid by the other we will immediately forward the reimbursed amount to the other.

10.   LIFE INSURANCE

As long as either of our children are financially dependent within the meaning of the Divorce Act, we will each:

(1)   Keep a life insurance policy in the minimum amount of $325,000.00 (or such other amount as we agree).

(2)   Ensure that our policy remains unencumbered.

(3)   Designate and keep, in the case of Jane's policy, Bill and Myrna Brown and in the case of John's policy, June Smith as beneficiary(s) of our policy on the following terms:

(a) Until the child ceases to be a dependant or reaches the age of 23 the proceeds will be used to pay all payments for the children including but not limited to, contributions to the joint bank account and post-secondary education. Any income from the proceeds not used in one year will be added to the capital. The trustee may use capital for the children's needs; and

(b) Pay to each child one half of the remaining proceeds when Dylan turns 23.

(4)   With 14 days of the signing of this Agreement, we will provide each other with a copy of our policy and the trustee designation. We will sign the Directions in Schedules "B" and "C" attached to this Agreement, permitting the other to confirm directly with our insurer that our policy is unencumbered and in force.

(5)   Each of us authorizes a lien and first charge against our estate for the full amount of the policy proceeds if the policy is not in force on our death.

(6)   If our policy is not in force when we die, in addition to any other remedy the surviving parent may have against our estate, the surviving parent may apply under the Succession Law Reform Act for relief for our child or children.

(7)   When both children cease to be financially dependent within the meaning of the Divorce Act, we may each deal with our policy as we wish.

11.   ISSUE RESOLUTION

Should issues arise in the future concerning the children or financial arrangements for the children, we agree to try to resolve them informally. We will:

(a) as a first step, communicate with each other by email.
(b) If the issue is not resolved under step 1, we will arrange a telephone appointment or personal meeting to discuss the issue.
(c) If the issue is not resolved under step 2, we will either attend mediation and/or return to the collaborative law process before pursuing any other dispute resolution process.

12.   SPOUSAL SUPPORT RELEASE

(1)   We are each financially independent of each other and release our right to spousal support. We intend this Agreement to protect us from any judicial review.

(2)   We know that our financial circumstances, health, employment or the cost of living may all change. We may be unable to work for various reasons, or earn less than we expect. These changes may be catastrophic, unanticipated or beyond imagining. Nevertheless, no change will ever entitle either of us to spousal support from the other.

(3)   We do not want any court to order a change which deviates from or overrides the terms of this Agreement, especially this release. We want the court to uphold this Agreement in its entirety because we are basing our future lives upon this release.

(4)   This Agreement recognizes all economic advantages or disadvantages to us arising from our marriage and its breakdown, has apportioned between us all financial consequences arising from the care of the children in addition to any obligation for the support of the children, relieves any economic hardship arising from the marriage breakdown and, insofar as is practicable, promotes the economic self-sufficiency of each of us within a reasonable period of time.

(5)   No change in our circumstances will be considered a material change justifying any spousal support. All changes will be considered immaterial to our rights and obligations under this Agreement. We have either anticipated all changes as possibilities or have decided to take the risk that there will be changes. This Agreement meets the objectives under the Divorce Act and is fair to both of us. For example, if one of us loses our job and for any reason cannot find work and therefore has no income, and the other's income and financial position have vastly improved from what it is now, these facts will not be a material change justifying any spousal support award. They will be considered and are considered now by us to be immaterial.

13.   MATRIMONIAL HOME

(1)   We hold, as joint tenants, the matrimonial home municipally known as 123 Any Street, Mytown, Ontario. The property is a matrimonial home within the meaning of the Family Law Act.

(2)   Currently with the signing of this Agreement, Jane will transfer all of her right, title and interest in the property to John. John will pay for the cost of preparation and registration of the transfer.

(3)   John will pay for all mortgage payments, realty taxes, insurance premiums, utilities, repairs and other expenses related to the matrimonial home, incurred from the date of transfer, and will indemnify Jane for all liability relating to the matrimonial home. John will discharge the current mortgage and Jane's name will be removed from any and all financing arrangements and obligations with respect to the matrimonial home.

(4)   Each of us will designate the matrimonial home as our principal residence as defined in the Income Tax Act, from the year of purchase until the year of transfer, which is 2002. If either of us becomes liable for income tax resulting from the other's failure to designate the matrimonial home as their principal residence, the one who failed to designate will be liable for the other's tax. Attached as Schedule "D" is the Principal Residence Designation.

14.   PERSONAL PROPERTY

We will divide the contents of the matrimonial home and our personal property in a manner satisfactory to both of us.

15.   EQUALIZATION OF NET FAMILY PROPERTY

Within 14 days following the signing of this Agreement, John will make an equalization payment to Jane of $160,000.00 by certified cheque. We agree that this payment, together with the other benefits given by this Agreement, fully satisfy any entitlement each of us has to an equalization of our net family property.

16.   PENSIONS

(1)   Jane has a pension with ABC Corporation.

(2)   John has a pension with XYZ Corporation.

(3)   Neither of us will make a claim to share in any pension of the other, including but not limited to any company pension plans, deferred profit sharing plans, registered retirement savings plans and registered home ownership savings plans.

17.   RELEASES

General Release

(1)   This Agreement is a full and final settlement of all issues between us and all rights and obligations arising out of our relationship.

(2)   Except as otherwise provided in this Agreement, we release each other from all claims at common law, in equity or by statute against each other, including claims under the Divorce Act, the Family Law Act, and the Succession Law Reform Act.

Estate Release

(3)   Except as otherwise provided in this Agreement, we release each other from all claims either of us may have against the other now or in the future under the terms of any statute or the common law, including claims for:

(a) a share in the other's estate;
(b) a payment as a dependant from the other's estate under the Succession Law Reform Act;
(c) an entitlement under the Family Law Act;
(d) an appointment as an attorney or guardian of the other's personal care or property under the Substitute Decisions Act; and
(e) participation in decisions about the other's medical care or treatment under the Health Care Consent Act;

(4)   Except as otherwise provided in this Agreement, on the death of either party, the surviving party will not:

(a) share in any testate or intestate benefit from the estate; or
(b) act as personal representative of the deceased; and
(c) the estate of the deceased party will be distributed as if the surviving party had died first.

18.   GENERAL TERMS

No Conditions

(1)   There are no representations, collateral agreements, warranties or conditions affecting this Agreement.

Reconciliation

(2)   If we agree to try to reconcile our relationship but cohabit for no longer than 90 days, this Agreement will not be affected. If we cohabit for more than 90 days, this Agreement will become void,

except that any transfers or payments made up to that time will not be affected or invalidated.

Severability

(3)   Except as otherwise provided in this Agreement, the invalidity or unenforceability of any terms of this Agreement does not affect the validity or enforceability of any other term. Any invalid term will be treated as severed from the remaining terms.

Headings

(4)   The section headings contained in this Agreement are for convenience only and do not affect the meaning or interpretation of any term of this Agreement.

Separation Agreement to Survive Divorce

(5)   If a divorce judgment issues, all of the terms of this Agreement will continue.

Applicable Law and Interpretation

(6)   The interpretation of this Agreement is governed by the laws of Ontario.

Agreement to Bind Estate

(7)   This Agreement binds our heirs, executors, administrators and assigns.

Amendments

(8)   Any amendments to this Agreement must be in writing, signed by us, dated and witnessed.

Execution of Other Documents

(9)   We will sign any documents necessary to give effect to this Agreement.

Non-Compliance

(10)   Any failure to insist on the strict performance of any terms in this Agreement will not be a waiver of any term.

Costs

(11)   We will each pay our own costs for the negotiation and preparation of this Agreement.

Where Consent is Required in this Agreement

(12)   Where consent is required under this Agreement, it will not be unreasonably withheld. If we cannot agree whether consent is being reasonably withheld, we will use our issue resolution agreement as outlined at paragraph 11 to resolve the matter.

Effective Date

(13)   The effective date of this Agreement is the date on which the last of us signs it.

19.   JOINT PREPARATION

We acknowledge that each of us and our lawyers have participated in the preparation of this Agreement. It is to be construed as if we are joint authors.

20.   INDEPENDENT LEGAL ADVICE AND FINANCIAL DISCLOSURE

We acknowledge that:

(a) we have each had independent legal advice;

(b) we have each read the Agreement and have full knowledge of the contents;

(c) we understand our respective rights and obligations under this Agreement, the nature of this Agreement and the consequences of this Agreement;

(d) we have exchanged all financial information which either of us believe important and necessary to resolve our property and support issues, including our incomes, assets and debts. We have exchanged sworn Financial Statements, our income tax returns for the last three years, and estimates of value of our home at separation and currently. We understand that we are relying on the accuracy and completeness of the information provided to each other and have instruced our lawyers not to independently verify our financial disclosure.

(e) the terms of this Agreement are acceptable to us both and satisfy our interests;

(f) we are entering into this Agreement without any undue influence, fraud or coercion; and

(g) we are signing this agreement voluntarily.

TO EVIDENCE OUR AGREEMENT we have each signed this Agreement before a witness.

Dated at Mytown, this 31st day of October, 2002.

SIGNED   )
)
in the presence of   )
)
)
)
)
_____   )
as to the signature of   )   **Jane Brown**
Jane Brown   )

Dated at Mytown, this 31st day of October, 2002.

SIGNED   )
)
in the presence of   )
)
)
)
)
_____   )
as to the signature of   )   **John Smith**
John Smith   )
)

APPENDIX "H"

What to do When Things Go Wrong

Problem	Possible Solutions
One party won't talk.	• Prepare the client to speak ahead of time by explaining the importance of each team member contributing to the discussion and giving him or her time to think about his or her ideas. • Ask why he or she is reticent to speak (is there abuse, intimidation?) • Ask direct questions to the quieter client in the meetings. • Create clear rules for taking turns talking. • When the client is simply unable to speak, the lawyer may speak on behalf of the client until he or she feels ready to do so.
One client verbally attacks the other.	• Do nothing. • Help the other client operate from a space of personal calm and centredness. • If the other spouse can deflect, rather than retaliate, it may stop the attacks and may even trigger an apology. • Never admonish either client in the group setting. • The attacking party's lawyer can discuss that person's conduct in private – explain the consequences of ineffective communication.

Problem	Possible Solutions
	• Consider referring the attacking party to counselling. • Take a break from the meeting or take a break from the process to allow emotions to cool. • If the attacking party cannot learn to treat the other with respect, consider terminating the process.
Both parties verbally attack each other.	• Allow the mutual jabs for a period of time to see whether the parties need to vent. • If neither party appears hurt by the conduct, consider whether or not this communication style is acceptable to the parties. • If the clients are OK with the method of communication, the lawyers can acknowledge that the parties are making mutual jabs at each other and state the lawyers' lack of comfort with this method of communication, but offer to deal with it if the parties wish. This may serve to awaken the clients to an entrenched method of communication that makes others uncomfortable and may not be effective. • Ask the parties if this style of communication is what their children are exposed to at home. • The lawyers may use their body language to demonstrate their lack of support for this method of communication – sit back, be quiet, withdraw. • Ask the parties whether this way of communication is taking them where they want to go, i.e. toward their best negotiated outcome. • Remind both parties of the communication protocol to which they agreed and ask whether they still wish to follow that protocol.

Problem	Possible Solutions
One party wants to move quickly but the other wants to go slowly.	• It is rare that parties move through the psychological stages of divorce at the same time. It is very common for one to be far ahead of the other and to be ready to resolve the issues and move on, while the other is starting at the beginning of the psychological process, struggling to come to grips with the separation. • Explain to the parties that this phenomenon is normal. • Help the parties understand that it is in their mutual interests that both parties are psychologically ready to make good decisions. • It may be necessary to slow the process down to allow the spouse who did not wish the separation to get counselling and process the separation. • Only decisions that are absolutely necessary are made while the process is put on hold for awhile until both parties are ready to make decisions. • Remind the party who initiated the separation that if the other spouse is pushed too quickly, the divorce process could become high conflict. The litigation route is usually much slower than the collaborative route, even with some pauses. Alternatively, a spouse who is pushed to make decisions too soon, may have *buyer's remorse* and seek to set aside the agreement in the future.
A client refuses disclosure of information, which the lawyer feels will affect the other person's choices or decisions.	• Remind the client that he or she and you undertook to make full disclosure of all information that will affect the other person's choices or decisions. • Explain that the lawyer has an ethical duty to ensure the fullest disclosure, to ensure the integrity of the CFL process.

Problem	Possible Solutions
	• Ask why there is reticence about sharing the information and brainstorm how it might be shared safely. • If the client still refuses to disclose the information, the lawyer must not breach solicitor and client privilege and therefore cannot share the information. • However, advise the client that you will need to terminate or withdraw and reality-check the consequences of that step. • If the client still refuses to disclose, terminate or withdraw in accordance with your local association's protocol.
Poor working relationship between lawyers.	• Debrief after each settlement meeting – have lunch, name the problems, and consider solutions. • Get help from other CFL lawyers or mentors. • Hire a mediator to conduct a five-way meeting to facilitate the lawyers' communication and problem solving as well as that of the clients. • Have each lawyer edit letters and progress reports prepared by the other before they are sent to the clients. • If relations cannot be repaired – transfer the file to another CFL lawyer who has a better track record with the other counsel.

One person continues to lobby for his or her position and won't share feelings or concerns.	• Remind the party that the goal is to create a customized outcome that integrates each party's subjective reality (wishes, concerns, worries) with the objective reality (available money, financial resources, number of children, value and extent of property).
	• Reinforce the rules of mutuality:
	  • each must be willing to share his or her subjective experience;
	  • each must be willing to hear the subjective experience of the other;

Problem	Possible Solutions
	• each must be able to acknowledge his or her own wishes without lobbying for a position or threatening, intimidating, whining, withdrawing, or pouting; • both people brainstorm options that account for both sides' subjective needs and objective reality. • Go back to exploring feelings and interests in individual meetings. • In a private meeting, explore why the client is unwilling to express underlying interests – abuse, intimidation? • If the lawyer can draw out underlying interests in a private meeting, the lawyer can share those on behalf of the client until the client is able to do so.

The parties keep arguing.	• The lawyers should model effective communication:
	• listen before you speak; ask if you can check out what you've heard with the other lawyer or party;
	  • ask if you've missed or don't understand anything; if new information is received, confirm again whether you understand;
	  • listen for something new; ask what new understanding you now have;
	  • focus on what might be desired by all the parties;
	  • invite the other side to do this as well.
	• The lawyers can model this form of dialogue until the clients can do so.
	• Name the behaviour and ask the parties if this form of communication is taking them where they wish to go, ie. toward their best negotiated outcome.
	• Consider referral to individual and/or separation counselling

APPENDIX "I"

Suggested Reading

Conflict Resolution

Deutsch, M. (1973). *The Resolution of Conflict: Constructive and Destructive Processes*. New Haven, CT: Yale University Press.

Kriesberg, L. (1982). *Social Conflicts* (2nd ed.). Englewood Cliffs, NJ: Prentice-Hall, Inc.

Mayer, B. (2000). *The Dynamics of Conflict: A Practitioner's Guide*. San Francisco, CA: Jossey-Bass Inc., Publishers.

Rubin, J.Z., Pruitt, D.G., & Kim, S.H. (1994). *Social Conflict: Escalation, Stalemate, and Settlement* (2nd ed.). New York: McGraw-Hill, Inc.

Communication

Binder, D.A., Bergman, P., & Price, S.C. (1991). *Lawyers As Counselors: A Client-Centered Approach*. St. Paul, MN: West Publishing Co.

Stone, D., Patton, B., & Heen, S. (1999). *Difficult Conversations: How to discuss What Matters Most*. New York: Viking.

Tannen, D. (1990). *You Just Don't Understand: Women and Men in Conversation*. New York: Ballantine Books.

Negotiation

Fisher, R. & Brown, S. (1988). *Getting Together: Building Relationships As We Negotiate*. New York: Penguin Books, USA Inc.

Fisher, R. & Ertel, D. (1995). *Getting Ready to Negotiate: The Getting to Yes Workbook*. New York: Penguin Books USA Inc.

Fisher, R., Kopelman, E., & Schneider, A.K. (1994). *Beyond Machiavelli: Tools for Coping with Conflict*. Cambridge, MA: Harvard University Press.

Fisher, R., Ury, W., & Patton, B. (1991). *Getting to Yes: Negotiating Agreement Without Giving In* (2nd ed.). New York: Penguin Group Penguin Books USA Inc.

Gifford, D.G. (1989). *Legal Negotiation: Theory and Applications.* St. Paul, MN: West Publishing Co.

Gulliver, P.H. (1979). *Disputes and Negotiations: A Cross-cultural Perspective.* New York: Academic Press, Inc.

Kritek, P.B. (1994). *Negotiating at an Uneven Table: Developing Moral Courage in Resolving Our Conflicts.* San Francisco, CA: Jossey-Bass Publishers.

Mnookin, R.H. & Susskind, L.E. (Eds.)(1999). *Negotiating on Behlf of Others: Advice to Lawyers, Business Executives, Sports Agents, Diplomats, Politicians, and Everybody Else.* Thousand Oaks, CA: Sage Publications, Inc.

Mnookin, R.H., Peppet, S.C., & Tulumello, A.S. (2000). *Beyond Winning: Negotiating to Create Value in Deals and Disputes.* Cambridge, MA: The Belknap Press of Harvard University Press.

Pruitt, D.G. (1981). *Negotiation Behavior.* New York: Academic Press, Inc.

Ury, W. (1991). *Getting Past No: Negotiating Your Way from Confrontation to Cooperation.* New York: Bantam Books.

Williams, G.R. (1983). *Legal Negotiation and Settlement.* St. Paul, MN: West Publishing Co.

Mediation

Bush, R.A.B. & Folger, J.P. (1994). *The Promise of Mediation: Responding to Conflict Through Empowerment and Recognition.* San Francisco, CA: Jossey-Bass Inc., Publishers.

Folberg, J. & Taylor, A. (1984). *Mediation: A Comprehensive Guide to Resolving Conflicts Without Litigation.* San Francisco, CA: Jossey-Bass Inc., Publishers.

Lang, M.D. & Taylor, A. (2000). *The Making of a Mediator: Developing Artistry in Practice.* San Francisco, CA: Jossey-Bass Inc., Publishers.

Moore, C.W. (1996). *The Mediation Process: Practical Strategies for Resolving Conflict* (2nd ed.). San Francisco, CA: Jossey-Bass Inc., Publishers.

Winslade, J. & Monk, G. (2000). *Narrative Mediation: A New Approach to Conflict Resolution.* San Francisco, CA: Jossey-Bass Inc., Publishers.

Collaborative Law

Tesler, P.H. (2001). *Collaborative Law: Achieving Effective Resolution in Divorce without Litigation*. Chicago, IL: ABA Publications.

The Collaborative Review (formerly *The Collaborative Quarterly*) newsletter of the International Academy of Collaborative Professionals.

APPENDIX "J"

Collaborative Family Law Protocols

These are the guidelines for members of the City in Ontario Association of Collaborative Family Law Lawyers. These protocols are designed to ensure that:

- Every collaborative family law client will receive the same information about the collaborative family law process; and

- All member lawyers are following the same collaborative family law process.

We recognize that some cases require some variation to these protocols, but all of us agree to abide by the intent and spirit of these guidelines:

A. INITIAL MEETING WITH CLIENT

1. Explain the three process options:

    a. Traditional lawyer to lawyer negotiation with possibility of court;
    b. Mediation; and
    c. Collaborative Family Law.

2. Explain how the Collaborative Family Law process:

    a. Client preparation meeting;
    b. Series of four-way settlement meetings in which parties decide issues, uncover interests, exchange all important information, develop wide range of settlement options; reach solutions acceptable to both parties.

3. Review Participation Agreement.

4. Help client decide whether CFL appropriate for him or her:

     a.   If client decides to use CFL, give client preparation hand-out, book client preparation meeting and sign CFL Retainer Agreement;

     b.   If spouse has not yet chosen CFL, send letter to spouse along with CFL information package.

B.   PREPARE CLIENT FOR CFL PROCESS

1. Review the CFL process again.

2. Review the Participation Agreement again.

3. Explain the expanded role of lawyers as:

   - Creators of a safe negotiating environment;
   - 60% advocates for client; 40% advocates for process;
   - Negotiation coaches;
   - Information resources;
   - Facilitators.

4. Explain the role of clients:

   - Assume responsibility;
   - Uncover own and other party's interests;
   - Voluntarily exchange all information;
   - Help create settlement options;
   - Take responsibility for outcome.

5. Explain the meaning of disclosure of all of the *important* information.

6. Discuss client's interests, concerns, and objectives and those expected of the other party.

7. Identify urgent issues for client and those expected of spouse.

8. Encourage client to avoid taking positions.

9. Explain agenda for first four-way settlement meeting:

   a. Review and sign Participation Agreement;
   b. Identify issues;
   c. Deal with urgent matters;
   d. Agree to exchange of information;
   e. Establish a date and agenda for next meetings.

10. Ask client whether any sensitive areas/issues for either.

11. Ask client to gather information needed to solve urgent issues.

12. Give client Financial Statement and ask to begin to gather disclosure.

C.   CONTACT OTHER LAWYER BEFORE FIRST SETTLE-MENT MEETING

1. Agree to place and time and for first meeting.

2. Set agenda for success for first meeting.

3. Discuss urgent issues.

4. Discuss possible pitfalls, flash points or sensitive areas.

5. Agree to bring information necessary to deal with urgent issues.

D.   AT THE FIRST FOUR WAY SETTLEMENT MEETING:

1. Commit to collaborative family law process:

    a. Read Participation Agreement, commit to process and sign;
    b. Agree to Guidelines for Effective Communication;
    c. Identify clients' mutual interests in protecting children, preserving ongoing relationships, achieving mutually agreeable outcomes; controlling costs.

2. Clients open the discussion to identify their goals for the process and the issues they wish to address:

    a. Create list of issues to be solved;
    b. Lawyers to listen actively so both clients feel heard and understood;
    c. Lawyers to assist and reframe where necessary;
    d. Problem areas of disagreement to be reframed as problems to be solved;
    e. Prioritize issues and order of discussion.

3. Resolve immediate issues:

    a. Identify interests;
    b. Exchange information;
    c. Generate options;
    d. Negotiate solutions as narrowly as possible so as to leave open future settlement possibilities.

4. Exchange of Information

       a.   Identify information/documents important to either party;

       b.   *Important* defined as affecting any of the choices either party needs to make about process or issues;

       c.   Decide most efficient way to gather information and prepare Financial Statements.

5.   Schedule next Settlement Meeting:

       a.   Agree to agenda for next meeting;

       b.   Schedule two or three future meetings (can be cancelled if necessary).

6.   One lawyer prepares minutes of meeting and forwards to all participants by email/fax.

E.   FURTHER FOUR WAY SETTLEMENT MEETINGS

1.   Review minutes of previous meeting – note any concerns or changes.

2.   Review agenda.

3.   Review homework.

4.   Negotiate issues using interest-based model:

       a.   Exchange information;

       b.   Uncover interests, goals, and objectives;

       c.   Generate settlement options, the sources for which are,
- the law (i.e. applicable statutory and case law),
- the external world (i.e. what others have done elsewhere), and
- the parties themselves;

       d.   Examine consequences of each settlement option for each client;

       e.   Help clients negotiate an agreement which satisfies the interests of both parties.

F.   COMMUNICATE WITH OTHER LAWYER BEFORE AND AFTER EACH SETTLEMENT MEETING

1.   Evaluate previous settlement meeting.

2.   Discuss clients' feedback and concerns.

3.   Critique collaborative skills and plan to improve next meeting.

**G.   COMMUNICATE OR MEET WITH OWN CLIENT BE-
FORE AND AFTER EACH SETTLEMENT MEETING**

1. Help client understand disclosure obligations and require-
    ments.

2. Invite client to express strong emotions.

3. Conduct reality check of client expectations.

H.   DOCUMENT AGREEMENT

1. Once agreement reached, lawyers prepare initial draft of Sep-
    aration Agreement.

2. Draft agreement provided to the parties.

3. Final meeting held to review, finalize, and sign Separation
    Agreement.

4. Signing ceremony and congratulations.

I.   FOLLOW UP AND CLOSING FILE

1. Register deeds, place insurance, etc. as required by Separation
    Agreement or ensure client does.

2. Send out client evaluation of CFL process.

3. Send in statistical reporting to CFL Association.

J.   NO COURT

1. Collaborative Lawyers may not ever represent collaborative
    client in contested court proceedings.

2. If a lawyer is a solicitor of record in a litigated matter in which
    the client wishes to switch to Collaborative Law, the lawyer
    will remove him or herself from the court record before signing
    a Participation Agreement.

K.   WITHDRAWAL

1. Permitted/appropriate if:

    • Lawyer and client cannot work effectively together;
    • Client wishes to retain new collaborative counsel;
    • Collaborative lawyer lacks the skills needed to support the
      collaborative client.

2. If lawyer withdraws, will assist in orderly transfer to new Collaborative counsel within 30 days.

L.   TERMINATION

1. Required if:

    *   Client continues to refuse to disclose important information;
    *   Client delays unreasonably;
    *   Client refuses to abide by interim agreements;
    *   Client otherwise acts in bad faith and contrary to principles of CFL process.

2. Withdrawing lawyer will advise other side but not disclose reason for termination.

Guidelines for
The Association of Collaborative
Lawyers
(Medicine Hat)

These are the guidelines for the members of the Association of Collaborative Lawyers (Medicine Hat). These guidelines outline the Collaborative Law Process each of us will follow. This is very important because each member needs to know that:

- every Collaborative Law client will receive the **same** information about the Collaborative Law Process; and
- all member lawyers are following the **same** Collaborative Law Process.

We recognize that in some circumstances it may not be possible to follow these guidelines exactly, but **all members agree to abide by the spirit of these guidelines.**

A. Initial interview with client:

1. Review the *Confidential Client Information* sheet

2. Explain the 3 process options:
    a) Collaborative Law Process;
    b) Mediation Process; or
    c) Court Process – Litigation.

3. Explain the Collaborative Law Process:
    a) Review the Association's form of *Collaborative Law Contract*;
    b) Tell client the goals of the Collaborative Law Process:
        - Create a safe environment;
        - Communicate effectively;
        - Provide full disclosure of information;
        - Explore wide range of possible choices;
        - Reach solutions acceptable to both clients;
        - Closure;

c)   Confirm your client wishes to use the Collaborative Law Process.

4.   Give client the Collaborative Law folder with handouts and review them with client:
- *Brochure About the Collaborative Law Process*
- *Process Choices for Divorce and Separation in Medicine Hat*
- *Collaborative Law Contract (Family or Civil)*
- *Expectations of Clients and Lawyers*
- *Guidelines for Parents During Separation and Divorce*
- *Effective Communication Skills*
- *Thinking About a Custody Battle?*
- *Suggested Ways to Divide Household Goods*
- *Who to Call For Help*
- *Parenting After Separation Seminar Information*
- *Information to Gather Checklist*
- *Average Monthly Budget Sheets*
- *Special Expenses for Children Sheet*
- *Canada Customs & Revenue Form*
- *Why You Need a New Will.*

5.   Give client a short, general explanation about the law, not how it applies to them specifically.

6.   Discuss costs and money retainer in detail.

7.   Get instructions:
   a)   If meeting with first of the couple to see Collaborative Lawyer:
      i)   Choices to enroll spouse in Collaborative Process:
      - client talks to their spouse;
      - neutral friend, counsellor or minister talks to spouse about Collaborative Process;
      - invitation letter from lawyer to spouse;
      - last resort if spouse does not respond to above, serve court documents and hopefully transition file to Collaborative Law Process;
      ii)   If meeting with second of the couple to see collaborative lawyer (ie. other person has expressed interest in Collaborative Law choice):
      - Set up Collaborative Law meeting and confirm in writing with other lawyer;
   b)   Court action or Mediation;

    c)   Do nothing and wait for further instructions from client.

B. Preparing a client for a first four-way meeting:

1. Get signed *Retainer Contract* from client.

2. Review the Collaborative Law Process with the client again.

3. Review the *Collaborative Law Contract* with the client again.

4. Go over *Expectations of Clients and Lawyers* thoroughly.

5. Explain how lawyers can be expected to act and of what is expected of clients.

6. Review what is important to client and client's concerns and what client thinks might be important and a concern to the other client. Help client identify fears, needs, priorities, goals and motivations for presentation to the other client.
    a) Talk about psychological needs
    b) Talk about procedural needs
    c) Talk about substantive needs

7. Discuss agenda for first four-way meeting:
    a) All four will review the *Collaborative Law Contract* and commit to the Collaborative Law Process;
    b) Identify what is important to the client (concerns, goals, priorities and fears);
    c) Identify what the client wants to talk about or what questions client needs to answer;
    d) Deal with any pressing issues;
    e) Assign *To Do List* for next meeting;
    f) Establish partial agenda for next meeting; and
    g) Establish date, time and place for next meeting.

8. Identify any pressing needs. A pressing need is a matter that must have a temporary solution in order to permit the couple to carry on to another four-way meeting. It is not intended to find anything other than a temporary solution.

9. Don't specifically discuss the law model in relation to their situation: "The Law Model is what we must resort to if we cannot agree

on something that works better . . . the Law Model is for people who can't agree".

10. Remind client to attend Parenting After Separation Seminar (PASS) – get client's commitment to attend PASS.

11. Ask if client has completed their *Information to Gather Checklist*. Confirm that client will bring their information to the meeting.

12. Encourage client to delay developing or promoting specific positions until all of the information has been shared and all options explored at four-way meetings.

13. Urge client not to negotiate prematurely.

14. Ask client to keep *Collaborative Law Folder* (given at Client Interview) updated and bring to all meetings.

15. Ask client to read again both *Collaborative Law Contract* and *Expectations of the Clients and Lawyers* immediately before first four-way meeting.

C. Meet with other lawyer prior to the first four-way meeting to:

1. Exchange anticipated client concerns.

2. Identify expected issues and areas clients have already reached agreement on themselves.

3. Agree on any procedures needed to accommodate client concerns.

4. Agree on location, seating and facility arrangements most likely to be effective in light of client's needs and concerns.

5. Identify pressing issues.

6. Agree on agenda and mutual goals for first session, ensuring pressing needs are addressed.

7. Commit to remind clients to bring as much information to first meeting as available.

D. At the first four-way meeting:

1. Review and commit to Collaborative Law Process:
    a) Introduce yourself and client;
    b) Renew commitment to Collaborative Law Process;
    c) Demonstrate interest and acknowledge the other clients' concerns and feelings;
    d) Review the *Collaborative Law Contract* in detail;
    e) Sign the *Collaborative Law Contract*; and
    f) Identify and agree on any further expectations of both clients and lawyers.

2. Identify client's mutual concerns and priorities, for example:
    - children's welfare;
    - safety;
    - need to be heard and understood;
    - protection from one-sided actions;
    - cost;
    - time;
    - privacy;
    - etc.

3. Identify what clients need to talk about or questions clients need to answer and anything clients have already agreed on:
    a) Assist your own client to effectively communicate their concerns, goals and needs;
    b) Reframe where necessary;
    c) Listen actively so both clients know they are heard and understood;
    d) Describe and note disagreements as things clients want to talk about or questions clients need to answer; and
    e) Normalize existence of disagreement.

4. Identify any pressing issues.

5. Attend to Pressing Issues:
    a) Reach short term, interim agreements without prejudice to either client for future discussion at next four-way meetings:
        - Identify the pressing issues as narrowly as possible;
        - Identify the underlying concerns, goals;
        - Obtain all readily available information;
        - Generate the most options in the time available;
        - Choose the best option;

- Document the temporary agreement in the minutes.

6. Organize Information:
   a) Share information clients have brought to meeting;
   b) Identify further information or documents needed for next or subsequent four-way meetings;
   c) Decide who will gather the information needed on a *To Do List*.

7. Discuss partial agenda for next four-way meeting and confirm date, time and place of next meeting.

8. Remind both clients to review *Collaborative Law Contract* and *Expectations of Lawyers and Clients* immediately before each four-way meeting.

E. At subsequent four-way meetings:

1. Identify what is important, the concerns and needs behind the issues for both clients.

2. Assist clients to understand what is important and the concerns, needs and priorities of the other client:
   a) Both lawyers help both clients to effectively communicate what is important, their own concerns, needs, motivations, goals and intentions and to understand the other client's concerns;
   b) Identify common concerns.

3. Exchange information until both clients are satisfied they have enough information to begin to look at choices.

4. Generate as wide a range of choices as possible to respond to each client's concerns and goals.
   a) Refrain from rejecting possible options prematurely;
   b) Review the law as only one source of an objective, reasonable range of outcomes;
   c) Recognize that the law has limited scope and flexibility and represents only one of many possible outcomes and may not generate the best outcome for the clients;
   d) Identify limiting factors beyond the control of the clients;
   e) Review the clients' and the lawyers' own creative options.

5. Examine possible consequences of each option for each client.

6. Encourage the clients to select the outcome that best meets the needs of both clients and is acceptable to both clients.

F. Communicate with the other lawyer:

1. Both before and after each four-way meeting.

2. Evaluate the previous session.

3. Plan how to improve the next meeting.

4. About any conversations you have had with your client before or after four-way meetings.

5. Brainstorm possible techniques to break impasse and how to assist clients in the development of options.

G. Communicate with your own client:

1. Briefly at end of each four-way meeting for immediate feedback on meeting.

2. If client calls between four-way meetings, note down any psychological process or substantive needs and concerns client raises.

3. Add clients above concerns to agenda to next four-way meeting.

4. Ask client for permission to let the other lawyer know about this conversation.

H. If an agreement is reached Collaborative Lawyers may assist the clients by:

1. Drafting and signing settlement agreements.

2. Implementing those settlement agreements in court proceedings on a consent basis only.

I.   The Collaborative Law Lawyer may not go to court.

At no time in a Collaborative Law Process may the lawyer appear in court or initiate court proceedings for the client. However, with the agreement of both clients the Collaborative Lawyer may be solicitor of record for the client **only** for the purpose of:

- processing the divorce in court with a consent divorce application;
- implementing the settlement agreement reached in the Collaborative Law Process.

J.   If a lawyer is solicitor of record on a matter which the client wishes to switch to a Collaborative Law Process retainer.

The lawyer may remain solicitor of record for the client but may take no further steps in the court process for the client except as set out in H and I above.

APPENDIX "K"

Websites

Canadian Collaborative Family Law Websites

British Columbia

Collaborative Divorce BC – The Humane Approach to Divorce.
Professionals practising Collaborative Divorce in Vancouver, BC.
www.collaborativedivorcebc.org

Collaborative Divorce and Separation.
www.divorcecanada.com

Okanagan Collaborative Family Law Group.
Representing practising lawyers
in the Okanagan area of British Columbia.
www.collaborativefamilylaw.ca

Collaborative Family Law Group – The New Wave of Law Without
Court.
Professionals practising Collaborative Divorce in Victoria, BC.
www.collaborativefamilylawgroup.com

Alberta/Saskatchewan

Collaborative Family Lawyers of Canada.
Practising Collaborative Lawyers in Calgary, Lethbridge, Medicine Hat,
Edmonton,
and the province of Saskatchewan.
www.collaborativelaw.ca

Ontario

The Collaborative Law Centre.
Representing practising lawyers in London.
www.collaborativelawcentre.com

The Collaborative Law Network.
Representing practising lawyers in Ottawa and Eastern Ontario.
www.collaborative-law.ca

The Collaborative Family Law Group.
Representing practising lawyers in Peel Halton region.
www.collaborative-family-law.com

The Niagara Collaborative Law Group.
Representing practising lawyers in Niagara region.
www.collablaw-niagara.com

The Collaborative Family Law Association of Ontario Toronto Group.
Representing practising lawyers in the Greater Toronto Area.
http://www.collaborativefamilylawassociation.com

The Collaborative Family Law Association of Waterloo Region.
Representing practising lawyers in the Cambridge-Kitchener-Waterloo
region.
www.collaborativelaw-waterloo.com

FLC Collaborative Family Law Centre.
Joel Miller's website with information about
Collaborative Family Law practice and other family law issues.
www.familylawcentre.com/collaborative.html

Nova Scotia

The Association of Collaborative Family Law Lawyers of Nova Scotia.
Representing practising lawyers in the province of Nova Scotia.
www.collaborativefamilylawyers.ca

American Collaborative Family Law Websites

The International Academy of Collaborative Professionals.
View this website for the most complete list of
Collaborative Law organizations in North America.
www.collabgroup.com

Stuart G. Webb, founder, practitioner, and trainer in Collaborative Law,
Minneapolis, Minnesota.
www.divorcenet.com/mn/webb.html

Chip Rose, Co-Director of the Mediation Centre and trainer in
Collaborative Law,
Santa Cruz, California.
www.mediate.com/crose

Pauline H. Tesler, practitioner, trainer, and author in Collaborative Law,
http://www.divorcenet.com/ca/tesler.html

Other Websites of Interest

www.iahl.org
www.restorativejustice.com
www.contemplativemind.org
www.therapeuticjurisprudence.org
www.transformingpractices.com
www.lawyercoaches.com
www.mediate.com

APPENDIX "L"

Disciplinary Procedures[1]

1. Disciplinary procedures are initiated by filing a written complaint with the Board of Directors.

2. The complaint should include the name of the lawyer against whom the complaint is made, the matter (if the client authorizes disclosure), the nature of the violation, the details and supporting documents, if appropriate.

3. The complaint will be placed on the agenda of the next regular Board meeting. Copies of the complaint will be distributed to Board members before the meeting.

4. If the Board determines that the complaint has no merit on its face, it will be dismissed and the complainant and the lawyer against whom the complaint was made will be notified in writing. Also, a copy of the complaint will be provided to the lawyer against whom it was made.

5. If the Board determines that the complaint has merit on its face, it will be assigned to a Board member or Board members for investigation.

6. As part of the investigation, a copy of the complaint will be sent to the named lawyer with the request that the lawyer respond in writing within twenty (20) days. A written report of the investigation will be made to the Board within sixty (60) days unless the time is extended for good cause.

7. The report of the investigator(s) will be considered by the Board at its next regular meeting. If the Board determines that the claim lacks merit, it will be dismissed and the complainant and named lawyer will be notified of that fact in writing. If the Board determines that the claim is

---

1 Webb, S.G. (2002). *Collaborative Law: A Training for Family Law Attorneys*. Unpublished manuscript.

meritorious, a representative of the Board will meet with the complainant and named lawyer, either individually or jointly, to reach a mutually agreed upon resolution of the complaint.

8. If the complaint cannot be resolved by mutual agreement, the Board will determine how the matter will be resolved. If the Board determines that removing the named lawyer from membership in the Institute is appropriate, the named lawyer will be notified and given an opportunity to appear before the Board to show cause why he or she should not be removed from membership.

9. After hearing from the named lawyer, the Board may either remove the named lawyer, impose discipline other than removal or refer the matter for further investigation.

References

Binder, D.A., Bergman, P., & Price, S.C. (1991). *Lawyers As Counselors: A Client-Centered Approach* (2nd ed.). St. Paul, MN: West Publishing Co.

Burger, W.E. (1976). Agenda for 2000 A.D. – need for systematic anticipation. *F.R.D.* 70:83-96. St. Paul, MN: West Publishing Co.

Burger, W.E. (1982). *Isn't There a Better Way?* Washington, DC: ACR formerly SPIDR.

De Bono, E. (1970). *Lateral Thinking: A Textbook of Creativity*. New York: Penguin Books.

Deutsch, M. (1973). *The Resolution of Conflict: Constructive and Destructive Processes*. New Haven CT: Yale University Press.

Fisher, R. & Brown, S. (1988). *Getting Together: Building Relationships As We Negotiate*. New York: Penguin Books, USA Inc.

Fisher, R. & Ertel, D. (1995). *Getting Ready to Negotiate: The Getting to Yes Workbook*. New York: Penguin Books USA Inc.

Fisher, R., Kopelman, E., & Schneider, A.K. (1994). *Beyond Machiavelli: Tools for Coping with Conflict*. Cambridge, MA: Harvard University Press.

Fisher, R., Ury, W., & Patton, B. (1991). *Getting to Yes: Negotiating Agreement Without Giving In* (2nd ed.). New York: Penguin Group Penguin Books USA Inc.

Follett, M.P. (1925). Constructive conflict. In H.C. Metcalf & L. Urwick (Eds.) (1940). *Dynamic Administration: The Collected Papers of Mary Parker Follett*. New York: Harper & Row, Publishers.

Gifford, D.G. (1989). *Legal Negotiation: Theory and Applications*. St. Paul, MN: West Publishing Co.

Gulliver, P.H. (1979). *Disputes and Negotiations: A Cross-cultural Perspective*. New York: Academic Press, Inc.

Knowles, M.S. (1975). *Self-directed Learning: A Guide for Learners and Teachers*. Englewoods Cliffs, NJ: Cambridge Adult Education Prentice Hall Regents.

Knowles, M.S. (1980). *The Modern Practice of Adult Education: From Pedagogy to Andragogy*. Englewood Cliffs, NJ: Cambridge Adult Education Prentice Hall Regents.

Knowles, M.S., Holton, E.F., & Swanson, R.A. (1998). *The Adult Learner* (5th ed.). Houston, TX: Gulf Publishing Company.

Kolb, D.M. & Coolidge, G.G. (1993). Her place at the table: a consideration of gender issues in negotiation. In J.W. Breslin & J.Z. Rubin (Eds.)(1993). *Negotiation Theory and Practice* (2nd ed.). Cambridge, MA: The Program on Negotiation at Harvard Law School.

Kuhn, T.S. (1996). *The Structure of Scientific Revolutions* (3rd ed.). Chicago, IL: The University of Chicago Press.

Lewin, K. (1947). Group decision and social change. In T.M. Newcomb & E.L. Hartley (Eds.) (1947). *Readings in Social Psychology*. New York: Henry Holt and Company, Inc.

Lewin, K. (1947). Frontiers in group dynamics. In K. Lewin (1997). *Resolving Social Conflicts* and *Field Theory in Social Science*. Washington, DC: American Psychological Association.

Mnookin, R.H. & Kornhauser, L. (1979). Bargaining in the shadow of the law: the case of divorce. *Yale Law Journal*. 88:950-997 New Haven CT: Yale University Press.

Mnookin, R.H. & Ross, L. (1995). Introduction. In K. Arrow, R.H. Mnookin, L. Ross, A. Tversky, & R. Wilson (Eds.)(1995). *Barriers to Conflict Resolution*. New York: W.W. Norton & Company, Inc.

Moore, C.W. (1996). *The Mediation Process: Practical Strategies for Resolving Conflict* (2nd ed.). San Francisco, CA: Jossey-Bass Inc., Publishers.

Pound, R. (1906). The causes of popular dissatisfaction with the administration of justice. *F.R.D.* 35:273-291. St. Paul, MN: West Publishing Co.

Pruitt, D.G. (1981). *Negotiation Behavior*. New York: Academic Press, Inc.

Rose, C. (2002). Wrestling with the model. *Collaborative Review*, v4, n1, pp1-4. Novato, CA: Journal of the International Academy of Collaborative Professionals.

Ryan, J.P. (1989). *Parents Forever: Making the Concept a Reality for Divorcing Parents and their Children*. A Report Submitted to the Department of Justice (Canada) on the Parental Responsibilities Legislation in Four Jurisdictions: Florida, Maine, Washington and Great Britain. Ottawa, ON: Government of Canada Publications.

Ryan, J.P. (1992). Mediator strategies for lawyers: the four-party settlement conference. *Family and Conciliation Courts Review*: 30:364-372. Palo Alto, CA: Sage Publications, Inc.

Sander, F.E.A. (1976). Varieties of dispute processing. *F.R.D.* 70:111-134. St. Paul MN: West Publishing Co.

Sander, F.E.A. & Goldberg, S.B. (1994). Fitting the forum to the fuss: a user-friendly guide to selecting an ADR procedure. *Negotiation Journal*, v1, pp. 49-68. New York: Plenum Publishing Corporation.

Schwarz, R.M. (1994). *The Skilled Facilitator: Practical Wisdom for Developing Effective Groups*. San Fransisco: Jossey-Bass Inc., Publishers.

Tesler, P.H. (1999). Collaborative law: what it is and why family law attorneys need to know about it. *American Journal of Family Law*, v13, pp. 215-225. San Fransisco, CA: Aspen Law & Business.

Tesler, P.H. (2001). *Collaborative Law: Achieving Effective Resolution in Divorce without Litigation*. Chicago, IL: ABA Publications.

Thomas, K.W. (1976). Conflict and conflict management. In M.D. Dunnette (Ed.) (1976). *Handbook of Industrial and Organizational Psychology*. Chicago, Il.: Rand McNally College Publishing Company.

Ury, W. (1991). *Getting Past No: Negotiating Your Way from Confrontation to Cooperation*. New York: Bantam Books.

Walton, R.E. & McKersie, R.B. (1993). *A Behavioral Theory of Labor Negotiations: An Analysis of a Social Interaction System* (2nd ed.). Ithaca, NY: ILR Press.

Webb, S.G. (1996). Collaborative law – a conversation: why aren't those divorce lawyers going to court? *The Hennepin Lawyer*, August 1996, pp. 26-28.

INDEX

shared parenting gaining ground, 161

role of CFL lawyer in focusing parents on ongoing parenting arrangements, 161

static labels, danger in applying, 161

PARTICIPATION AGREEMENT, 61-65, 84-85, App. E *See also* **AGREE-MENTS**

POUND, ROSCOE, 22-23, 28

PROPERTY REGIME
CFL in practice, 195-202
  agreement, separation, 202
  alternatives, 201-202
  calculation of division of property, 196
  financial statements, preparation of, 195
  interests, 196-198
    business enterprise, 197
    family residence, 196
    personal use property, 196-197
    retirement assets, 197-198
  issues, 195
  options, 198-201
    business enterprise, 200
    family residence, 198-199
      mortgage, increasing, 198-199
      option generation in maximizing satisfaction of interests, 199
      rental of second property, 199
      sale and purchase of two properties, 199
    personal use property, 199-200
      final offer selection, 199
      items in dispute, identifying, 199
      replacement of property, 200
      sentimental value of certain property, 200
      unequal division, and valuation of difference, 199-200
    retirement assets, 201
      division of pension credits at source, 201
      lump sum payment representing interest in pension, 201
      retirement plan, preparation of, 201
        supplement income of spouse lacking pension plan, 201
  principles, statement of, 198
  production of financial information not condition of attendance, 195
  valuation of assets or debts, 195
complexity in determining property issues, 193-194
equal division of property acquired during marriage, 193
  credits or exclusions possibly applying, 193
generally, 203